How my river runs

runs

An autobiography of survival

Helen Mary Barr

chipmunkapublishing
the mental health publisher

Helen Mary Barr

Published by
Chipmunkapublishing
United Kingdom

http://www.chipmunkapublishing.com

Copyright © 2017 Helen Mary Barr

ISBN   978-1-78382-337-6

How my river runs

Dedicated to

My parents, who are always standing on the riverbank
with a life belt

My husband, who Captains the lifeboat

My sister, who will never let me drown

My children, because they swim alongside me

Sarah Brenig and Anwen for crossing the deep beside me

Xanthe and Clare for sandwiches, scones and laughter

David Charles Leonard William Hogan
for letting me swan about with leaves

Kathleen Anne Hogan, for her mountains

Helen Mary Barr

How my river runs

Introduction

I hear that life flashes before your eyes when you drown.
That it pours itself over and around you, completely
uncensored. I have drowned, and I have resurfaced.
The colours of my madness; mania that scratches the sky
and death, ever the undertow holds me like a child with
rocks in my coat. I jump into puddles without knowing how
deep they are and the river dazzles me when sunlight leaps
into the sky, making tiny sails from the moving surface. I feel
the rainbow spray touch my face and I close my eyes with
the power of it all. These are the inks of my life, that swirl
their way into the river.

My name is Helen Mary, although my friends often call me
Nelli. Either make sense to me.

Sometimes I laugh with hysterical joy when I realize that the
world is mine to command. I love fiercely yet I fall so hard
that disbelief is my executioner.
My first fifty years are offered now and lay a rainbow against
oily matt black. My stories have chosen their own order, the
full Gestalt moment. The whole being far greater than the
sum of these pages.

I have a sister, Elizabeth (also known as Liff) who is four
years younger than I, both parents living and two children;
Michael, born August 1986 and Lucy, a January baby, in
1988. I also have four husbands but I am using only one, the
last and the best.
Married life began with John (1986), who is the father to my
children and gave me seven years of growing up. Closely
followed by Francis (1993), John's friend who gave me
twelve years of climbing and falling, following and leading.
Charles (2006), came out of my computer and was not
known by anyone at all. Bringing me nine years of a life
rebuilt and a world without history, Charles gave me a future
and a life of worth. Finally, Anthony (2015). A friend of both
John and Francis, and my dearest friend. My true love, the
love of my life.

Other than Charles, we were all bound together by a motorcycle pub in the heart of York City Center. A place of meeting and leaving, a world within the City walls where we were both damaged and rescued and sometimes made strong.

In 1986 Anthony and I rode Francis's bike through town. I was wearing a full length white dress and I was pregnant with my first child, John's son Michael. Anthony rode Francis's bike, as he had done so often when taking me out and away from the noise inside my head. The shouting in my veins again raised to screaming pitch by my undiagnosed psychotic illness. I stretched my arms high in the air as we passed through the crowds of tourists, my open faced black helmet and flying goggles fit for any journey into the realms of madness.
Michael took his first turn on a motor bike before he was even born.
I have auburn hair and hazel eyes, I am also tall (five feet eight inches) and apparently I don't look fifty years old but this is changing along with everything else.

I was born in York by the river Ouse and brought up in a house built in 1936, bought new by my grandfather, the same house my mother grew up in. The same bedroom also. The house, along with its beautiful windows dressed with stained colour was closed up in 1939 when Grandad was called up, two weeks before the declaration of war. He was a poet who worked at Rowntree Chocolate Factory packing sweets into boxes. This he did beautifully, along with the fine jewellery he hand-made at home, skilfully bending gold wire into delicate shapes.
My grandad made my mother, my sister and me a bracelet each, crafted from horse-shoe shaped links. I adored him and he visited us every day after work, when my parents bought the house from him after Grandmother died. I didn't know my grandmother, who died at sixty years old, unexpectedly and tragically. She passed away after shingles was mistreated by her elderly doctor who also diagnosed the pattern of her wallpaper as the reason she felt ill. The heart attack took everyone by surprise. The doctor retired not long after.

How my river runs

I was seven years old when Grandad married Gladys, a woman from London who lived to be almost one hundred and always wore cream slacks, pencilling in her eyebrows and her opinions every day. Each Sunday morning, my dad, my sister and I cycled to visit 'Auntie Gladys' whilst Mum made the Yorkshire puddings.

The little house in the heart of the City walls became home to Grandad and Auntie Gladys, when Gladys moved in and it was here that my grandad began to suffer a progressive stroke. The small brain tumour had most probably been there since the war. I remember clearly the terrifying way my grandad lost the use of his arms, legs and his voice, drifting slowly away over time. Auntie Gladys tried to encourage him to recite nursery rhymes, but my grandad was a poet. When he couldn't write, Grandad grew very frustrated and so Mum found him a small portable typewriter, thinking he might be able to press the keys. His fingers didn't have the strength. The inability to communicate was an incremental death in its own right. Grandad became so distressed that he was found at home, on the floor, with all his liquid medication in his dressing gown pocket. The effort to take it all at once in itself causing him to let go. After being taken to hospital in Hull, his agitation increased and only began to subside when Mum arranged for the Methodist minister to pray for him. Grandad died in 1973.

The Sunday morning visiting ritual continued for many years after my grandfather passed away. I developed a love for strong cheddar cheese and butter on cream crackers, with sweet creamy coffee in a china cup. I was not given this, but my Father and my Mother's brother who also visited Gladys, once Granddad had gone, had the delicacy placed before them every week, along with a sherry. I can't remember what I had, but it wasn't cream crackers. What I do remember is that as I grew older, judgment fell upon me more and more. I was never old enough for sweet coffee, but I was always available for criticism and blame. Still visiting Auntie Gladys at nineteen years old, and pregnant with Michael, Auntie Gladys spoke openly in the street about her magnanimous gesture, that of standing with me at the front door where she could be seen.

On arriving at Auntie Gladys's little terraced house in the heart of York, one Sunday morning ten minutes before my father arrived, a hot plate had shattered onto the kitchen floor. As my father came in, he immediately assumed I was responsible for the breakage. 'What has she done now'?

These words might seem to echo across the years, and I could assimilate their motto for the worst and my undoing. Yet my hope is that the question never leaves my life, because if I can carry it above my head, 'What has she done now'? will forever keep those around me guessing and expecting a rabbit of a different colour out of the hat. Or perhaps some crackers.

The thing I have come to realize with terrifying clarity, is that anything at all can happen to you, to me, to us. I know that we say this all that time, 'Anything is possible', but we don't expect that anything WILL become possible. We don't expect that the unthinkable will happen to us, in our own lives. For example, we don't expect that our husband will die eleven weeks after feeling ill, only nine years into the marriage. We don't expect that our university graduation plans will make way for a hospital bed right in the middle of the living room. Even then, we don't expect our husband to actually die in it. How could these things be possible? We don't think that we would ever allow ourselves to be drenched publicly in vegetable oil to chase away our demons, or that we would climb a stairway to an uncertain violation. We would never believe that our mother–in–law could outlive all six of her adult children, but when she does, she has six lifetimes of nurture for six coffins. The truth however, is a beautiful one. Anything is possible. This means that despite loss, humiliation and violence we can also be healed, educated, elated, loved and accepted. Any of it, some of it, all of it.

I was seven years old when Grandad died, and beyond my grandfather we cannot trace as there are no records. When he was born, he was placed in a drawer on the floor, a draft stung his eyes and although loved, he grew with the feeling that he ought to prove his worth. Granddad was my mother's Father. The following year, my father's mother died. My Cumbrian grandma lived in a tiny house in Bigrigg, Whitehaven. She never knew what it was to have an inside bathroom, despite living into the 1970s. The tiny Cumberland house was owned by Jefferson Rum Importers. The office where my Father went as a boy to pay the rent is now a museum. My grandma brought up three sons alone, of which my father is the eldest. She lost both her husband, an iron-ore miner in his early thirties and also her mother within six months. My father worked from an early age to help support the family. The visits I made with my dad to Bigrigg are very precious to me because they are the strongest memories I have of my father outside of our home. I see the jug with a bowl standing in the window and I hear a horse nearby, very different from the sound of trains I grew up with.

My mother and father met as pen friends when my father worked for Rhodesia Railways. They wrote beautiful letters, discovering one another through pen and paper. Not so different from an email relationship, only slower. My parents would not agree, but Charles and I are testament to the computer romance.

My dad showed my sister and I how to make paper cones in which to sell sweets, just as he had done when he was a boy working at the Co-op a few doors away from his childhood home. We can always work for sweetness and hold it dear. There is no shame in simplicity, in fact simple dedication is by far the greatest skill there is.

My life as a child at home was not particularly easy. I began to sink and to sail at a young age.
The river reached our house when I was very young after a great deal of rain. I saw it bubbling up the drains and I waited for an army boat to take me up the road to school. It is always advisable to stay dry, or at least know that the river is coming. Flooding makes such a mess.
It is 2009. I am sitting on a bed, which is part of a larger ward holding three other beds. We four are partitioned from one another – which makes me smile. What kind of things

are shut out by an ill-fitting curtain? Not many. A chirpy teenage girl just turned eighteen slept next to me. With her short blond hair cut neatly round her ears and curled on top, she decided to read me some of the poetry she had written. Carol was round and cheerful, cheerful to the point of being painful to the ears. Two people with Bipolar Affective Disorder will either burn one another's thoughts faster than a hummingbird's wings, or build a suicide pact. At that time, I was far from high. Carol swept aside the curtain between our beds and we sat facing one another. As she began to read her verses, I wanted so much to encourage her. An unstifled need for acceptance poured from every pencil stroke. Again that day, her Mother had phoned the ward to say she couldn't make it in to visit. I listened and then tired, I lay back on my bed to untangle my own thoughts. I was dipping in and out of sleep, my medication heavy but welcome, when I heard many pairs of feet running on the hard floor. I turned my head to the right, as nurses pulled at Carol, using scissors to cut the elastic from her neck. She resurfaced to a bed free from dangerous sheets and clothes with which she could not end her life. I watched. The curtain was rubbish.

I'm not sure why I chose to start this book with Carol, she did manage to end her life.
I think it is the right time to open the curtains so that people can see me.
I have written and performed award-winning projects exploring art and mental illness and trained for seven years to get here, a place where I can both heal and be healed. I am a bride four times over and a widow once. I have been taken up and away by evangelical Christians, then admitted to the psychiatric ward which is by far the safer place to be crazy. I have entered a cult, a terrifying place filled with God-praising soldiers wearing camouflage jackets in vivid blue red and green (defeating the object somewhat – or maybe not). My sanest hours have been spent supporting people with a bag full of stones and tarot cards, laughing with my sister and being hugged by my friends.

I have been exorcised twice and been saved by God multiple times. I am a person with Bipolar Affective Disorder and also Schizo-Affective Disorder. In my struggle to find peace inside my head, I have been drenched in vegetable oil whilst stranger folk than I did battle with demons on my behalf. I have given away all my worldly goods three times, twice willingly and once not so willingly. I have changed my life with internet dating and watched my son battle with heroin. Sometimes I climb into a boat to avoid drowning. I don't blame anyone else when the river floods.

I am now a practicing Shamanic therapist and a Tarot and Crystal Diviner. I believe that the last fifty years have taken me to places I would die in rather than explore but I have fettled the noise inside my head so I can finally know what it is to swim.

After falling backwards onto concrete during an erratic evangelical worship evening in Northampton, I was slain in the spirit, with the help of a good Christian soldier. Nobody thought to catch me. I'm not sure where Jesus was that day, but my bruises were not healed. I was told that God wanted me to feel the pain. He didn't have to push me over to do that.

I have witnessed behaviour that would be certifiable in everyday life yet unquestionably appropriate in a community church. Lining up to reach the front of the hall, an orderly queue of worshipers formed because God wanted to free them from the spirit of masturbation. Writhing, even flipping on the floor was highly recommended. Seriously, my lovely pagan rituals are tame in the presence of this bunch even though I am branded by the Devil. It's the word 'pagan' that worries folk. Thrashing away masturbation publicly is nothing to worry about.

Trust me, the stories get stranger and stranger.

I would like you to walk with me through the weird and the weirder, the sad and the devastating. Hopefully you will find something that makes you laugh.

Helen Mary Barr

How my river runs

Chapter One
The Christmas Eve Meteorite

Barwell is a strange place. Christmas Eve 1965 at around
4.20 pm - a 100lb meteoroid hit the large village, breaking up
and scattering less than a mile from where my husband
Charles and I now lived. Every time I walked to the shops, I
laughed at the Parish Council offices, nestled between an
odd place selling handmade greetings cards, home knitted
baby clothes and parts for pushbikes. Also one of around
four hairdressers in the main street. The Council Offices had
chosen a logo consisted of a dark blue night sky and a
number of meteoroid parts hurtling towards the village. All
my life I have wrestled with paranoid ideas of apocalyptic
destruction, so this new life, a move in 2007 definitely had
the eve of destruction stamped upon it's brow. I had never
even heard of Barwell, neither had any of my family or
friends. However, the weekend Charles and I moved into
Barwell it was plastered all over the main news. A few
streets away from our house, a lady had killed both herself
and her disabled daughter, ending their lives in a car
consumed by flames. The daughter had loved jumping in
puddles, the youths who tormented them day in day out took
away all the love of life they might have had. A disabled son
was also left behind. Suddenly everyone knew where
Barwell was and where it was we were moving to. For a
number of years after moving in we were called on at least
weekly by the police, wanting to make sure we weren't
experiencing any anti-social behaviour. I came to love
Barwell with its quirky shops and pubs and it had begun to
feel like a kind of home.

The first time I saw Sarah and Brenig, Sarah was carrying a
bunch of Avon catalogues and Brenig leaned against the
gate post, with his long dark platted beard and enormous
boots, waiting for her. Wanting to add some eyeliner to my
order, I telephoned the number on the front page of the
booklet and heard the message that changed my life. 'This is
the Sacred Voice, please leave a message'. For six years I
had lived in the Midlands with no friends whatsoever,
nobody like me, nobody to meditate with, to look for spirit

with, to wear rainbow clothes with. Sarah arrived later that day to collect my book and I seized the moment to ask her about the Sacred Voice.

Sarah had bright pink hair and she wore purple skirts with leggings and dolly shoes. I loved her immediately and knew we would be friends for years to come, if not forever. She explained to me about her chanting and how she played the singing bowls. Sarah's bowls were in three sizes, all large and a subtle rose quartz, pink in colour. Every Friday evening, she and Brenig took the bowls and other instruments to the local community centre where she gave a 'sound bath' to a few of us who lay out on the floor, just like being in a school camp. As the sound from the singing bowls vibrated around the room, Sarah began to chant multiple notes at once and to sing beautiful mantras in Sanskrit. I had finally come home in a place where I didn't belong. I loved Sarah's Sound Baths. One Friday evening I had been unable to make it as I was tied to an essay for my Masters degree needing to be submitted. The Bath was due to start at around six in the evening and I was surprised to see a Facebook message from Sarah, during what I knew to be the chanting phase of the evening. Another couple of messages later (all happy ones, chatting about the session) I became even more confused. I knew how much concentration it took for Sarah to chant the mantra she had chosen and how powerful the result always was. Baffled, I waited until Sarah got home and rang her immediately. 'How in God's name did you manage that?' I rattled down the phone … 'I have to keep myself grounded during the session or I would disappear off and not be able to guide it for everybody else' she laughed. The skill it must have taken to evoke deep throat chanting and sound therapy, to the degree that a whole room of people were whisked away, yet to keep grounded by messaging on Facebook is an enigma to me even today. Sarah's ability to ground a situation became the backbone of my final years in Barwell and we developed a friendship that would go on to see me through the darkest hours of my life to date. She saw the 'funny' in me, and both she and her fiancé Brenig, gave me space to find myself, the self that had been lost in the reinterpretation of my life as I slipped from the North, Southwards.

How my river runs

I was asked one morning, to wait at Sarah and Brenig's house for an Avon delivery, whilst the pair of them were at work. In the kitchen, were a jar of biscuits, tea bags and a mug. Alongside the biscuits was a pair of tongs. Looking around the room, I was suddenly struck by the thought that someone might be watching me. I made a cup of tea and believing that the tongs were to pick the biscuits out of the jar with, I carefully carried a single rich tea with them into the living room and on to my plate. I was fastidious in my use of the tongs, just in case the observation meant that I might be in trouble for spreading germs by handling the biscuits myself. When Sarah came home, I told her I had used the tongs and she almost doubled over in hysterics. The tongs had been to squeeze out the tea-bag. I rolled up in laughter too, but secretly I was a little afraid that I had thought myself being observed.

I was reminded by this secret fear, of a client I worked with from home in York, 2005. The young lady came to me for Cognitive Behavioural Therapy, so that we could work on her fear of germs and eating outside of her home. Up until that time, Sally was only able to use paper cups which she brought with her to the house. After a couple of sessions, I was able to support Sally in the idea that the mugs in my house might be safe. It was a real breakthrough. Leaving her in the living room, I went into the kitchen to make Sally a mug of tea. As I put on the kettle, I was suddenly struck by a fearful spike, that my mugs might not be clean enough. I looked around the room, feeling the old familiar paranoia that I was being watched. I placed the mug onto the draining board and poured boiling water all over it. It still didn't seem clean. I looked around for the hidden camera.

Making the tea, I took the mug in to Sally, who bravely drank it all and beat her fear of germs, for that day. I however, was wracked with fear in case I had poisoned her, and had been filmed in the act of doing so.

The friendship between Sarah and I grew. She knew me as I genuinely was and she became my closest friend. Driving from Barwell to Leicester where the final days of my Master's degree were taking shape, Sarah was on her way to her teaching job. A skilled Sound Therapist, she also taught saxophone, flute and clarinet. As we arrived at the point in the road where King Richard the Third's bones were said to have been tossed into the river, (now known to be untrue) an enormous swan flew right in front of the car. It was incredible.

The following day, I was at home in Barwell when Sarah rang me up. 'Guess where I am and what's happened?' I had no clue at all but Sarah quickly went on 'I'm at the Richard the Third stop and all of a sudden, 'Ride a White Swan, by T-Rex' came on the radio. The exact same point that the swan flew in front of us yesterday'.

Swans flew around quite a bit after that initial sighting. I learned in late summer 2014, when I went to the 'Mercian Gathering' festival, where Sarah was lecturing on chanting, that swans are often seen as a Celtic symbol of passing over, a flight to the otherworld. In Autumn of the same year, I had the Celtic symbol for love and a swan tattooed on my upper right arm. Within the blue and green inks, I had my late husband Charles's ashes added to make a memorial within my skin.

Two weeks before Christmas 2013, Charles and I were visiting his Mum in Coventry. Dot was eighty years old and a small yet very strong minded woman. At the age of twelve, Dot's Mother died leaving her to care for three young brothers. Dot loved being a Mother and rarely returned to full time school. Her Father was unable to cope and so the running of the house fell to her. The three brothers were a handsome bunch and in the 1960's and 1970's, wore lovely greased back hair and Teddy Boy suits. The youngest brother was only two years old when their Mother died and the older two under ten. Dot married in her late teens, and she gave birth to Charles in 1956 (my husband, who was ten years older than I). Then came Kathleen, (less than two years younger than Charles). The youngest child was William, roughly six years younger than Charles.

How my river runs

After meeting on an internet dating site in September 2005, Charles visited York and I travelled to see him in Coventry. I think he found me a strange but interesting person. Charles was eccentric to those who knew him well and he was never afraid to hurdle conventions. In the final year of his business degree, which he studied two nights a week after work, Charles was due to sit his final examination and he was very nervous about it. I gave him a piece of quartz crystal, telling him that he needed to leave it outside overnight for the moonlight to cleanse it and then to charge it, with his knowledge and confidence. At the time, it transpired, Charles was still speaking online with his ex-girlfriend. I had no idea about this.

The morning of the exam, I was at home when my telephone rang right when Charles should have been at college. An almost accusatory voice explained that he hadn't made the exam. Charles's car it seemed, had broken down in the middle of Coventry ring road and he had been unable to move it. He had missed the exam. In a rather suspicious tone, Charles asked me if I had given him the crystal on purpose to make the car break down. I couldn't believe what I was hearing, but I also realized then, that I was someone who deserved to be taken seriously. I would no more have wished the car to fail and the exam to be missed that I would have bought a large cauldron and sat in it naked! I also had no idea that Charles was still speaking with his ex. It had been proved that where there is a hint of the unknown, the mind will believe anything it is told. Fear is a great leveller. However, when true vision and light are manifest, anything is possible.

I packed up lock stock and barrel, moving into Dot's house with Charles for a few weeks. We then squashed everything I owned into a van to take from York to the tiny terraced house we had rented. Whilst Charles and I loaded the high sided van between the two of us, my son Michael stared at me in anger. I had made provisions for him to communicate with the City Council so that he would be offered a bedsit or flat. I was unable to cope with life in York any more, it had become dangerous and toxic but I had done my best to leave it intact. Whilst Charles and I were packing, my ex-husband Francis turned up on his new motorbike, wearing a bandana. He grimaced at Charles and handed me some post that had arrived at the house we had shared. I was aware that I looked very different from the previous year, albeit a secret monsoon hiding behind the smile. This was the last time I saw my ex-husband number two. He quickly moved a young woman into what had been our house and they went on to have a child.

Charles and I moved into a multi-cultural part of Coventry, with the help of Charles's best friend Marco. A body-builder, I watched him carry the great slab of rock from the back of the van, that I used as an altar for my ceremonies. 'I could have dug a chunk of concrete up for you in the building site over there', he gave me a sidelong smile. 'Saved you the bother of packing it'. He helped us carry everything in… the sofa really did have to be forcibly squashed into the door, which opened straight onto the street. 'I was surprised you came with him in the van', Marco laughed, 'I expected you to follow behind on your broomstick'! I loved the little house and the African take-away shops selling a selection of differently sized snails. I went every day to the nearest internet café, also run by a kind African man. I was fascinated by the combination of hair pieces, afro hair products, brightly coloured telephone cards and computers. It was a weird time. Being completely alone in a new city had its thrills and for me and this involved the freedom to roam and discover new possibilities. The expectation that I would fit in as a wife, get a full-time job and go to the pub on Sundays made me feel a little out of my depth, but I believed Charles to be more than he portrayed. Sometimes I felt a high-pitched terror at the life I had walked away from and the one I was determined to believe in. The year I had spent without a relationship, between Francis and Charles had given me the freedom to do whatever I wanted. Yet still I filled it with failed attempts at finding the man I wanted to marry and weeks in the psychiatric ward. Not a great combination for stability. I wasn't so great in the running of our house either. Dot had done everything for Charles. The only socks Charles wore, were 'Pringle' socks. When we first moved in together, the socks were neatly placed in a drawer of their own. Gradually, the sock situation began to suffer and one morning, when getting ready for work, Charles opened his drawer to find only one single sock… not even a pair. He laughed and realised then that he would have to make adjustments.

Now in Coventry, I was occasionally choked by the lack of a river running always, through the streets. Being landlocked made me want to scream. I walked by the canal when I could but it wasn't a safe place to be alone. In later months, I persuaded Charles to take on an allotment which backed onto the canal. An old fence separated the unworkable plot from the water and I was prepared to push a chair through to sit on the two feet high, five feet wide bank. Even the sight of a narrow boat was a connection home. Marco laughed when he saw the allotment and told me that Charles would probably bring his secret women into the ramshackle shed. I laughed too but I didn't like the suggestion as I was a long way from home and still didn't really know anything about the man I had invested everything in.

For Charles's fiftieth birthday and my fortieth, we decided to take a trip to Holy Island. I have a particular affinity with the place and also a fixation with the statue of St Aidan. Checking into one of only two hotels on the island, I was really excited. Charles and I had only been together a few months and this would be our first expedition together. We had a brilliant time, the weather was sunny and although Charles was a little the worse for wear, it wasn't a problem. We stayed only one night, but Charles had found us a breakfast table looking right over my favourite statue. I was thrilled with this and couldn't wait to sit eating, looking at it. When our alarm went off, Charles began to panic, shouting that we had slept in and would miss the tide that would prevent us from travelling over the causeway. We had also missed breakfast. I dragged a comb through my hair and we ran down to the breakfast room. Sitting there, hair in knots and last night's eyeliner making me look as though I had been punched, we realised that the cereals and juice were untouched. I looked at St Aidan. A waitress came in to us and explained that we were half an hour early for breakfast.

Realising that our clock must have been wrong, I tried to find serenity and connect with my spiritual brain but it was too funny. When the waiter arrived to take our order, I looked at the menu and saw several lines of writing each with different things on them. Not used to eating out, I figured that a full breakfast wasn't an option, but various combinations of food were. So I chose hash browns and baked beans. The waiter looked at me as though I had gone mad (hair, eyeliner) and I insisted, that this was what I wanted. As he left the room, the penny dropped and I shouted 'Can I have an egg please'?

Back home in Coventry, I was in the African internet café and I received an email from the Guardian newspaper. The researcher had found my website on Google, which linked to a project I had built in the year 2000, involving mental health and the arts.

A journalist came out to visit me, followed by a photographer. So there was I, living in a city I didn't know, with a man I barely knew, absolutely no family or friends (Dot was completely against Charles and I for many months), and standing posing in the middle of a multi-cultural road. The photographer sat on the ground looking up at me and took photographs for an article in the Guardian about sex and mental health. The article appeared in the Guardian Weekend Magazine, Easter Saturday 2006. I was terrified because the journalist had spoken more candidly about my mental health than I had hoped for and I didn't want my Mother to read the article. The subject matter was not what I had expected and clearly I had chatted away too much. The day before had been a Sunday and therefor a Charles, Marco and crew afternoon in the pub. I was still hungover. I knew my Mother was shutting the article out, when I rang to see how many copies she had bought. 'Just the one'. I wasn't surprised. The photograph showed me holding a cat. I don't know who's cat it was. It was just a cat in the street.

After Charles read the article, I thought I had better explain to him about the difficulties I had experienced when I was sixteen and vulnerable. I told him but his response was amazing. My words didn't appear to register on his face at

How my river runs

all. When I spoke, he spoke about something else. It was like putting on a CD and nothing coming out. This continued for the whole nine years of our marriage and in the end I decided to think the same way and close the box again. But boxes filled with water will leak. In my case, the box poured had poured from all its seams many years before, with thoughts of damaged health and a paralyzing fear of HIV. I had stitched up the seams but the thread didn't hold for long.

Little wonder that my original diagnosis alongside hyperactivity was that of Obsessive Compulsive Disorder. No amount of reason or sanity could raise the truth that I hadn't done anything to make something terrible happen. My paranoia began to spiral out beyond any kind of control and only when I was prescribed anti-psychotic medication did the pain and fear stop their chase. These were not subjects I could share with anybody, they made no sense. Nobody would have understood.

The Gift of Flight

I crouch down low and try to hold my soul intact. My fears outrun me and I lay wounded,
Hunted, haunted and heavy with despair. Where can I run? Where can I hide?
This terror has a form that is all its own. It splits into many faces and waits
at every corner, speaking ancient languages and laughing at my screams.
Towering darkness, split open your clouds and show me merciful sunshine.
'Run, and run again', commands the demon, 'What use have you for light and yellow?'
Dragging, crawling, rising now running, the voices mock, but I look up to the sky.
With outstretched arms, I lunge from the edge and fall from the day, to silence my vicious captor. Expecting to be tossed forever by the charcoal hurricane inside my head,
I feel oxygen rush past me, and the morning, so bright that I fear my opening eyes.

Silence and space, a calm sea washes through my mind and
I am covered by feathers,
and the feathers are wings, and the wings pour healing oils
into every pore of my body.
The beating of wings, so loud in my heart, I dare not look
into my Saviour's face.
He gently places me in the calm waters, and pours the
diamond bright salt
over my head with his cupped hands.

Wild geese circle in the light and a swan flies across the sky.
'You are whole, you are free, they are silenced' he says, and
I am still for the first time ...
... the first time this time. My sadness slides from my brain,
away into the sand.
He covers my face with his hands, and I am resting,
watching the sky.
Only the sound of wings.

As I touch my cheeks I feel the memory of him, and I find
that my hands
are drenched in blood. Deep red blood from the palms of my
Saviour, where he stroked my stricken face.

I did not know I was worth so much.

I think people were rather bemused. I split up from Francis,
my husband of twelve years in February 2005 taking a near
fatal overdose of anti-depressants, then not leaving the
family home until April. I then met Charles online in October
2005, taking the second overdose of that year, in December,
only to split up from Charles and receive a proposal of
marriage from another internet dalliance. I refused to
acknowledge Christmas altogether, and got back together
with Charles in February. I left everything I owned in York
and took my worldly goods to Coventry, moving into our first
rented home, March 2006. At Easter 2006 I appeared in the
Guardian Weekend Magazine, contacted by them for my
insight into Obsessive Compulsive Disorder and sex. For the
next sixth months, I was offered job after job. This run of
employment started as a call centre operative with Jaguar,
on through to a teaching role in adult education, with

assorted jobs in between. For several weeks, I worked as a teaching assistant for a school supporting children with complex and emotional needs. This was one of the worst jobs I have ever encountered. Having spent some of the final year of my Counselling degree gaining a teaching diploma, I found myself running around the school daily chasing children intent on escaping the confines of the classroom. I loved supporting children on the autistic spectrum, but many of the children knew exactly what ADHD was and how they ought to be treated. I don't think I have ever heard such disgusting insults aimed at a teacher from a pupil. On one occasion, two brothers barricaded me into the school hall with them, where they embarked upon a tirade of abuse that left me speechless and distressed. This was not the teaching I had set out to enjoy. Having been recently diagnosed with bipolar, I had disclosed this to the head teacher, who was more than positive about my contribution to the children needing more support than others due to mental health issues. I was asked to attend a meeting with the occupational health department of Coventry Council and I wasn't in the least concerned about what they would say. I should have been. The nurse was rude, even offensive. I was told in no uncertain terms not to return to the school until a psychiatric report had been prepared.

The head master was livid. He needed me in school, even though school was challenging indeed. Refusing to wait for the report to be requested, the head teacher paid for the report to be done privately. I was humbled by this and it made me want to get back to work. The psychiatrist who had diagnosed my bipolar wrote a glowing report and I was given the green light to return to school. The only problem was, I had lost all my confidence. When a child dangled himself from a second-floor window ledge, I began to feel it might be my fault. The words of the occupational health nurse rang in my ear, 'We can't be sure you wouldn't put the children in danger'. I left the school, telling the other teachers I had a bad case of haemorrhoids.
Charles and I embarked on a second house move in September 2006, when Charles bought the property from a good friend. Every employment ended with my leaving within

weeks, hysterical and wandering the local streets. So terrified was I of everything around me that even roles that I knew backwards became unthinkable. I began to realize that I couldn't reinvent myself as someone I was never meant to be. I knew that the process would finally kill me, or break me to the point that I would be better off dead. I began work as an Addictions Counsellor at a Christian Rehabilitation Centre, which was in a pitiful state of affairs. Left alone on my first ever shift, with no induction or case notes for the men I was put in charge of, my first client was a chap out on license for violence, but I was never informed of the risk assessment.

 I could have been in danger, in the large walk in pantry with a man who wanted a bag of crisps but I was incredibly lucky, and got on well with him. However, I still needed to call for an ambulance as his leg swelled beyond that which I deemed safe, due to deep vein thrombosis. For this I was reprimanded as the journey out of the centre fell outside of the license dictates, with only me to accompany him. No-one else was there.

Charles and I married on December 9th 2006, exactly one year since I had taken an overdose whilst he was with me in York. I was then asked to cover both Christmas Day and Boxing Day at the Rehab, along with another female counsellor working in Coventry on a work visa. Together we tried to manage an impossible situation as we were seriously understaffed. We were told to lock the office door and pray if we felt unsafe. Unsafe wasn't the problem, absconding addicts who put themselves in danger was the problem. By the Spring of 2007 both Manager, under Manager and I had walked out. My fellow counsellor was unable to leave because of her visa. However, she took months off sick, so terrible was the job. We were highly skilled counsellors but in the end, only a person with a counselling certificate would take on the job, and this was simply wrong and unethical.

I thrive on change and extreme situations. Rather I should say that my illness thrives on change and extreme situations. I do battle with it daily in my fight to enjoy the calm and the steady, but to be out at sea (although landlocked) I was up the canal without a paddle.

How my river runs

Living with Charles and getting to know him was a scary business. I needed to learn to drink for one thing, and to sell myself to his friends and family, especially Dot who thought I was the evilest woman alive for leaving my children (now eighteen and twenty) back in York. Dot and I did become good friends as the years went on, but initially I felt as though I had to explain every single word action and deed to the whole of this unknown city. Moving away from everything I had known was dangerous. My mental illness had brought me to my knees and yet was not properly diagnosed. I found myself at least twice a week in the café below Coventry Cathedral. The doctor gave me a counsellor but when I rang her from the café, to tell her that I couldn't move because I thought that Charles hated me, there was little she could do. Especially when I explained that there were cameras capturing our conversation.

Both Michael and my daughter Lucy were struggling with deep emotions and we had reached a point of impasse over so many things. The twelve years of marriage to Francis had left both myself and the children damaged – not beyond repair but the healing would take at least another ten years to bring us all home. During my marriage to Charles, both Michael and Lucy endured pain that I honestly thought would never go away. Michael's drug addiction and Lucy's lack of self-confidence and fear took us all further into the depths and we almost didn't make it out again, any of us. Today, Michael, Lucy and I are swimming freely together, and I am now so blessed. (But not in an evangelical way ;>)

Charles and I bought a large semi-detached house in the Leicestershire village of Barwell in 2007. The house had a massive garden and neighbours who would come to see so much of our lives that the relationship was positively raw. I was so excited by the move because I had wanted to leave the house we had bought in Coventry, 2006, which was dangerously close to Dot's home. It was also in the same street as several of Charles's good friends, each with the equivalent of their own purpose built pub in the garden. It didn't take long to organize a pub crawl in the close. After seven years together, we had made our Barwell house a real haven. Our neighbours turned out to be skilled in just about everything (especially pinching anything they fancied from the while my back was turned). This was a mutually humorous situation and they were good friends however, right until the last week before I moved back to York in 2015, when I left without saying a word. Unable to handle Tony and Janice's opinion of my leaving and marrying Anthony, I chose to make it go away. Anthony's brother and his partner Tessa came to collect me in the car and to follow the van back to York. Having to walk away, leaving many things standing in the front garden because they wouldn't fit into the moving van felt like a devastating fracture. We bundled six cats, each in their own box into Mark and Tessa's car. Henry in the front footwell, Charles on Tessa's knee, Albert and Luna next to me with Lotte and George on my knee. As we drove away I couldn't look at the house. I had accidentally left Michael's money tree plants sitting on the window sill and we couldn't open the car doors again for me to get them. They were the only things that Michael had kept with him throughout his difficult journey with addiction and now he was living away from our safety again, seeing them grow smaller as we drove away broke the back of my strength. Life in Barwell was over. I didn't have long to be devastated because Luna broke out of her box and began slithering around the car like a demented baby rabbit. We were near the local charity shop for rescue dogs and so Mark pulled into the main Barwell high street. Carefully opening the door, Tessa forced Luna back into the car and ran out to get a pet carrier. How she managed this without Luna flying into the road I will never know. The shop only had a dog box and so little Luna was piled even higher next to me on the back seat. I began to feel hysterical but without Mark and Tessa I would have jumped into the road myself, after waiting for a suitably large lorry. They kept me alive that day, without a doubt.

Arriving at our new home, Mum was waiting in the empty house, showing us how lovely it looked. This didn't last. It was pouring with rain and the removal men I think, were in shock when they saw the size of the house we were moving into as opposed to where I had come from. As they slid down the front hallway, Mum, Tessa and I were slowly

barricaded into the far corner of the sitting room. The cats were put in the spare bedroom and sat quietly throughout the whole process. Box after box kept coming and bearing in mind how much I had left behind I began to realise just how much of a life I had actually brought with me.
Anthony arrived early evening to find Tessa and I eating sandwiches and staring at a wall of cardboard. He moved in the following day.

Right now, I want to take you to December 2013.
Charles and I pulled up in our car outside Dot's front garden, ready for our Sunday Lunch. Sunday's were hard because Kathleen, Charles's sister had passed away eighteen months previously having fallen downstairs at her home, opposite to Dot's house. I got out of the car and turned to speak to Charles. I was utterly dumb struck. My husband had turned a vivid shade of yellow; in the forty minutes it had taken to drive from Barwell to Coventry. I grabbed onto his arm and said 'You are completely yellow'. Stating the obvious I know, but what else could I say? I wanted us to drive to the hospital immediately, but Charles refused. 'We'll have dinner and I will sit in the shade so she can't see me'. Charles had his reasons for trying to divert his Mother from any possible serious event. William, Dot's youngest son had died more than thirty years earlier. He was part of 'Satan's Slaves' motorcycle club and had passed away in his sleep after a prolonged period of celebration for the birth of his son. William was wild but loved and adored by Dot. Two of Dot's three brothers had also passed away from cancer when I joined the family and the third brother died just after we married. He was the only family member to turn up to our wedding, as for the first part of our time together, Charles was battling (but won) his fight with throat cancer. Something I had to fight on his behalf as nobody believed that what I saw in his throat was true. We cancelled our wedding because of Charles's surgery but kept the date for ourselves. We almost cancelled the ceremony too. Charles had become terrified of being, what he termed a 'chin man'. When we visited the hospital to see his consultant, we sat in the waiting area along with other people in various stages of throat surgery. Some of the men we saw had lost their jaw

line and looked very poorly. Charles and I always sat away from other patients so that he didn't have to watch them. The shock came when I received a phone call at home, to let us know that Charles needed further surgery, this time through the jaw. I was given the task of telling Charles the news.

In the end the operation was not needed but Charles contracted an infection, meaning that I had to put him back in a taxi and take him to the consultant again. I don't think I have ever seen such pain in one person's face, as he was forced to take antibiotic tablets. I bought baby food for Charles to eat but that didn't go down too well as he felt humiliated. Slowly, a bit at a time, Charles got better. Life was very busy as I tried to feel at home, having only left my life behind a few months earlier.

Michael telephoned me, as he was afraid of some physical symptoms he was experiencing. After sending my son a CD containing over two hundred photographs of himself as a child with the family that adored him, and pages of writing telling him how much he was loved, I had no idea that this was to become the slide into heroin addiction.

Charles and I tried very hard to make our lives mundane, and to give ourselves the chance to live an ordinary married life. This didn't come easily. One night, Charles had been drinking whisky. We were talking and listening to music. Suddenly, he became angry, shouting and although not physically aggressive, I found it hard to fight my corner, especially as he wasn't making sense. Charles ranted on for hours, and it became clear that he did not know what he was doing or saying. I tried to get him to sleep as I felt that this would break the episode, but he wouldn't. Swinging between biting anger and being unaware of his state of mind, speaking gently and calmly, I felt I needed to lock myself in the small bedroom. I did this, but Charles lay in front of the bedroom door, threatening me to try and leave. I didn't have my phone on me or I would have rung the police or the hospital. I didn't want him to get into trouble however, as I thought his job might become at risk. I was afraid, and yet not afraid as I didn't believe I was in any danger. I now know that this terrible experience was a mix of stress and alcohol.

How my river runs

It continued right through the night and didn't begin to slow down until the following late morning. During this time, I left the bedroom. Charles was shouting about having his sword on him, which would have been funny had we not experienced a whole night of incoherent ranting. My financial advisor rang at around ten o clock that morning and he could hear Charles shouting. He asked me if I was safe, and told me to leave the house. I managed to finally get Charles into bed, but he shook it about and wouldn't let me leave. Finally, at approximately three o clock in the afternoon, Charles became coherent again. He could not believe what had happened. We did experience something similar several times over our married life, but never to the intensity of that day. I learned very quickly, what a powerful man my husband was and how hard it was going to be to stay so far away from home. Gradually though, the joy of our relationship and the strands of hope I had held on to in 2005 began to outweigh the unstable fear. My illness began to develop into a monster of its own and we learned how to lean on each other and survive.

In December 2005, Charles had inadvertently saved my life from suicide, but our relationship ended until February 2006. For a while at least. A tumultuous game of 'Shall I shan't I go with Charles or move to Bridlington with Simon, another man I met online?' An amazing turnaround after the previous year, when Francis blamed my brainstorms for his desire to end our marriage. I don't think I have ever felt so worthless. Indecision took over until I finally packed up and moved with Charles to Coventry in March. I had managed to hide Charles's identity from Simon, telling him he was a pig farmer from Dorset (instead of a Midland Commodity Manager in Aerospace). Our wedding, a year on, was a scary experience for me. I was alone at Coventry Register Office, which is stunning, but empty when about to get married with no family or friends. Only Dot, Kathleen and Kathleen's son Wayne were present, apart from Charles's Uncle Sam. Our families had never met and after the ceremony our mothers spoke on the telephone outside the registry office, for the first time. From outside Coventry Register Office, we all jumped in a taxi and went to a lovely

hotel doing two meals for £10.00. I walked into the ornate
and rather beautiful door, wearing my gold and cream mini
dress, my cream suede boots and a gold headband with
pearls in it. I was carrying a large bunch of daffodils and
gypsophelia, tied with a long cream silk ribbon. The magic of
being 'just married' began to feel like an imposter's joke.
Nobody in the restaurant knew that we had just got married,
and the fizzy sensation made me feel stupid. Charles and I
didn't even sit together, I sat next to Dot. I wanted to throw
my bouquet at somebody but didn't feel it was wise to
perform a floral assault on my unsuspecting reception
guests. Dot's remaining brother who was late, almost
arriving half-dressed as Santa Clause on his way to
entertain the children from his club. We cheered him on
when he appeared at the door. Dot's final brother, he too
was to pass away within two years. We drove back to our
house and our family group, all five of us now, had a glass of
wine and some cake. The family looked quite honestly like a
funeral party, from the moment they arrived to go to the
Register Office. After an hour or so, they all left apart from
Wayne. He too had become drunk and was trying to make
me dance with him. He also had a nasty side when drinking
and he began to accuse me of taking Charles away. His
language and accusations were beyond forgivable. Charles
didn't seem to hear him. I went upstairs and I started to
download the pictures we had taken at the Register Office.
My parents and my sister had all got together and had raised
a glass to us, the same minute as Charles and I married. I
had sent them cake and wine, the nearest I could get to
them being with us. Whilst I downloaded the images, they
appeared an inch at a time in my parent's house, on their old
computer. All of them cheered as each new inch appeared.
My sister was a bit concerned as I had told her I was going
to wear leopard skin tights. As the image revealed ordinary
plain tights she laughed. The pictures were in fact beautiful. I
asked Wayne to leave and Charles didn't seem to know
what was going on. I left him to his wine and I lay on our
bed, with enormous tears pouring down my cheeks. That
night, I seriously doubted that I had made the right decision,
but I decided to find the good and to make it work. Two days
later we went to Gran Canaria for a honey moon. This was
the first hot holiday I had ever experienced. Sadly, our first

night was spoiled by Charles's drinking and he was asked to leave the restaurant having worn the wrong clothes. The following night, he was still angry about this and I misplaced him. I looked everywhere in the large, plush hotel. Eventually I found him asleep on a sofa in reception. As a big man, Charles was hard to manage, but I threw his arm around my shoulder and got him into the lift. I daren't sleep however because we had a very high balcony in our room and I was terrified he would fall over it. As an all-inclusive hotel, it was difficult to keep Charles sober, but when he was, our time was wonderful. I had never sunbathed by a pool before and I clung to those moments of normality. I almost got the pair of us thrown out of the airport on our way to the holiday, as for some unknown reason I had put a long pair of sharp kitchen knives in my hand luggage. My body became one massive 'gulp' when I realised what I had done, and I was terrified to bring them out of my bag to hand in. I honestly thought I would be thrown to the ground. So between my bag of weaponry and Charles's whisky drinking at seven in the morning, we were all set for a great life together!

Again I digress, forgive me.
The final reason Charles didn't want his Mum to see that his skin, the whites of his eyes and nails were all yellow, came in the final blow to hit Dot. Kathleen, her middle child and only daughter had fallen downstairs in her own home eighteen months earlier and died on her birthday of a brain stem injury. Charles and I sat by her bed as she died. I had experienced nothing like it, having never been present at an actual passing. The letting go and the obvious shell. Dot had wanted me to bring in some Elvis songs on an mp3 player. She seemed to think that this would wake her up. At one point, over the three days it took Kathleen to pass away, Dot handed me a shopping list for food she needed at home. She passed it over Kathleen's bed and it was clear to me, that Dot did not realise Kathleen was dying. Even when the organ donation person talked to us, Dot still believed that Kathleen would get better. It was rather like being in a constructed world where what was happening, was not happening. Kathleen was a woman in her mid-fifties but the youngest mid fifty that you could ever meet. She was small

with the same dark hair as Charles and loved football, wearing tomboy clothes every day. She bounced about and loved gardening, particularly her wild birds. I think the most surreal moment, was when Charles and I headed for the hospital right after the accident had happened. It was in the early hours of the morning and the road was silent. As we approached the turn off, we saw a stationary car in the middle of the road with what appeared to be two figures in the front. We then realised that the police were in the process of marking off the area. We later discovered that the two boys were dead, having driven too quickly and crashing into a tree. On our return from the hospital around 7.00 am, there were flowers round the tree. It seemed eerily appropriate. Kathleen died that night too. I was able to plan a lot of her funeral and I wanted to make sure that her sense of fun filled the church. Kathleen always wore lots of coloured bracelets and three or four watches. She loved a tin of beer and we would often go to Coventry Market for a bacon sandwich. Social phobia had caused her to avoid many situations and on more than one occasion whilst we were sitting in the market café, she leapt over the barriers and hit behind the fabric stall. The smell of fresh market cotton and fried bacon lets me see Kathleen again, flying over the temporary fence and hiding like a cheeky child. Her take on many things, even history was truly unique and often hilarious. One Sunday lunch she explained to me that the Midlands had once been just like the Yorkshire Dales, and the Lake District, but the Romans had taken down the hills and mountains to make their conquering easier. (I actually felt the need to go and check this, so fervent was she in her belief).

So, here we are at Dot's house. A Mother who has lost five of the six children she called her own. Dot had deep brown hair despite being eighty. She had divorced her husband when he chose to take up with a local barmaid. The embarrassment was dreadful for her as he moved into her house, right opposite the family home, where he eventually died. Charles's Dad passed away downstairs in an area that was to become his daughter Kathleen's kitchen. After he died, his new wife (the barmaid) swapped houses with Kathleen so that she could be closer to Dot. I always think of how Dot made me laugh when she told me 'He always missed my crisp sheets'. Kathleen would die only feet away from her father, at the bottom of the stairs. Telling Dot that day about Charles's sudden change in colour would have been catastrophic, so we decided to leave it until we had seen a doctor.

Arriving home, it was obvious that we needed to see a professional so we rang the emergency clinic. We called at the small surgery and were immediately asked in. The Doctor and Nurse seemed jovial and not concerned. They mentioned that Charles might need stents in his bile duct and they made us laugh because they assumed that I was Charles's daughter. Their advice was to see our own doctor first thing in the morning and they sent their findings across electronically. So we were upbeat. It was the X Factor final that night. I remember closing the partitioned doors so that I could listen to 'Sky Scraper' full belt. Charles settled down to watch his history channel. I glanced at him through the glass doors. He had been a large robust man. A rugby player. Apart from the thick brown hair at the back of his neck, he was mostly bald. His face could erupt into a frightening demand or an angry stare but mostly, it held a gentle expression. I called him 'Ratty' as his cheeks and little glasses reminded me of the child's TV program 'Tales from the River Bank'.

The following morning, we were quite bright as we went to our local Doctor's practice.
Our doctor had received the report from the previous day. He was worried. 'This appears to be your liver', he said, 'We just hope it isn't linked to the shadow that has shown up on your recent lung examinations'. Charles had been receiving ongoing monitoring as he had experienced several chest infections. I'm not sure what happened to me, in that moment. Due to the medication I need to take to treat my Bipolar Affective Disorder, I rarely cry or feel the need to cry. However, on that morning, in that office, on that chair, I could not stop the terrified hot tears. They simply poured down my face. I managed to gasp a request for the Crisis Team to help me (part of my mental health team) because I

was suddenly afraid for the future. I felt helpless. Something terrible was happening and I couldn't prevent it from hurtling towards us.

Charles was admitted to hospital and Sarah took me backwards and forwards to visit over the coming week. Despite being yellow and losing some weight, he seemed fine. I took him in a funny cat hat to wear and surrounded his bed with icons from every religion I could think of. 'I'm hedging my bets' I told Sarah. So many hours that week, Sarah sat in the corridor waiting, insistent that we have our time together. Charles had two stents placed into his bile duct and a liver biopsy. All of which hurt him a lot. When Christmas arrived, we looked forward to our plan of driving up into the Yorkshire Dales to spend Christmas with my family. Mum and Dad from York, Charles and I from Barwell and Liff, Neil and Adam (my sister, her husband and son) who's house we would get together in and enjoy a vegetarian Christmas dinner. In the days after Christmas, Charles and I would laugh at the fact that his last Christmas lunch was vegetarian. We laughed about a lot of things that week, because it really doesn't matter anymore when the finish post appears.

On Christmas Eve, Sarah and I arrived at the hospital to take Charles home. We knew the results of his biopsy wouldn't be ready, and that he was sore, but we all wanted to get out of the waiting area and go home to organize Christmas. The waiting seemed to take forever. I made a computer animated version of Charles and several other fit bodies with Charles's head on the top of them. I had them doing an Irish dance like the Chippendales. We laughed such a lot because the nurses were having a Christmas party in the next room and every time one appeared we thought it was for us, with the medication – but always turned out to be a cake instead. I began to steal some magazines in my anger at our being left without any answers as to Charles's discharge. The longer it went on, the angrier we got and Sarah, as a joke, picked up the entire stack of magazines and tipped them into her bag.

It seemed sudden. A man came over to us introducing himself as a member of the Palliative Care Team. I was

utterly flummoxed. I knew what the term meant, but I had no
idea why Charles would need it. The man himself seemed
confused, looked from Charles to me, he asked 'Is it OK to
talk?' 'What difference does it make now?' I thought, we are
in a public waiting place. The man, a bit shaken it seemed
proceeded to talk about his role as a pain relief specialist.
'OK' I thought. 'Can we just get the pain killers and go
please? Family are expecting us before tomorrow at least.
The palliative care representative left the room and another
much chattier doctor arrived, finally, with Charles's
medication. The three of us left, got into Sarah's car and
began rabbiting about managing to get up to the Dales by
lunchtime the following day, after all the fiasco with late
discharge and even later medication. Charles sat in the front
passenger seat and Sarah drove us home. In the back, I
held the large bag of medication and the discharge letter.
When I took out the envelope with the letter inside, there
was no writing on it and it was unsealed. Thinking I was
browsing Charles's pain relief plan from the bile duct stents,
I idly began to read. Thinking more about how soon we
could drive to my sister's home, I glanced down at the
printed information. As I started to read, I began to feel my
whole body had fallen down through my legs and out of the
car. The letter was not only regarding pain relief; it was a
diagnosis of terminal lung cancer. Cancer that had spread
into Charles's liver and into his bones. I looked up to see the
thick brown hair curving around the nape of my husband's
neck. I heard him brightly chat to Sarah. I tried to move my
head back down to the letter, but it seemed that my neck
had somehow seized up and I couldn't breathe. I couldn't
speak. In that moment, I knew the exact size of my
husband's tumor, the size of the area in his lung and liver
and all I could do was to smile about our journey for
Christmas. I could hardly hear Charles, as though his words
were being spoken to me through water or from a far distant
planet. I couldn't tell what I had just read, yet my life had
completely fallen into pieces. Sarah pulled up into our drive
and Charles went inside as it was cold. I closed the front
door after him and I stopped Sarah from getting back into
the car. 'It's cancer', I told her. 'Now you don't actually
KNOW that, do you? She smiled – knowing my propensity to

see the dreaded in everything. This time, the dreaded had manifested and I didn't know how to say the words. 'I do'. The words seemed to come out in a kind of drawl, and I thought I might be having a stroke. 'It's all in here', I pointed to the letter. I could feel the cold hard sting of what had begun and nothing else made sense. Our life together was over. Probably within weeks. Sarah was concerned and confused. I could feel the tears begin to ache out of my face but I waved her off. I carried the letter into the house. Charles was sitting on the reclining end of the sofa, looking at all the presents we had packed ready for the following day. We had supposed to have been driving to my sister's house that day, Christmas Eve but it was too late now, and Charles was tired. I tried to dissuade him from driving to the Yorkshire Dales at all, but he was determined. In his mind, we were already delayed. I didn't know what to do. I held the letter in my fist, wanting to burn it on the cooker. We had a window between our kitchen and sitting room, as the sitting room was a recent extension to our home. I shuffled up and down, moving around the kitchen with no purpose. I knew that Charles had not seen the diagnosis and if he had been told it, it was without my knowledge and he hadn't grasped what had been said. I held the thought, for a minute, that if I didn't give my husband the letter, then somehow it wouldn't be real and not the start of a fast track to death. I reasoned with myself however, that the information belonged to Charles and so I needed to hand it over. It wasn't my place to keep it from him.

'Do you want a coffee?' I shouted, putting on the kettle. 'OK' he shouted back. Such a simple transaction yet now it was priceless. Worth a thousand coffees. I took in his drink and without showing any emotion (as far as I can tell), I gave him the letter. 'Your discharge letter is here', I struggled to say, knowing I was handing my husband a death sentence.

I walked from the room and let him take the letter out of the envelope. I could see, through the kitchen window, how he read the indescribable words. He didn't look up. He simply put the letter down and drank his coffee. 'We'll drive up tomorrow as we agreed' he finally spoke. I was confused but I think I realised in that moment that this was how Charles would play the greatest role of his life. His death. He didn't cry and neither did I. We knew what was happening and we spent all our moments together. I knew we would never plan another hot holiday, never drive to my parents in York again, never go to another aerospace fun day and meet the Red Arrow pilots. In fact, we would be lucky even to watch a full season of our favourite drama and I doubted he would read another book.

The following morning, our neighbour Tony warmed up the car, I had told them our news. Charles helped me load the Christmas gifts, but the suspension on the boot of our car had broken and so lifting the boot was impossible. I struggled to do it, with Tony's help. As we drove to the Dales, I could not believe how beautiful the morning was. So clear so fresh and new. I wanted the weather to stay like this always. We arrived at Liff's house just in time for our vegetarian lunch, still not having spoken about the diagnosis. Mum and Dad were there at the house too and we all laughed, especially after our Christmas dinner. We sat in the three-hundred-year old living room. It was dimly lit by candles and the beams on the ceiling were hung with tinsel garlands and coffee pots. The wood burning stove seemed to beat out a surge of life for us as we played the word games we always did at Christmas. The laughter was the same and at that moment, it was easy to pretend the nightmare hadn't happened. We knew that this would be the last gathering with my family but we chose to make it timeless. I suppose that when Dot found out she was probably angry that Charles's last Christmas was spent with my family and not with her, but we had shared our time between the families well. We had taken Dot on holiday with us more than once and this Christmas, being the second one after the death of her daughter, she was happy for us to come back and spend time with her out of the festive season. Kathleen had always loved Christmas and Dot missed her beyond all else and couldn't even put up decorations as they caused her so much pain. Dot wasn't left alone however, she spent Christmas Day with her nephew (Sam's son) and his family. Sam, being the last brother to pass away had known he was dying too. The day we found out about his cancer, I cancelled my visit to York to be at home with Charles. It was a hot day and I had planned a picnic by the river with my good friend Cathy. Charles seemed irrationally angry that I had cancelled, as though he was refusing to allow death to change our plans. When Sam became very ill, the working men's club where he was Chairman held a large party in his honour. Dot, Kathleen, Charles, Lucy and I sat at the back of the room and watched Sam in his wheelchair and oxygen. We couldn't reconcile the party with the coming of Sam's death. How could we ever have imagined that both Charles and Kathleen would give us the same vigil. Charles and I tried to protect Dot from the coming tragedy. She didn't know what was about to descend on us as we had chosen not to tell anyone until we had all the facts in front of us. In fact, we didn't tell Dot until late January, after she had given her son the shirts and ties she had bought him for Christmas. We chose for Charles to wear the favourite shirt and tie from Dot's Christmas gift as his final outfit, when Dot, Sarah and I went to visit him in the Chapel of Rest. He held the pork pie hat we had laughed about so much, with the silk sprig of Ivy in it. Charles and I had been turned away from a restaurant when he wore the hat. Combined with my striped tights and vivid pink dress, we realised that they thought us travellers from a nearby traveller site. Charles also held the photo of me in a little frame which he carried round the different jobs and desks he had worked in since we got together.

In the month before Charles's death things seemed to strangely calm down. I struggled a great deal with Dot. Understandably she wanted to spend every moment with Charles. She had lost all her children and Charles was her last and her first-born. Charles decided when he wanted family and friends to know. Nobody believed my phone calls. We didn't want Dot to be any more stressed than she needed, but when the time was right, I had the job of ringing all the family and friends to tell them that Charles was dying and wouldn't be around for much longer. That day was one of the worst in living memory (which is saying something).

Charles was offered a form of chemotherapy to help the pain but sadly didn't get the chance to have it. The same day, a

problem occurred with our transport home from the hospital and we waited more than three hours for the hospital taxi. We had a relatively relaxed evening (as much as we could, knowing that he was fading fast). The following morning, my husband appeared to be freezing cold. His lips were blue. I bundled him up to bed and piled as many blankets and duvets as I could find. Then I rang the paramedics. When they arrived upstairs in the bedroom, I think I had my first small breakdown. His temperature was through the roof and the two lovely lady paramedics pulled all the covers from him. Charles was still the same to me. He hadn't deteriorated mentally at all. Even at Christmas he had held his mind still. My family had watched him walk to the car on our return journey home from Christmas and Mum said they had never seen a person deteriorate physically so fast yet be so mentally active. They had also known that it was the last time they would ever see him. How do you handle that? Knowing that the person before you – a big man, so deteriorated, would be leaving your friendship, your family forever. I held his feet in my hands, as the paramedics worked at the top end of his body. I kissed his feet and looked at him, knowing this was rapidly turning into the end. One of the paramedics turned to me and asked 'Do we have a DNR?' I didn't know what she meant. My husband was still alive and mentally fit. Then it struck me, that she was asking whether Charles should be resuscitated. I started moaning about the mess in the bedroom. Charles was carried downstairs on a stretcher and I was asked to prepare to accompany him in the ambulance. I became agitated at that moment and pointed out that I couldn't come to the hospital as I had ironing to do. I also had no socks on. Our neighbour Janice stood at the foot of the stairs as the stretcher came down. I stood still, staring at my feet. It's surprising how important feet become in a crisis. No socks. I couldn't possible go without socks on.
Janice took the socks from her own feet and put them on to mine.

Helen Mary Barr

Chapter Two
Leaves on Canvass

The phone calls started not long after Charles was admitted. I was due to graduate from my Masters degree in Humanities, in January 2014. My plans for the day had been long in the making and I was looking forward to them. My good friend Rob, a lovely man in his early twenties who made me laugh like a lunatic with his plain speaking, was due to meet myself and my family at the Graduation Ceremony. The year had been incredible, and lectures where usually only four of us participated found my brain crackling as it expanded. My first day at the University of Leicester saw me queue up for the induction, wearing a shocking pink denim skirt and leather jacket. When I found my room, I was shocked to find only the four of us, two student doctors, Rob and myself. The first thing Rob ever said to me, on that first day when I was convinced there had been a mistake and I was not really a Masters student, was simply 'You've got to be a mature student. Aren't you?' I creased up at the sight of his face, not knowing whether I looked like an old sheep, or a lamb to the slaughter. My painting, poetry and audio work based around the theme of sexual violence against women was being exhibited at the 'Speaking Out' exhibition, Embrace Arts Gallery in Leicester. I found the subject a bit revealing as I read my pages in the gallery catalogue.

Excited more than I can say to see my painting exhibited alone and lit on a white wall, and the wonderful write up of my work by the exhibition curator, talking about my use of autobiographical collage and a house hold squeegee didn't feel real somehow. It reminded me a little of my interview with the Guardian Weekend Magazine a bit too revealing, but on this occasion, within my control.

'Helen Mary Barr is an artist, published poet and author. She returned to education after bringing up her two children and studied Media (word/radio), Communications, English Literature and English Language, obtaining special commendation for her work by William Sterling (BBC-TV

Helen Mary Barr

Film and Television Producer/Writer, September Film Productions). She is a qualified counsellor and completed an MA from the University of Leicester in 2013. She was presented with the Lifetime Member Award of the Millennium Association by Rt Hon Tessa Jowell in 2001 in recognition of services to Mental Health through the Arts. Her radio programme was first aired in 2001'.

On first moving in with Charles in our tiny rented Coventry home, before we were married, he made it quite clear 'You can have a full-time job – there won't be any swanning about sticking leaves on canvass'. When my picture for the Leicester gallery was finished, eight years on, I made a point of sticking two leaves on the canvas, just for Charles.

As an apology for one of Charles's outbursts, he bought me a year's membership to the Tate Modern. The museum soon became my own hide-away. I could get on a train at Nuneaton, arrive in London and be on the door of the Tate Modern in under two and a half hours. I filmed myself on my first visit, chattering away into my camera and playing with the reflections as I entered the main entrance. I had come to see Damien Hirst, prepared to hate his shark and his pharmacy. Before entering the exhibition I took myself to the café where I ordered a plastic bowl of salad and a coffee. Sitting at the table, looking out towards St Paul's Cathedral from the Member's Gallery, I examined the images on the wall and all around my plate. I looked at them over and over, trying to decipher the art. I counted four forks on the dish, perhaps I thought, this was a tribute to the late great Ronnie Barker? After all, being in the Tate could mean anything. I felt a sudden surge of creativity from my perspective as a member. It took around ten minutes before I realised that I was attempting to do an academic reading of the food information. I gave myself a laugh as I pondered my perspective (but hastily stopped this before I became too much of an art arse). I loved Damien Hirst.

How my river runs

January came and I decided not to attend the graduation
ceremony. Mum and Dad had been due to come, along with
Charles and Dot. We were to visit the gallery, have lunch in
the café and then go on to the ceremony. I couldn't stomach
it. Charles had supported me through my Masters degree,
picking me up late in the evening after a day driving home
from Luton and eating fish and chips with me as I didn't have
time to cook. So I made a decision. Sarah picked up my cap
and gown, Lucy came over to stay and I 'swanned' into the
ward where Charles was hooked up to monitors. I got a few
odd glances but I didn't care because I just wanted my
husband to see what he had created – leaves on canvas
and all. Lucy took the pictures and it was the best graduation
with a black red and silver gown, that I could have thought
of. No ceremony, just us and what we had achieved.
Afterwards, I went home and snuck into Janice and Tony's
garden. They had a small pond with a bridge. I stood on the
bridge and with tears streaming down my face, I posed for
my photo's, with my daughter.

At least three times I was called into the hospital as Charles
was fading. I sat by his bed until morning. I watched how
hard it was for him to use the commode. At first I had
thought that his mind was beginning to falter very quickly,
which it did. However, this was only hours since he had
spoken quite coherently. During the night, a nurse came to
catheterize Charles. I was sitting between his bed and a
large window, looking out over Leicester city centre. In the
dim light from the bedside lamp I looked the other way
because I felt compelled to respect his privacy and dignity.
He didn't know that I could see him clearly in the reflection of
the glass. It broke my heart to watch his life stripped away
and to see it happening from the remote place I had now
arrived at. This quiet moment showed me the end.

In the early hours of the morning, I would answer the phone
to hear the now familiar beeping of hospital equipment. 'I'm
desperate to see you', he said. 'There's a man here with a
gun and he is going to kill me'. I talked and talked and then a
nurse asked me to come in to the ward. It was around three
in the morning. My angel friend Sarah, despite having work

the following day, came to pick me up. I don't drive which limits things for me, and how I would have got through this journey without her, I will never know. We arrived at the hospital just as dawn began to tickle the sky. The Ward Sister took us immediately to one side. 'He's fading now, and it would be good if you could just be there and help us to know how he feels'. Sarah and I sat beside Charles's bed. He opened his eyes and smiled at us. 'Hey … ladies, what are you doing here?' 'We missed you', we said 'and thought you might like the company'. The three of us sat chatting. Morning began to take over and it seemed that Charles still had plans for it. We needed to get some rest, for what could be Charles's last day. Sarah took me home and then told me that I was to go to bed. She would wait by the phone to take the call. Her Mum arrived too to help with the situation. They didn't want me to get the news of his death first hand, they wanted to tell me themselves in a gentler way. I will never ever forget that kindness. Never.

However, the call didn't come. I received telephone messages many times and each time, Sarah took me into hospital. Charles was a proud and strong man. He didn't want his food cutting up for him, in fact he choked himself trying to eat a sausage. We both laughed at that in a more lucid moment. As the cancer went to his brain, the requests became more and more strange. He wanted me to make him a picnic, which I did, knowing he would never eat it. He began to accuse all the nursing staff of trying to kill him and he launched at them with his walking stick. On ringing his Mum one night, with the story of another intruder on the ward, Dot rang the police. I knew I shouldn't be angry but it was so ridiculous and made things so much harder. Dot was a lady in permanent grief and had been from the moment I met her. How do you console the woman who has lost everything and yet deal with your own loss at the same time?

My Father came from York to visit Charles. He is a softly spoken Cumbrian man with an infectious humour and a family history washed in tragedy too. This having been washed new by his tiny, beautiful mother (my grandma) with her love, sunshine and dedication to her family. He had wanted to see Charles one more time, after our Christmas get-together. He had also come to try and help me with the finances as I didn't have a clue about any of it. Dad and I hadn't seen eye to eye for much of my childhood yet I never doubted his genuine love for our family or the fact that he would always do everything he could to keep us safe. I don't think I realized until the day of his visit, how deeply he felt everything and how the depths could rise in him too.

None of us could keep Charles safe, we could only be with him as he left us.

I decided to buy Charles lots of airplane magazines, as his first love was aerospace. He had worked his way up to the top of his career as a commodity manager with sheer grit and determination. Just four months before his terminal diagnosis, Charles had started his own business and so we rented a flat in Bournemouth so that he could be near to his first contract during the week. It had been an amazing summer. The beach was hot and shiny and I studied for my Master's dissertation from a deck chair. I recall it as a strange and beautiful time, almost a preparation for what was to come. I spent hours on my own walking and thinking, just enjoying the beach and the sea. On the hottest day of the year, I walked along the shore from Southsea into Bournemouth. I even went into a bar alone and ordered a large lemonade … something unheard of (not the lemonade, but the idea that I might order at a bar)! On my birthday, I treated myself to breakfast at the 'Luna Lounge' (our favourite place) I had pancakes with blueberries, and I took a picture on my phone. Then I had a large tattoo of a hummingbird drinking from a lotus flower inked onto my shoulder blade.

It feels almost comforting to have loved this day as one I spent alone.
As I have moved forward with my Shamanic therapeutic studies, I have taken to having my power animals inked onto my skin. Alongside the swan, now surrounded by leaves of every season, I have a stag on my left arm and a passion flower on my left shoulder blade.

The day Charles and I moved into the flat, I had a very strange experience. Due to my medication, (Lithium at the time, plus Quetiapine) I don't often feel moved to tears. As we unpacked the things we needed for our time there, I was suddenly moved to near hysteria. Tears streamed down my face and I grabbed Charles. 'I feel like I'm going to lose everything' I yelled at him. 'I'm not going anywhere' Charles looked at me oddly.

The day we hastily packed up the flat, it was a cold, dark January afternoon. In the pouring rain, Janice and Tony rushed the things we had bought into a mini-van belonging to Janice's brother. I ran into the café up the road that I had loved having breakfast at so much, and bought four pieces of my favourite flapjack. As I finished emptying the flat's freezer, I found a box with two chicken portions inside. Something in me broke and I slumped onto the kitchen floor. Janice pulled me up and at the same time, Tony was holding Charles, who too, had slumped onto the floor in pain.

Dad and I went into the ward to find Charles. He never actually made it onto the oncology ward, and I still don't know why to this day. When he saw us, Charles started shouting 'We need tea here, these people have come from York'! Dad and I smiled as Charles had forgotten that I had only come to see him from our home, a couple of miles away. Mind you, he winked so I think he was doing what was necessary to get us all tea.

He looked intently at the magazines and I found that look heart-breaking. I couldn't wrap my head around holding interest in something when your life was ending. I had felt this first on Christmas Day. We had all given our gifts out and Charles, knowing for only a few hours that he was soon to pass away, began to read his book and put on the scarf he had been bought. I didn't know how to talk about life with him let alone death. I did it, but conversation felt strained and pointless.

Dad and I drank our tea and went to wait outside for Sarah to collect us. When we got home, I was coming down the stairs and my dad was in the front room. He didn't see or hear me. My Dad is very deaf and so I could move around without disturbing him. He was on the phone to my mother. I could see and hear that he was crying. I also heard Mum asking him to stop and to be strong for me. He was.

A week before Charles died, he was discharged to come home.
My husband arrived home in a wheelchair, at eleven o'clock at night. Exactly one week prior to this, the consultant had given him a hip replacement, for palliative pain relief. Of course, Dot jumped on this as a sign of hope. Charles, eloquent as always, told her about the treatment he was being given and that he would be home soon. I have never in my life seen anything so ridiculous. A terminally ill man, in his last days, a hip replacement – discharged home with not a single aid that would be normally put in place for a discharged hip replacement. By then, I had the hospital bed set up in the living room. I could see it from the kitchen window and it seemed a lifetime ago that I watched my husband read the discharge letter through it, telling him he was going to die. I was left alone with no support, no help, no night nurse.

I tried to lift Charles into the bed but of course he was in agony. I had not been supplied with any male bed pans and was expected to move him (still a dead weight) backwards and forwards to the toilet. I rang the number I had been given to call and was told to wash out a milk bottle for him to use. My strong and clever husband, reduced to peeing in a milk bottle. I don't think I will ever understand how we went from New Year's Eve, 2013, where I remained downstairs watching Jools Holland (something we always did together), and Charles sitting upstairs at his computer, to his death nine weeks later. I had simply joined him in the office, looking at telescopes. Charles had always wanted one and not knowing how fast death would find him, we decided to buy one for him. We smiled, as the model he chose was not yet in stock. 'That's no good', we laughed 'You haven't got time to wait for it to come in'. That was the last time we shared a joke, albeit macabre. From then on, the jokes were no longer funny. The moldy picnic Charles had me make for him, the nurses who were trying to kill him, the many calls to come for his last hours only to find his smiling face instead. Not funny. I clung on to it all, to every spark of life left in him.

That night we gave no acknowledgement that 2014 had arrived, because it would be the year of the end.
I had planned the last days before Charles passed away with great care. His bed was facing our large TV and I recorded many of his favourite programs in the naïve belief that we would watch them together, lying on the comfortable mattress and talking. I don't know what we would have talked about. How can you chat about anything when every hour could be your last? Charles however, couldn't talk. He was absent and his eyes were empty windows. The TV was never switched on and the mattress had a rubber cover over it. We did laugh, as I tried to manage the raising and lowering of the bed, but he slept most of the time. Dot, who had come to stay until the end took over completely (and I know that this should have been a sacred time between us both) was overwhelmed by her desire to mother her eldest child and this completely took over. She said to me 'I've got him back', and I remembered the days when Charles and I had laughed as she tried very hard to split our relationship up. I have chosen to talk about our beginnings after the ending because it will make more sense and will bring him alive again.

I was sitting next door with my neighbour Janice and Dot began hammering at the kitchen window holding a pint glass full of blood, fluid and phlegm. 'We have to show this to the nurse' she shouted. Janice, a trained care nurse took the glass from her and firmly responded 'The nurse doesn't need you to give her this, she knows what is happening'. I could see the terror in Dot's face. 'Please come with me' I asked Janice and she threw her apron on, a bit like a superhero and ran with us to make Charles more comfortable. Later that day, Dot, Janice and I were sitting in my front room. Dot began to speak to me in a nasty tone of voice. She could barely form her words and spat out the opinion that I was responsible for taking Charles away from Coventry to Leicestershire. Right at that moment, for good or for bad, I let lose my anger at this pathetic idea, made far

How my river runs

worse by Charles's nephew, Kathleen's son. Wayne had never forgiven the relationship his uncle and I had made, and he ruined what could have been a happy family with his drinking and his aggressive behaviour. The sad thing was that Wayne could have been a big part of our life in Barwell, but his inability to let Charles be his own man and move away into his own life made holidays and visits difficult. Three years down the line, Wayne still sent me evil messages on the internet and only the intervention of Michael put this right. I have remained in contact with William's wife who was also treated shabbily by the family after William's death more than twenty years prior to Charles and I getting married. Most recently, I contacted Dot at Christmas as I felt it was right to acknowledge the water that had gone under the bridge, and to make a new bridge. She was happy about my telephone call and Charles's ashes are now back at home with her in Coventry.

The day Charles died, I took full control of the event. We had care nurses washing him every couple of hours, Dot, who I couldn't move from the bedside and my daughter who had arrived to help. It's odd, because I don't remember Lucy arriving at all. As we were nearing the end, and we were medicating him with syringes into his mouth, I suddenly became very clear and focused. Charles was bringing up blood and it was intolerable for him, he knew we were all there. It began with the urge to call our family doctor, who had supported us through so many situations. 'Can I move him to a hospice Doctor'? I pleaded. 'Normally I would say he won't make the journey, but I advise you to take him. Go.' Within minutes (or so it seemed) an ambulance was outside and only I could accompany Charles. It was the first time we had been alone and I knew this was the last. I held his hand and I talked to him about all the things we had done, in the nine years we had been together. I laughed and told him we were eloping away from his mum. At the start of our relationship, Dot had made it her business to send me packing back home to York. I also knew that some of Charles's friends felt I had somehow stolen him from Coventry and taken him away to Leicestershire.

Helen Mary Barr

We arrived at the hospice and on entering, suddenly, everything became calmer. I know I can't have imagined it, but a choir of children were singing the song 'Titanium'. Charles was put in a beautiful bed, with a patchwork quilt the colour of Spring. I was given a chair and a cup of tea. Peace. Within minutes, Dot, Sarah and Lucy arrived. We all sat calmly around the bed. It was then that a nurse came to us and asked if we would like to see the chapel. Dot, Sarah and myself went, leaving Lucy to read to Charles. Charles was an avid reader and we had picked up a history book about the Roman Empire (his favourite period). The chapel was beautiful, circular with shafts of coloured light and gentle music playing. We thought it fascinating that the music was that of Tibetan Singing Bowls, Sarah's expertise. Quietly, a nurse guided us back to Charles's bed. He was letting go. Lucy was struggling as she had seen it first. The nurse lifted my husband up into her arms. I couldn't believe how fragile he was, and how I hadn't seen the change take place. She felt his pulse. 'Have we lost him'? I asked. 'Yes'.

I walked across to where Dot was sitting and I knelt before her. I took her hands in mine, and I said 'He's gone'. 'He's with Kathleen and William, Albert, Wall and Sam. They will take care of him now. At this point, two of Charles's nephews, Wayne and Ali arrived and Dot began the process of ringing people. Charles was washed and dressed. We all sat in a comfortable room filled with large brown sofas. A small picture hung on the wall next to the light switch. It was a painting of a swan.

Wayne refused to even acknowledge my presence and looked right through me. Suddenly, Dot grabbed my hand and also Wayne's hand. She pushed us together. It was a strong gesture but I knew it wouldn't change how he felt about me. We were then able to see Charles. Fresh flowers had been picked and placed around his head on the pillow. However, it was clear to see that he had not died peacefully. I am positive that my husband became at peace immediately after his passing, but the sight of him was distressing for us all. His face looked twisted and agonized. Sarah, Dot and I visited Charles a few days later however, in the Chapel of Rest. We were warned that Charles was slightly raised up and facing us. Having only ever seen one body, eighteen months earlier, that of Charles's sister Kathleen, I was afraid. Sarah had also no experience of viewing a body.

I felt that I couldn't get near to him and yet there were only the three of us in the room. Sarah tried to help me to touch his skin but he was too cold. I slipped the bell from our cat Mildred, who had also died into the coffin. I immediately worried that it would ring during the funeral and I hadn't told the funeral director. We decided not to say anything and keep it a secret. Despite looking peaceful, even down to his beautiful crooked smile, and the ring of thick brown hair, it was clear that he had left and we were looking at an empty shell. It was at that point that I knew, for sure, that there was a heaven and I was not deluded.

Lucy, with all her amazing support, her little notebook and pen with which she sorted out the estate came with Sarah, Dot and I to arrange the funeral. We chose 'Let it Be' sung by Paul McCartney and the Beatles instead of a hymn, 'You are not alone' by The Eagles and a coffin painted with a sunset and Spitfires all over it. When the hearse arrived and stopped outside the front of our Barwell home, Michael came to tell me. 'Is he here'? I asked. Michael nodded. I walked to the car and put my hands on the glass, close to Charles. I had asked for a single wreath, made from wild flowers, shaped like a heart. I couldn't feel him there, he wasn't there. Lucy, Michael and I climbed into the front seat with me in between them. Dot and Kathleen's two sons sat behind. I know I must have made them angry. I couldn't stop talking, raised by mania resulting from the enormity of blocked pain. I gave a running commentary as we drove to the crematorium, pointing out places we had been for meals, even supermarkets we shopped at. Michael on my right and Lucy on my left, held my hands and it was all very strange. My parents travelled with Janice and Tony. We arrived, and all I could see were crowds of people standing waiting for us to arrive. My lovely friend Rob, who I had studied for my Master's degree with, had travelled on his own to support me. He raised his hand to greet me as I saw him through the glass. I was moved beyond belief to see a number of my good friends from York who had come to be with me. Mostly, the crematorium was full to the brim with Charles's friends and family. As I got out from the car, Marco came straight to greet me. He had organized six of Charles's closest friends to carry the casket. I felt as though I was handing him back to them, to the Mercians, to lay their own to rest.

Charles had good friends, and a number of them called themselves 'the halfway round the world' club. They certainly had visited many places, from New York to Turkey. We filed into the crematorium and Sarah played 'Spring' from 'The four Seasons', Vivaldi on her flute. Marco had asked if it was Ok for him to say a few words. I was so glad that he did. Without prompts, Marco spoke about his friendship with Charles. He told the packed room that he believed Charles to have been happier in the last nine years than he had ever been before. His words raised a spontaneous round of applause as he finished with 'I am privileged to have known Charles, I would have liked to have travelled around the rest of the world with him, but if I can be half the man he was, I will have succeeded'.

I had written a poem and as the vicar read it, a plane flew over, almost on command.
I stood outside the crematorium with Michael and Joy, the Funeral Director who had done so much for us. 'When do they cremate the body'? Michael asked. I felt a little exposed by this question, not sure if I wanted to know. 'Now,' Joy answered. We need to do it straight away. Michael and I looked at one another and took a deep breath.
It was done.

Chapter Three
The Doll's House

E mail transcript, Internet Dating Site.
'I am looking for a lady albatross. I have many camels and will travel'.
'Morning Nell, I must have come across as a complete idiot last night, nervous, stupid and coming out with some real nonsense at times! Anyway …;>) All I can say in my defense is …. I've been trawling the BBC/Nature websites for albatross DVDs. ;>) No luck yet, but I'll keep trying. It was a bit like a "live" version of your bat emails ;>) (I keep losing the plot)!   & …… I truly would like to meet Helen Mary Barr. Love Charles. Xxxxxxxx (Your bat)'.
You see, this is what happens when you try to email the guy you've just met on a dating website and you attempt to write 'Dear Babe'. Bat appears in its place. A lot can go wrong on a little computer in a little bedroom in York – whilst trying to reach someone you don't know in Coventry.

'I'm going to hang upside down in the loft for an hour now – like a good little bat, it might do me good')!
' Nell? Are you OK? I am worried about you, is your mobile OK? I have sent you two texts and you haven't responded. Please let me know you are alright'.
Charles xxxxxxxxxxx

'What do you do on a Friday Night? It varies with me but this weekend (tomorrow night) I am in with my nose in a book and a beer in the fridge. I could call you then? Let me know? If you are out that's find (really fine, please don't change any plans????) – we can arrange Saturday or something. We need to talk sooner rather than fall victim to email failures or even email misunderstandings. Some things can only be said live on the phone. (wow this all sounds serious)! Let me know what you think please my little bird that soars the southern oceans)'!
'Good morning Nell)! I hope you are feeling a very positive young lady today because I love you :>) I will always love you. Your Charles xxxxxxxxxxx'

October 2005. After two unsuccessful meetings via internet dating, I had just about given up the search. The first, Jason, was a man who took every single hair from his body so that he could reach higher speeds on his racing bicycle. I allowed myself to feel something other than rejection so I went to his bedsit without knowing what kind of person he was. When I arrived at his flat and he opened the door, I was bemused to see a line of candles right down either side of the hallway. More candles were neatly arranged in the living room and a tall, rather beautiful fish tank stood in the corner, with one elegant fish inside of it. As I looked around the room in the shadowy candlelight I began to feel a little out of place. Jason had prepared a meal and I felt even more out of my comfort zone, when he handed me a tray with neatly folded kitchen paper and a perfectly round plate of curry on an even more perfect circle of rice. After the meal, Jason came to sit next to me on the black leather sofa. I had begun to get used to the lighting and I was aware that the whole room was decorated as perfectly matched as the curry. Only black and white framed photography of trees were on the walls and every image matched the next.

As he began to pull me towards him I felt the untimely sobs begin to pour. Needless to say, after Jason returned me home to my haphazard little house, I realised that I wouldn't be eating any more round curries.

A week or so later, I received another message from the dating site. Vic wanted to meet me. There was no picture but I immediately and naively gave out my telephone number. Vic began to ring numerous times every day and I told him about my experience with Jason. We arranged to meet in my favourite Bistro, Habitat, right in the town centre. I hadn't wanted a relationship with Jason, but every failed attempt at grabbing something worth keeping left me more engulfed by the end of my marriage to Francis. When I walked into Habitat I spotted the man I thought was Vic. Tall and much older than I had imagined he bought me a glass of white wine. I couldn't work him out. He didn't say too much but looked at me in the eyes for most of the time. Without much conversation, I decided to end the date and go home. Vic however asked to see me again so I agreed thinking that he might need more time to talk about his life, himself and what he hoped for. Vic gave me his address, which was a flat not far from my parent's house. I don't know why I thought this would be safer but I do believe that I wanted desperately to find something genuine.

I took a taxi to the flat and knocked on the door. Looking back now I can see that my mental state was not at its best. In my bag, I had packed a pair of hand knitted slippers, rather like those a child would wear. They had monkey heads stitched onto the front. In my mind, I believed that Vic would not be dangerous because he would see by my slippers that I wasn't visiting him for sex, but for companionship.

Vic opened the door (bearing in mind that he knew all about Jason and his candles) and I almost laughed and cried at the same time. This had all the hallmarks of an opening to a horror film. Vic stood at the door, wearing nothing but grey boxer short underpants and holding an old jam jar with a tall battered white candle slumped in it. Vic had promise me something nice to eat and as I looked at the bag of crisps in the middle of the table I really ought to have turned and run. However, I didn't. Desperation and trust are a lethal combination. 'Let's go listen to some music,' Vic said, without raising so much as half a smile. 'What bands do you like?' I asked him. 'The Killers', he answered. Now, bearing in mind that I didn't know that the Killers really were a band, I should have fled. Still I didn't. 'Where is your CD player?' I looked around the room. 'It's here', he pointed at what I assumed was the bedroom. At that point, I sat down and put on my slippers. Following Vic into the bedroom was probably the single most stupid thing I could have done (and trust me, there have been lots of them). 'Lie down,' he said, 'I'll but the Killers on'. I lay there, on the bed, wearing my slippers.

Vic, a large man, tall, as I have said, began his rather forceful attempt at kissing me. I began to feel overwhelmed and unsafe. He continued his moves and I continued to try and prevent him, by commenting on the Killers and how much I liked their music (having only heard them that night for the first time). I began to feel as though I owed this man something and that if I was prepared to go to his house, and lie on his bed, then perhaps I was in the wrong place at the wrong time, but a mistake of my own making. Vic began to demonstrate the belief that I was in his bedroom because I was prepared to have sex with him. I was confused, having come out of a twelve-year marriage where sex had dwindled to almost nothing, in the last five years. I wondered if this was how real life played out and perhaps I was acting like a child.

So, I attempted to respond to Vic and he hovered over me like a bison, ready to reach his grunt. I fell away before he did. The tears began to fall all over me, once again and only stopped as a frozen shock when I realised that this man had no sympathy for me or my slippers. I pulled myself onto the floor and said 'I'd better go'. 'Yes', he answered, free of all emotion. I got to the door and let myself out, running onto the main road. I dragged the phone from my bag and rang my best friend Xanthe. 'Get a taxi over to my house, now', she ordered, worried – I could tell. So by midnight I was at my friend's house, on her sofa, with her pet rat and her cockatiel 'Birdy'. I still wore my slippers and I had a large mug of tea. Safe, I began to feel even more sad and didn't see the darkness appearing over the horizon. As I slipped into the hands of deep depression I vowed that I would take my name from the internet dating site.

I was sitting at my computer, up in the bedroom, in the process of deleting my file when I

received a message from 'Lord Asriel 500'. He sounded rather arrogant I thought but also more than a bit interesting. I returned his email and was especially interested that a female friend had written his profile for him. Messages passed backwards and forwards, unable to meet easily because he lived in Coventry. Tentatively we arranged to speak on the telephone. Lord Asriel 500 was in fact a well-travelled, respectful man named Charles. The first night we spoke, he was so nervous that the messages kept arriving 'Any minute now, I will ring. Any minute. I promise, any minute'. When Charles did manage to pluck up the courage to ring, he held the phone against the little waterfall he had built for his Mum's garden. I think he had had a few beers as he kept walking around instead of sitting still. He told me that

he owned two houses, that his Mum came to visit and his sister lived opposite, a house he owned also. Within a few weeks, I discovered that Charles didn't own a house at all, and lived with his Mum. It made me smile however, as Charles took good care of both his Mum and he sister, also his nephews. Charles had a great job in aerospace and could easily have owned a house. Within the next three years, Charles bought two houses and worked his way from the ground up, to owning his own business, 'Pantheon Supply Chain' (my idea for a name).
We spoke on the telephone for seven hours one night during which I drank a full bottle of Lemon cello, smoked a packet of fags (I didn't smoke), became rather lude and then sobered up. Charles's Mother appeared at some point and announced in the background rather aggressively, 'You will have a bill'!

We decided that Charles would come to York at the weekend and he asked me to book him into a 'good' hotel. Right, thought I. The Churchill Hotel, where we had enjoyed my Sister's wedding and lots of other family occasions sat at the end of the road where my little detached rented house was situated. The house looked as though a doll lived there, one room wide. At the time, Lucy (then seventeen) and I lived together. Lucy wasn't speaking to me for most of the time as she hadn't forgiven me for my first suicide attempt. She couldn't understand why I would want to leave her and was traumatized by our journey to hospital in the ambulance. February 2nd 2005 marked the end of my twelve-year marriage to Francis and it wasn't pretty. It was messy and excruciating, revealing and horrifying. Having been at work teaching in the family school, 'Premier', I had come home to cook tea. I sat on the sofa. I had put on so much weight as a side effect of the anti-psychotic medication, and I was so tired, but Francis had begun to treat me like a stranger and not even a stranger that he was decent to. The nastiness in his voice and the horrible things he said were devastating to me. Comments about being a 'fat mad cow' and 'not getting off my arse to work', when I had just completed a BA in Counselling, a Teaching Diploma and worked two days a week teaching, also cleaning the school, were distressing and confusing. As I sat there, I looked at the man I had been married to for over a decade and I realised that I didn't recognize him. 'You don't love me any more do you'? I asked him, sitting on the large coffee table with short legs as I had decided to cut them off.

'No'. He answered. After everything we had been through together, the nonsense and the serious, I was lost. I didn't know what to say. Lucy had her friend staying over to tea and the two of them were upstairs in Lucy's bedroom. Francis began looking for his passport. I became hysterical. It turned out later that he only needed it for identification on something connected to his work. I didn't know this. Outside Lucy's door, I lay on my side screaming. Francis stepped over me and I felt him sneer. Part of me wanted to bite him and make him bleed.
I gathered my thoughts, became focused and went to the bathroom cupboard.
After swallowing every tablet I had in the cupboard, I called Michael and Lucy into the bedroom to tell them what I had done. I was calm and unemotional, thinking only that I did not have a life worth living and that they would understand this. Lucy called the ambulance and the only contact made with Francis was his attempt to put my shoes on. I kicked at him and told him I refused to die in the shoes he had chosen. Feet, again.

Beyond that, I tore my wedding ring off in the ambulance and Lucy was on her knees trying to find it. She spent the rest of the journey and many hours in the hospital trying to convince me that I had a life worth saving. Not what you want for your child.
My good friend Clare, who had seen the ambulance arrive, went to collect Mum and Liff who arrived at the hospital and obviously, things were very sombre indeed. I needed the toilet, so my sister helped me from the bed, where I had been drinking the charcoal milkshake needed to absorb the poison of the overdose, prior to their arrival. We got into the loo, and my Sister said 'I don't want to upset you, but did you choose to put on black lipstick as a gesture to us of your intention to die?' I didn't have a clue what she was talking about until I looked in the mirror and saw my black lips,

caused by the charcoal –What on earth must they have thought of me… that I would make such an artistic statement with lipstick?

When alone and attempting to help the nurse feed a drip of fluids through the arm of my nightdress, the river rose beyond my nostrils. I was in an ordinary ward in the general hospital as opposed to the psychiatric hospital. Most nurses are beautiful in their ability to care no matter what the cause of pain. The nurse who attached the tube for me was silent. The black lips gesture makes me feel out of control, even hysterical. Even in the midst of death, there is art to be had. (Especially in the midst of death).

Ten months on and I repeated the scenario, only then, 10th December 2005, it was Charles who got me to the hospital. That same tunnel vision and resolute focus seeped into my veins, but when he left to go back to Coventry from York, my room was empty with no visitors. My sister arrived later and I was never more glad to see her face. My nephew blocked up the sink with toilet paper and I felt just like it, stuffed and dammed.

I suppose that families get sick of trying to convince you that your life is worth saving.
One by one, I took the tablets with a glass of milk. Then I heard Charles coming downstairs. In my desperation to get the rest of the tablets into my stomach I began to shove handfuls into my mouth as fast as I could. Charles launched himself at me and thrust his hand into my mouth in an attempt at dragging them out. I bit him. Hearing all the noise, Michael ran downstairs and taking one look at me, rang an ambulance.

When the paramedics arrived into our quiet cul-de-sac, I was appalled. I refused to leave and didn't want to be seen. The paramedics told me that if I didn't leave with them they would have no choice but to make me go. I left because I didn't want Michael to be embarrassed. He'd seen it earlier that year and I didn't think it was fair to give him more of my suicide memories. Charles got into the ambulance with me.

His nephew, who was visiting with Charles hadn't yet arrived back at the house from town so Michael waited for him. I am so glad that he wasn't around for my overdose as I later discovered that in his teens, he had tried to save the lady next door as she lay unconscious and full of pills. He had been unable to succeed.

As I got to the hospital, the cot sides on the bed were put up and I was given the charcoal to drink. This time though, only Charles was by my side. He telephoned my family but as it was so late at night, nobody took the call. A forceful nurse with short grey hair told me in no uncertain terms that if I didn't drink all the charcoal then I would die. Charles, now gentle and caring begged me to drink it. Which I did. Charles and his nephew stayed at my house that night. Despite later years when we took six cats into our home, Charles was not a cat lover. When he woke the following morning, my cat Willow was sitting on his chest staring down at him. I loved that image and it helped me cope when Charles seemed unsettled. He came to the hospital the day after and asked me what I needed. When I asked for underwear, he asked me, in a state of genuine confusion 'Does it have to be matching'? I laughed and laughed. I don't think I owned any matching underwear but the question made me realize how vulnerable Charles was also.

When he left that day, with his nephew in tow, the darkness had begun to settle in. I had brought a crochet blanket into hospital with me, as some kind of comfort. I got out of bed, got dressed and folded up the comfort blanket. A doctor came to visit me. She asked me if I ever felt elated or high. I looked at her and with a strange kind of anger I shouted 'I do not have Bipolar Disorder. I am leaving'. I immediately discharged myself, left the blanket on the bed and walked out, in my miss-matched underwear.

Whilst waiting for my taxi, I telephoned a new friend Kirk whom I had met through my own website which I had built as a support for mental health through the arts. Kirk lived in Bristol. 'Come and see me', he said. And I did.

I'll tell you later.

How my river runs

Lucy and I had moved out of the family home into the 'doll's house' in April of 2005, after Francis and I broke up, February 2nd. My family and a few friends, also Michael's friends turned up to help Lucy and I move in. Francis stood by the van and did not venture into the house. I think he was afraid of the reaction he might get. At that time, he was a coward without honour.

Lucy and I went to Gibraltar for a week on holiday. The role reversal had really come into play and was never more obvious than when we visited Morocco. It rained and the narrow alley ways were slippery and dangerous coupled with the intrusive (abusive) shouting of the men and their jewellery items. I could not stop laughing and giving money to anyone who entertained me at all. Arriving at the café with no proper floor where we were due to eat, a little band of musicians each wearing a fez gathered around to play. I wanted to tip them, so I opened my purse and handed each musician a ten pound note. Before Lucy could snatch away my purse, the musicians devoted themselves to following us around smiling and hoping for more cash. I loved Morocco but I managed to purchase a large rug, which had to be brought home with us and also to buy a baby camel. Nobody else on the coach wanted a camel ride, but I did. I love camels. The ground had turned to mud but leapt off the coach and was greeted by bangles and rings, plus a fez of my own. I got on the camel, happy beyond hysteria whilst the coach watched, dumfounded. I paid another ten pounds for a fifty pence request, and was given a baby camel. Lucy managed to get me back onto the coach. We also went on a dolphin watch where I became very angry at the Spanish schoolchildren who I believed were frightening the dolphins. We had a great time though on the whole, eating afternoon tea and spending money. After Charles died, Lucy and I went to a wonderful spa hotel in Tenerife. I became obsessed with spa treatments and spent every day having massage therapy and floatation experiences.

Whilst newly single, and prior to my internet adventures I decided to take a life drawing class. The college was not far from the house I had shared with Francis and I thought I would call over to collect more of my stuff and see the cats. My cats were an important part of my life. I was only able to take one cat with me, so I chose my black and white lady, Willow. I began walking to the house and on my way, Francis sent me a text.

'There might be a young woman in the house cooking my tea. Please be nice to her'.

I was so angry that I think I flew through the streets. Letting myself in, thankfully the house was empty. I looked around and saw the trappings of another woman. There was a trifle in the fridge and clothes in the bedroom. I checked the size. I contemplated putting the trifle all over the bedsheets, in what had been my bed. In the end, I telephoned Michael (from the house phone) and asked him to come and collect me. John had bought Michael a little car and it was proving a Godsend. I waited for him to arrive and then loaded as many of my belongings into the boot as I could. I chose not to smear trifle as this would simply illustrate that I was a nutter. I was tempted though, really tempted.

Not long after this, Francis's 'young woman' decided she wanted to meet me.

I arrived at what had been my house and knocked on the door. It was a knocker I had chosen with great care, as I had also chosen the door, not that long ago. In fact, it was only six months since it was the door to my house. It seemed as though I was knocking on the door to my past and asking for permission to enter. I didn't know how to feel. Rosy appeared and gave me a hug, more out of nervousness I suspect. She invited me into the kitchen, the one I had lovingly painted and rebuilt just the year before. Picking up the kettle, I think she realized the strange situation we found ourselves in, and she said, 'You know how to put this kettle on'. I laughed. I had brought her a present, a book about Children's drawings and their possible significance. Rosy worked with children. As we went to sit down in the living room, I noticed additions to the shelves that made me shiver in an odd way. Rosy had created clay models of herself, Francis and the cats (my cats). There were also cards addressed to Francis, wishing him a wonderful three-month anniversary, and in child's paint, the words 'Francis for Rosy' was written in the top corner of my lovely French windows. The scene made me smile and I had already begun to feel released.

My own memories of the living room were tinted with the colours of mania. As a wedding present from Francis's boss, we had received a large, very old pine dining table. I loved the table but it had been bought for our first cottage at Nestleton. I desperately wanted it to fit in our new house but couldn't find a way. I decided it would be a good idea to cut the legs down to the height of a small coffee table and then to fill the centre of the room with it. I am not known for my spatial awareness or my gift as a mathematician, so the new coffee table had a slight wobble. Left with four legs, I decided to use them to prop up a dark wooden book case. Pleased with my work, I waited for Francis to get home. On seeing my creation, Francis said very little and simply put his cup down on the large coffee table, along with his feet. Whilst Francis worked nights, I had the opportunity to decorate the house in ways that only an artist in abstraction would appreciate. (One with bipolar disorder at least). The week Michael, Lucy and I had moved in with Francis at the cottage, I decided to strip the wallpaper from the large bathroom and then flick as many coloured paints as I could find right across the room. I liked the effect and decided to do the same again when we next moved house (which would be many, many more times).

Remembering this, I used a bath sponge and pouring paint all over it, I very quickly made prints all over the walls, down the stairs and through the hallway and landing. I also pulled up the stair carpet and poured brown paint down the three different sets of stairs. I worked from the ground up so that I could go to bed leaving the paint to dry, which of course they didn't in time for Francis to get home from work. Realizing my mistake, I planned to get a new stair carpet.
A few weeks later I received a phone call from a friend, asking if I would go along to the sheltered housing area at the end of the street, as a cat had left a litter of kittens and the four of them were running around the gardens. Known for my rescuing instinct with cats, I set off with a small

cardboard box and a pair of heavy duty gloves. When I got into the garden, elderly folk were looking out of their windows and doors, I began trying to capture the babies. I remember one lady trying to hand me a plastic carrier, asking me if it would be useful. Managing to capture all four kittens, all teeth and claws, I set off back up the road to get them into a proper carrier. As I walked, a car slowly appeared next to me. Inside, I could see a woman in her late thirties, early forties, and a boy of around twelve. 'Do you need a fantastic quality carpet'? She asked me. Not sure if this was inside my head or if it was really happening, I asked 'What sort of carpet'? The woman stopped the car and got out.

'Here in the boot. I have just finished carpeting an airport lounge so this stuff is indestructible'. 'OK' I thought … 'This could be a synchronistic event. I do need a carpet'. Opening her boot, I looked at the green roll of carpet which did indeed seem to be hardwearing material. 'I'll take it', I confidently announced. Bearing in mind that I hadn't asked the size of the roll and therefor had no clue whether it would fit, my triumph was somewhat misplaced. The woman didn't stop there. I know now that she realized she had a 'live one' and was going to exploit me as far as she could. 'Also', she beamed 'I have a beautiful silk rug'. Pulling out a largish rug from behind the roll of carpet, she began to demonstrate how to care for it. 'All you need to do, is to rub the surface of the rug across the grass first thing in the morning, because the dew will gently clean the silk, which has been woven together by silk worms'. Thrilled at this idea, I immediately agreed to buy the rug. Now, bearing in mind that I was still holding the kittens and had no money on me, this was quite a conundrum. 'Can you go home and get some cash'? The lady asked. 'I have to get my son to the doctor's as he isn't very well'. A light bulb suddenly lit up the inside of my head and showing her the house I lived in, I asked her to pull up outside. Having just started my Counselling degree, my student loan was sitting untouched in my bank account. Taking the hardwearing carpet and the silk rug, I struggled up the path with my kittens and the key for the door. Once inside, I ran to find my cheque book and promptly wrote a cheque for one hundred and forty pounds. 'Who shall I make it out to'? I asked. 'Just write cash', the lady said 'I won't be going near my bank and if you just write cash, I can get the money quickly before I take my son to the doctor'. 'OK' I grinned, beginning to laugh at the Dr Zeuss moment. 'Cats in a carton and carpet in a car', I sang to myself. The woman and child drove away.

This time, Francis had lots to say about my purchase. Looking at the carpet roll he showed me how it could be torn using just bare hands and how it would never pass as airport carpet. The silk rug, it seemed was a cheap acrylic mix and wouldn't require the use of morning dew to keep it clean. I felt so stupid but knew that I had genuinely felt as though I was doing the right thing. The woman had appeared out of nowhere with a carpet and I needed a carpet. We couldn't stop the cheque I hasten to add. When I legitimately bought a sofa, my friends laughed and asked me where I got it from. The roof of a passing car perhaps?
I have been conned a number of times, but this one stands out as particularly spectacular. This is a memory that rose to hit my face, as I sat in my kitchen, which wasn't my kitchen. Drinking tea with Rosy, I began to offer her pearls of wisdom from my twelve years with Francis. 'When he's drunk', I began 'He will say nasty things. Don't worry, he won't remember them the next day and he probably doesn't mean them'. Suddenly, I was filled with the need to go into my garden, down to my grove, where I had enjoyed so many ceremonies, as a Druid, often including more than thirty people from university. 'I need to close down the grove' I smiled. 'You don't need to come; I know exactly where I need to be'. Leaving Rosy in the kitchen, I knew that she was watching me. Rightly or wrongly I decided to give her a bit of a scare. Knowing that Francis would have cast me in the role of the crazy woman in the attic, I didn't see any harm in letting Rosy know that she was in fact dealing with a woman who saw and heard the madness in everything. My altar stone was still sitting right at the bottom alongside my weathervane, a brightly coloured cockerel on top of the four compass points. I began to walk the circle, backwards, knowing that the mystery of it all was protecting me once again from the direct hit of an abusive situation. I spoke the

ritual out loud, waving my arms about, genuinely closing down the sacred area, but being more animated than necessary. I then rang Charles, who as yet, I had never actually met in person. I recited the ritual to him on the phone, walking backwards and forward, closing down my history and sealing the memories, cauterizing the pain. I walked back into the house. 'I think it would be a good idea to do a small ceremony, we should mark the end of our marriage and the beginning of your relationship'. Rosy looked at me with incredulous fear, but we were spared the ceremony because Francis came back from work.

I knew every sound, every word. Francis did not deviate, ever. Walking down the hallway I could hear the familiar rattle of the carrier back and the thud of the bottle of red wine onto the kitchen worktop. He then spat his chewing gum into the bag. As he walked into the kitchen I knew exactly what he would ask. 'Have you lit the fire'? he looked at Rosy. In that one moment, I felt free. I didn't have to light the fire or cook tea. Lucy lived with me in the doll's house, and Michael lived with his friends in a shared home. I picked up my leather coat, knowing that I looked a million times better than when the kitchen was mine and I said my goodbyes. The days when I could do very little except mark the hours by BBC Radio Four and do my best to cook and light coals had melted away with the sound of pounding clay and anniversary cards. I was touching the sky but I didn't want to remain in that place for another second. Fizzing, I caught the bus back home. I called for Lucy and we went to an Indian Restaurant for tea. I could do anything, it seemed. Anything I wanted to.

A week or two later, Rosy invited me for a drink one Saturday afternoon. I'm not sure why, but I agreed to meet up all the same. It was a cold day and I suggested we go to the 'Evil Eye', one of my favourite haunts and the pub Charles and I first kissed in. (Now a favourite of Anthony and I too). I had a glass of cider, a couple actually. Feeling the need to make myself feel more than the woman who laid on the sofa every night, drugged on meds and without a hair brush in sight, I had begun to visit a beauty parlour. Here too, I managed to 'lose' a lot of money but I did enjoy the new world of waxing. In terms of pain, I think it comes second only to falling over my altar and breaking both arms and legs. Lucy and I tried it together at first, (waxing, not falling over the altar) on a small holiday to Gibraltar, but I went on to neaten more and more of my womanly assets. Thinking this a good subject to chat with Rosy about, I soon found myself in the uncomfortable position of discussing the best way to present pubic hair for my ex-husband. Feeling kind of angry and embarrassed, I amicably got up to leave. I think it was at that point that I scared Rosy away for good. Not far down the road from the Evil Eye, was a fantastic sword and armoury shop. I wanted an athame (a ceremonial knife) for use in my Solstice rituals. I chose a gorgeous wooden handled dagger, sharp but safe within a stitched leather sheath. Rosy took one look at what I had planned and decided it was time to leave. I did wonder if she had thought my new acquisition part of my female tidying regime. Either way, I wandered happily off to find my great friend Basil, who was busking on his piano in St Helen's Square. I showed him the athame and we went off for coffee. We laughed a lot that afternoon.

October 2005
I booked Charles into the Churchill Hotel. We were due to meet on the Friday night.
My heart was in my mouth and I jumped around the bedroom not knowing what to do. My body had changed shape so much in the last six months due to the fact that I had stopped taking my medication (anti-psychotic medication to treat Schizo-affective Disorder). I had in fact lost three stones in weight and far from feeling like a physical failure (as Francis had pointed out) I was now on top of my game. I chose a black and white vintage skirt with silver sequins and black net underskirt. On top, I went for a green halter neck fit and flare with a large pendant of the moon. (Appropriate). I also wore my thigh length leather boots and leather Matrix style floor length coat. (I had bought the leather boots and coat on a crackers shopping trip to Oxford Street in London, with my crazy friend Debs (from the Counselling Degree) after one too many large wines in

Covent Garden. Debs was and still is an enormous inspiration to me and is capable of literally, anything. Anything at all. She would always come out on top, shining like the sun and she made me feel courageous and safe.

Email Transcript
'I am heading off now in my car. Please don't message me as I am going to be driving. See you soooooooooooon lady Albatross'
'I will see you tonight at the hotel Mr. Albatross. It would not be amusing to give me the co-ordinates of another guest, I will guess who you are. Your Nell'
In his first email to me, Charles had expressed his desire to find a lady Albatross, to mate with for life.

So, I chose the 'pulling gear' as we had named it. I arrived at the Churchill Hotel. It was around eight o'clock and dark. I wandered into the sweeping driveway and began darting around the outside, trying to see into the bar area. I should mention also, that I was wearing mirror sun shades for some reason. Not a homage to the Blues Brothers, I assure you, more a homage to my own lost little soul, attempting to hide in plain sight. After around five minutes, the smart young man on reception came out to me. 'Can I help at all Madam'? he asked, looking quite rightly at me and thinking, 'this one's either crazy or on the game'. 'I am meeting a guest here' I replied. 'Come and sit in the bar' braved the young chap. I followed him in. Sitting down and taking off my leather pulling coat, I crossed my legs this way, then that, then not, then up to the bar to buy a large white wine. That was when I heard it.
'Mr. Hogan, your guest has arrived'.

Six simple words. The arrival. It was at that point I realised that I didn't really know who Mr. Hogan was, or even what he looked like. I had only seen a fuzzy computer print of Charles at a barbeque. I sat. I waited.

When he came through the door, I knew him immediately. I don't know how, because he looked nothing like the blurred print. I stood up, I laughed like a loony and I squeezed his head. After telling me that he didn't smoke, he pulled out three packets of cigarettes and promptly bought me another large wine.

We walked into York town centre and I remember that it was slippery with wet leaves, not the ideal underfoot for my pulling boots. We ended up in the Evil Eye Lounge, a place of dark sweeping colour and Moroccan sparkle. After standing near the bar for a while making small talk, Charles suddenly said 'I fancy you'! Feeling a bit confused by this new interest in me as a person and not as a done-with mental health cock-up, I replied 'I fancy you too'. We sort of lunged at each other, and Charles, a large imposing forty-nine-year-old man, (although he told me he was forty-seven) met my face, the face of a rather lost thirty-nine-year-old woman, and we fell on the floor – on top of our coats. After that we just didn't care. We talked about things that I would never have thought talk-worthy and a couple of girls in the toilets of the bar expressed concern for me as I explained to them that I was with a man I had met on the internet.
The evening was a strange one. I hadn't been in a position where it was necessary for me to 'big myself up' to anyone. I had known all my previous partners well from the bike pub. So much had happened over the previous twelve years that the idea of telling my life to someone new just felt exhausting. Walking back to the hotel, I turned to Charles and in the corniest of voices I mustered the words 'Would you like to come back for coffee?' It had begun to feel rather surreal and my life with Francis began to seem like a nightmare lost in some video game.
'Are you sure?' Charles looked at me sideways. He had already begun to take the mickey (in a nice way) out of my Druid beliefs and experiences. I didn't mind that he had done this as it showed that he at least cared enough to think about it. It didn't seem right to spend the night one street apart, now, when he had come all the way from Coventry. My months on dating sites had changed the way I felt about things and I would be the first to say that I had taken chances when I shouldn't have. Charles felt different though somehow. So we walked back to my little doll's house. We spent the night listening to Owls singing outside the bedroom window. I got no sleep at all, and we talked all

night. Charles didn't try a thing other than to tell me about owls.

I agreed to visit Coventry in two weeks' time. It was exciting. The chance to get dressed up and to meet a whole new city of people, without anti-psychotic medication in my system pushed me up into the realms of mania. My diagnosis was incomplete and anti-depressant tablets were making my mood swings much worse. I began an attempt to control my fear of the unknown by drinking enough wine to match Charles's beer consumption. Bad idea. Charles drank a lot of pints.

Arriving in Coventry, late into the evening was both exciting and scary. Nobody knew me or anything about me and that meant I could be whoever I liked. Charles had been invited to the eightieth birthday party of his former father in-law. Charles was married to a lady a few years his elder, around twenty years or so ago. As an invited guest, he decided to bring me with him. This was not such a good idea. Charles's ex-wife did not quite know what to do with me and I didn't know what to do with myself. I attempted to fit in with Charles's friends but the large glasses of white wine began to prick at my paranoia and before long I was dancing around Charles like a woman with complete self-confidence and a desire to move like a lap dancer. I became fiercely territorial and all my dreams of enigmatic mystery were overtaken by my usual swift rise to mania and the always predictable fall into hell. Always a lot of crying and vomiting. Not good in a new relationship and an even newer city.

The following day, Charles took me for a walk into a wonderful park with heron nesting. Being the end of October, the air was as visible as it was cold. I decided not to wear my coat as I wanted to look pale and interesting in my shawl collar jumper. It didn't take long for me to realize that I was headed for hyperthermia. We watched the herons from the wooden hide and then Charles drove back to Dot's house, where he lived also. We walked to the pub. Had I known that this would become the routine for the next two years I would have headed in the opposite direction. The gnawing need to be part of a couple however overrode everything and it took a great deal of time to make sense of my life.

How my river runs

The following week, Charles came over to York to watch the light display projected onto the Minster. We didn't see too much of it however as I was matching him again, pint for pint. The sudden flood of alcohol through my life began to turn the tide that night. As we walked back to my little doll's house, I only made it as far as Woolworth's shop front. I lay down on the ground and simply didn't want to move. Charles picked me up and carried me the rest of the way home. I will never know how he knew the way, but he was, such a clever chap.

On getting back, Charles ran me a bath and sat on the toilet making sure I didn't sink under the water. I remember looking at him, not wanting to change anything from that moment. He put his hands over his cheeks and breathed out 'I've got a crazy one', he said.
The days of attempting to control my illness with alcohol were tough and dangerous. They lasted for around three years until I was properly diagnosed with Bipolar and Schizo-affective disorder and given Lithium. They have never returned.

By the end of November, we had only seen one another one more time and this visit was the deciding factor for the next couple of months. I decided to have a party at my house so that my friends could meet Charles properly. I had begun to have more self-confidence mostly because I had stopped taking my anti-psychotic medication after my marriage to Francis had ended. I had done this to lose the weight the tablets had given me. I was, however, a ticking time bomb. My little house was filled with all my friends, also Michael and Lucy who were nineteen and almost eighteen. I bought a couple of cases of beer and wine (something I had never done before). As I ran down the road, a young chap got out of his van and started shouting 'Will you come out with me for a meal'? I felt fizzy with it all and such mania radiates around everyone who gets in the way. Diamond eyes can be such a magnet mostly for all the wrong reasons. Charles and his nephew arrived. I noticed that Charles was being rather obnoxious and saying things that I didn't like. As he drank, he became more and more hard to handle. I began to feel very disorientated. A couple of my close friends noticed and some even made their excuses to leave. As the night wore on and wore on, friends were expressing their concern to me. I didn't know what to do.

Eventually, the old familiar grip of sinking fast grabbed me. Most people had gone home except for a couple of friends who were staying over. I felt so ill that I knew I had to lay down. Leaving Charles downstairs, I lay on my bed. When the gut wrenched crying started followed by the convulsing, my oldest friend Basil came to find me. I was unable to stop. Basil took my face in his hands, holding my head against his shoulder to try and calm things down. He knew me best and how to keep me safe.

The following day, I tried hard to make everything right. After losing my twelve years of marriage to Francis (albeit the best thing I lost that year by far apart from the three stones), all I wanted was a stable home life, one I didn't have to struggle with. Charles, his nephew and me went into town to see to ice sculptures and some other happy Christmas displays. Eventually we went into my favourite bistro, in the centre of town. Basil played piano here on an evening and I was hoping he would be there to bring a sense of calm. A couple of friends from the night before turned up, more as a gesture of support I think. I was so shocked at Charles's sharp tone of voice and the things he said, that I began to feel that my chance at a new life was slipping mercilessly away. I realised I had to get him out of the bar and back home. Tension was gripping my stomach and I just wanted to feel safe.

We arrived home and immediately went to bed. Stupidly I began to ask Charles about his ex-girlfriends. I think I did this to feel secure, but he didn't realize this and didn't answer with the required information to give me the feeling of safety I needed. I realised then, that I didn't know this man at all and he seemed very different from the emails we had shared. If I had known that he too was nervous and reacting in the light of this, then I would have understood. In the years after our marriage, Charles allowed himself to let go

How my river runs

and to be the amazing man he really was, but right then, that night, all I saw was my dream of home disintegrating.
There it was again. The clarity, the tunnel vision. I got out of bed, wearing my pink pyjamas. I put on make-up and platted my hair. I could hear Charles snoring loudly, and Michael too – as he had lived with me for a couple of weeks now.
Charles stirred and I whispered, 'It's OK, there's something I just have to do'.

I crept downstairs and lay out my tablets on the floor in front of me. One by one, I took them out of the foil packets. I counted around forty-three tricyclic anti-depressants.
One by one, I took them with a glass of milk.
When the episode was over, crotchet blanket left behind and a phone call from Kirk within hours.

I packed lots of nonsense into a suitcase and got the next available train.

Kirk met me at the station. He was twelve years younger than me and an artist, living with his parents. I arrived, in my long coat and boots and he smiled at me, waving his business card so that I knew who he was. We walked through the graveyard (which gave me a strange chill), passed a large garage to where his parents lived and saw Shane Ritchie filming an advertisement. When I met Kirk's parents they were so kind and wonderful. They didn't once make me feel sad even though I had turned up in shocking pink tights, and a bright green dress. Along with the shades. Looking back now I can see how I must have appeared but at the time, everything felt normal. I stayed with Kirk in his single bed and he put his arms round me every day and every night. Kirk's Mum brought up home cooked food on a tray, she knocked at the door and slid the try inside. We did think about having more of a romantic relationship but two of a kind doesn't always bode well. The website I had created with the purpose of finding support through mental illness brought me this great friend, but fear bounced between us and the idea that neither one of us could promise to always be there for the other made a relationship too dangerous. Such kindness, and genuine honour. Kirk's Dad, a carpenter made a table for us to use whilst I stayed. We watched horror films that had been remade in 3D. We stared at the screen disappointed, until we realised that we needed glasses.

After a couple of weeks, Charles began to ring most days. However, the calls began to trail off. I decided to go home for Christmas (although I had decided that Christmas didn't exist). Kirk took me to the station and I wept as I left him because he had been one of the kindest and the most special of friends who had asked for absolutely nothing in return. As we waited for the train, a Druid Priest and Priestess, hand in hand with a bunch of mistletoe gracefully walked across the platform. The Winter Solstice had become one of the most powerful of days for me and my journey as a Druid, which I will tell you about soon, had given me reason to live. Seeing the pair (real or acted) was a sign for me and it gave me hope.

After an arduous journey home across London, diverted all ways due to the festive time, I arrived back in York. By this time Charles had not rung for a few days. I rang him and he answered. Nothing. So I simply said 'Goodbye Mr. Albatross'. 'Goodbye,' he replied.
The next time I saw Kirk, was Charles's funeral nine years later.

How my river runs

Chapter Four
Man on the fence

I still felt like I needed to find somebody, as it seemed that Charles had gone from the map. I picked up my laptop and logged in to the dating site. Charles had left his boots behind and the ring I had given him to wear. I half thought of giving them away, but pushed them into a box instead. Pretty quickly I came across Simon. No photograph, but a good profile. Simon was a teacher with a specialty in languages. I sent him a message.

Before long, my mobile phone rang. I had given Simon my number and I was sure it would be him ringing.

'Hello' he said, turning the word into a question with his unsure intonation. 'Hi', I replied. 'What are you doing?' I'm buying some last-minute Christmas presents for my nephews', he went on. Simon sounded like a decent person I surmised, as he was buying gifts for children. He also sounded intelligent. 'Would you like to meet up the day after Boxing Day'? he said further. 'OK', said I, already climbing the tree like a capuchin monkey hell bent on fruit.

Christmas Day was a disaster. I had made it clear that I would not acknowledge Christmas, but my family arrived in the car and I was bundled into the festivities. I had no gifts for anyone so I gave my sister the gold cross and chain Francis had given to me the year before. Michael and Lucy spent the day with their Dad. During the afternoon, Simon began to send me texts. To my surprise, Charles also began to text. I knew that Charles always made a joke when the Queen's speech came on the television. He loved the Royals and spent lots of his time reading history books about the Monarchy. So when the Queen's speech began, I sent him a text message, 'The Queen is a lizard'. (I referenced the New Age conspiracy theory that I found rather entertaining). I didn't hear from him for a while, but I had come to terms with the fact that I wouldn't hear from him much more.

That evening I began to receive rather saucy texts from Simon. Now, call me stupid, but I could not resist replying because the idea of being alone was abhorrent to me. I enjoyed watching the television I wanted to, and eating what I liked, but I know that I simply don't function well as a single person. I was always looking for my perfect other half. I know that I need to work at a relationship and I am fully ready for that, but at that time, in that place, my other half had not revealed himself. The following day, I put on my long coat and boots again and set off for the station. The train to Bridlington was frequent and I was excited at what this new man might bring into my life. Bearing in mind, that I did not have a clue what Simon looked like, and all he knew of me was a small photo and red hair.

I got on the train, and for some reason, I rang Charles from my mobile. He answered and I chatted about the date I was heading for. Charles sounded quite narked about my date and almost jealous. This made me feel a little confused about what I was doing, but I did it anyway. At the small station, I got off the train and walked to the exit where Simon had suggested we meet. I knew him immediately and he knew me too. He told me that it was my hair waving about that told him I had arrived.

Simon was a very large man. An ex rugby player, he had put on a lot of weight after an injury. He was also tall and a lot older than me. I liked his smile and his voice. We left the station hand in hand. After a couple of drinks in the pub, we walked by the sea. I suppose it was then I realised I didn't feel much in the way of romance. Internet dating had led me to expect instant results and it just wasn't happening. Stupidly I went back to Simon's house, where he had a pizza ready for us to eat. I sort of felt like I didn't care anymore. Simon became overly amorous whilst we sat on the sofa and out of nowhere, the physical shaking began. I just wanted to leave, so Simon took me back to the station. He was a genuinely nice chap and for the next month or so we formed a kind of relationship. On New Year's Eve, Simon did everything that should have made me feel all the sorts of things I wanted to feel, but it was the wrong place, the wrong person and the wrong time. A bath filled with bubbles, grapes and Champaign with specialty cheeses should have been the absolute moment of perfection but it just made me sad.

On New Year's Day, Simon came over to meet Mum Dad and Liff.
Simon's main subject was German language and literature. He loved Germany and as my parents had enjoyed many holidays in the area, they began to talk. As I sat on the sofa, I watched the scene unfold, dumfounded at the behaviour of both my parents and my sister. First off, my Mum brought in a plate of German cheeses and crackers for Simon to try and pass judgment on. My Dad then launched into a monologue on the Third Reich and rise to power of Hitler. My sister completed the group by singing a selection of songs from 'The Sound of Music' through the half open door as she left. I honestly felt that my family had gone completely nuts, but it made me feel safer in my relationship with Simon. I was sent into a tail-spin by their acceptance of the situation. Perhaps he was due to be my other half?

On our way back to Bridlington, where I had decided to spend the night, I popped into the local supermarket. Simon stayed in the car. As I got to the racks of fruit and vegetables I had a sudden urge to ring Charles. He answered straight away and I ducked down so that Simon couldn't see me on the phone. 'This isn't going away' he said. 'I know', I replied. It was obvious that I needed to visit Coventry again. I tried to explain to Simon who was understandably upset. The following couple of weeks were farcical to say the least. Simon began arriving at my house, talking about the 'sword of Damocles' hanging over his head. I explained to him that I needed to know for certain whether Charles was the man I was meant to be with. I didn't expect him to embrace the idea but his obsession with our being together forever began to get hard to cope with. I understood how he felt because I was capable of behaving in the same way, just not with him.

One evening, Michael and I were at home. I was in my pyjamas and not looking my best to say the least. Suddenly we heard a heavy knock on the door. I could see Simon's

shape through the glass and right then, I just didn't want to see him. He continued knocking and began to shout through the letter box. I knelt and shouted back through 'I have lost my key'. 'I'll come around the back', he carried on. 'I have lost the back-gate key and Lucy has it' I called. 'I want us to be together, I am going to kidnap you and you are going into the boot'. I looked at Michael and we didn't know quite what to say or do. I took a step back and I looked at what was happening. Last year, exactly this time, I was on the scrap heap. Francis had ended our marriage and I didn't think I would live to see another Spring. Whilst we were pondering, out of nowhere a loud bang and a rattle happened at the side gate. Michael and I rushed outside to see Simon half hanging from the six-foot fence with one leg in the wheelie bin. 'I love you' he bellowed. 'For God's Sake', I shouted, but Michael and I couldn't stop laughing. We hauled him back over the fence, to the outside of the garden. 'I will marry you'! he screamed.
'Not now' I answered. I asked him to leave, he grabbed at me, not in a nasty way but it wasn't welcome. 'I promise I will ring you as soon as I get to Coventry and I know what is happening' I yelled as he got back in his car.

I felt mean, I really did, but in some ways, I also felt strong. I was making decisions, maybe not the best ones, but decisions all the same.

A couple of days later, I took the train to Coventry. I was a little early so I sat in the Pumpkin café, my bright pink suitcase on wheels and my hair braided. I looked up to see Charles trying to open the wrong door. I picked up my bags and raced around the front to meet him. He swept me up in a way that oozed with relief. I felt it too. I was still quite nervous of him after the last time we had seen one another and being in Coventry didn't make sense, but I knew that I had made up my mind. I didn't know what to say to Simon, I wanted him and his Champaign bubble baths to disappear because I had enjoyed our time together. I couldn't walk away from Charles again and no matter how tough it was going to be, I knew that I was in for the long haul.
Getting in the car at the station with Charles, on route to Dot's house, it became clear that we were going to be

together. Dot was not pleased about this at all and the following week, Charles moved some of my stuff into his bedroom. He had however omitted to tell his mother that we would be living together. This information, he had left to me. Dot was very angry and made it plain that I was not welcome. In fact, when Charles went out, she began to tell me that he wanted me to go back to York, but couldn't tell me himself. She also told me what a terrible mother I was to leave Michael and Lucy at home. Maybe so, I thought, but I am putting back the pieces of my life and I can only do it one way. Dot then stopped the cable TV into Charles's room, which made us laugh. He asked me to marry him.

I asked Charles how he would feel about a Druid Hand fasting ceremony at the nearest stone circle or in the beautiful parkland on the outskirts of Coventry. We moved on to discuss inviting some of Charles's late younger brother's friends, who belonged to the Hell's Angel bike club where William was a prominent member. It had been a couple of decades since his death but every year, a black and white wreath would appear on the grave with a half full can of beer. It seemed a good idea, and Charles even went so far as to think about including items that had belonged to his beloved late uncles. We went to Charles's local pub that night, where everyone knew him and nobody knew me. Charles began chatting to his good friend who was also the landlord. He took one look at me and asked me if everyone had to wear Christopher Lee masks. So, it was decided. Tough though it was (the accent barrier was problem enough; I have lost count of the number of times that I had to ask for a glass of Coke and not cork) I chose Charles.

Simon was angry. He shouted a lot and kept my wellies. I knew I had made the right decision. So, I packed my life into many sized boxes and got in the van.
After Charles's death eight years on, Simon came to Leicester to visit me.
I knew instantly that I had made the right decision nine years earlier and I didn't ask him to stay.

Helen Mary Barr

How my river runs

Chapter Five
The Golden Hour and the best Fish in the sea

I lived in the Midlands for ten years and most days, it felt like a thousand lifetimes. There I was at Hinckley rail station, wearing a full length black coat with a fur hood, boots to match and clutching a wooden ornament of a motorbike. The train was held up, one minute outside the platform where I was standing. I was so nervous and couldn't stand still, sweeping my hair this way and that, staring at my phone and answering the messages from Anthony who was sitting in the train, just a minute away. One more minute should have felt like nothing, but Anthony and I hadn't seen one another for almost fifteen years.

I had lived in York all my life, but physical and emotional disaster, coupled with a serious desire to end my life found me riding the winds of mania. Packing up everything I owned, I had said goodbye to my children and jumped into a van, with Charles and my cat Willow. I believed that I had no choice but to escape. Everything around me was turning to poison and the choice was a simple one, reinvent myself or die. So, in March 2006, I landed in Coventry in the small rented terraced house, where my furniture didn't fit and with a man I knew nothing about. Nothing.
Sarah and Brenig were married three months after Charles died. I performed their Hand Fasting ceremony in a beautiful and very old barn. I also created all the flowers in shades of pink and lilac which sat beautifully amongst the wonderful tea lights nestled in jars, put together lovingly by family and friends.

Wedding floristry was born in me during a major manic episode. I was in hospital after surgery to repair the damage done to my womb, bladder and fallopian tubes. Basil and his wife Katy, best friends of mine came to visit me. Their large, sumptuous wedding was coming up in a few months' time. As we chatted, for some ungodly reason, I offered to make all the flowers for them. I had no experience, training or skill in floristry, yet I was as confident as a professional in my ability to give them what they wanted. I was separated at the

time from John and as he took care of our two children, I
filled the house with silk flowers, ribbons and several library
books explaining how to make a wedding bouquet.

Basil and Katy's wedding came around and I took my fresh
and silk creations to the church. I was terrified that the roses
would drop dead, now fully aware of what I had offered to do
and no longer manic. Miraculously the baskets and bouquets
made it through the ceremony and I was announced at the
lavish reception as 'The Florist'. I re-laid the swags along the
head table, lifting the cake to keep them in place. Katy's
Father, a talented film producer and writer, smiled at me
'Very pre-Raphaelite', he said. Months later, he endorsed my
poetry by writing me a beautiful reference which I used to
enter Media College.

How I got through the day I will never know, but as soon as I
could, I looked up the meaning of 'pre-Raphaelite. I was
twenty-three years old and alone with Lucy and Michael,
then two and three years old. I felt I could do everything and
nothing, launched and dropped, praying I didn't fall too far
into the water. I returned the library books, but carried on
with the weddings.
Sarah's wedding had given Charles and I the opportunity to
stay in the gorgeous hotel, set in large grounds filled with
trees of every type. We had first thought to carry out the
Hand fasting ceremony outside, but chose instead to use the
large barn. I felt empty sleeping in the double room meant
for Charles and I. Sarah was fantastic at keeping me upbeat,
even giving me a t-shirt with the slogan 'Priestess of Honour'
in bright pink letters. I didn't wear it as I felt very self-
conscious and I regret this. The wedding went so well that it
made me cry a lot. Lucy and her fiancé came to the Hand
fasting, as did Michael. As I walked bare foot around the
large area, with my broomstick and wand, I shouted and
clapped. Pouring myself into the ceremony, I tried hard to fill
the empty space, where Charles would have sat, drinking
whisky and being outrageous. Probably wearing the top hat
Sarah had bought for him.

I booked a holiday for Lucy, Michael and myself to go to
New York, at Christmas, but when the time approached I

couldn't face it. I booked a cruise and chartered a plane to take me to Luxor in Egypt. I cancelled this also. I bought lots of things I didn't need and every day I opened my door to a nurse from the psychiatric Crisis Team. In the end, Michael and I spent Christmas on our own, as he moved in to stay for a while. We watched a film. I don't remember what we ate.

As the anniversary of Charles's death approached, I felt like downing would be a good idea. Out of nowhere I saw clear images of him sinking into the dark water. He was on his back, arms and legs stretched upwards as he disappeared. His face, the last part of him to remain clear was bright with eyes open. I felt that Charles was moving further and further away from memory and very soon I wouldn't remember his face at all.

My friend Anthony, known also as Fish (Mr. Fish to me) however, had surprised the hell out of me by telephoning in March 2015, having found my number on Facebook. One year exactly since Charles had passed away, I was waiting for Anthony at Hinckley Station, a Yorkshire woman lost in the Midlands.

I had forgotten how safe Anthony's voice sounded. Thirty-two years ago, Anthony and I had cuddled in the corner of my small flat. I was eighteen years old, with no decent life experience other than as a struggling outsider, damaged by the wrong place and the wrong time. Anthony and I would hold hands and enjoy the lack of expectation. Anthony was twenty, with cavalier black ringlets down his back and a softness I was completely unused to. As we cuddled, my boyfriend Paul slept on my bed. One hour out of time, with which we could have changed so much of the future that went on to hurt us. Anthony took care of me in a way no-one else ever had. A group of us rode the bikes into Cumbria to visit one of Paul's family members who owned a bakery. The front of the shop looked amazing with so many different motorbikes in a row. It was even funnier as next door rented out push bikes, so the sign 'Rent your bike here', looked very strange but appropriate. I was the only female in the group and on the back of Paul's bike. Francis and his then fiancé were due to come but had recently come off their bike so they weren't in a fit state to ride. That night, we all went out for a drink. We ended up in the local rugby club and it wasn't long before the rugby crowd were giving our group nasty looks from across the room. We decided it would be best to go. After getting outside, a little the worse for wear, we started running and shouting. I ran too, but the boob tube I was wearing under my jacket fell round my waist and I didn't realize until we reached the road that my boobs were bouncing with the rest of me. It was very funny and I didn't feel upset about it. After finding the only pub that would let us all in, we had a few more drinks. For some reason I decided to eat the daffodils in a vase on the table. Had I been educated and diagnosed, I would have seen the signs. I hadn't drunk much, but the mania was beginning to soar. I walked outside of the pub and sat on a stone wall. Without thinking, I simply allowed myself to fall backwards onto the concrete slabs behind. It felt like I had fallen into soft pillows. By this time, my friends had decided to go back to the bakery. I simply couldn't keep still. I lay on the living room floor but could not stop myself from shaking and involuntarily jumping around as I lay there. Paul decided to look incredulous at me and to leave me in the obviously distressed state. Suddenly, a Police van pulled up outside. I was aware at everyone laughing out of the window. Anthony got out of the van, waved at the Policemen and came into the bakery. He had got lost and asked them for a lift back.

When Anthony came inside, he took one look at me, and put me into his sleeping bag. He put his arms around me and held me secure for the whole night, helping me the following morning when the awful thirst set in and the low had me pinned to the floor. It's when I remember times like that, I can't understand why I didn't grab him and marry him right then and there. We could have had our family and built a lovely life. My life has so many 'what if's?'. So many choices I could have made. I like to think that Anthony and I were positioned as friends and kept that way until we had both ridden the rocky roads that were to come. Only then would we be allowed to live our lives together, for the rest of the second half. Anthony's first partner was killed in violent circumstances, and the son she had born a few years earlier has become like my own, as has Anthony's step-daughter from his second partner (and first wife). His ex-wife and I are best friends.

So when we sat in the corner of my flat, there was so much good still to come for us both, along with the pain.
Shocking cold shook us out of our lovely place however, as Paul poured a whole bottle of wine over our heads. How I despised him for that, years down the line. There were so many points at which Anthony and I almost made it, but for more than thirty years we slipped through one another's fingers and took up different paths.

I remembered the sunny times, when as a young, rather lost girl, Anthony would take me out on his motorbike. Both of us spent our time away from the more frenetic biker lifestyle, at that point anyway. Although we had biker friends and spent many nights sleeping on their floors, something between us was always special and safe. We rode to Knaresborough and hired a boat. Going around in circles because we couldn't decide which way was up, on the gorgeous river under the bright sky. The day became a joke as I split my skin tight red jeans trying to get out of the boat. Anthony wrapped his baggy jumper around my waist. Ever the knight. We spent the day in Knaresborough a couple of months ago, as a middle aged married couple.
I should point out right now, that on the day of writing this comic strip, I am fifty years old. I turned fifty in June of this year (2016). I am a woman with four weddings and a funeral, so far, to date. I don't want any more of either. I landed in the Midlands, from Yorkshire, under circumstances most folk wouldn't have touched with a barge pole. Before meeting Charles, who promised by email that he would 'travel anywhere as he had many camels', I was in recovery from the breakup of my second marriage.

Watching Charles die changed me. Charles changed me. He gave me so much life that I could make the journey back home to York, dressed in new and powerful colours with memories that were both searing and sweet.

Coventry, a painful, ecstatic odyssey that I wouldn't have missed for anything, despite the times that I wished myself away …anywhere.

Anthony and I reconnected on Facebook in 2012, and he told me that his marriage had ended many years earlier. I had become reclusive in 2003, after my first full diagnosis of psychosis. The dreadful side effects from the anti-psychotic medication, hailed the end of my marriage to Francis (we had married on 27th March 1993, the same day it turned out, as Charles's funeral).

By the end of December 2005, I had survived two suicide attempts. In contact with a Charismatic church group, the first overdose was explained to me as 'Devils inside me attempting to end my life'. I survived the demons not least because of the care my daughter Lucy gave and not because I prayed at them. She became very angry at my attempts to leave her and we spent the next few years working this out. Lucy – tall, striking, with a fierce intellect and her father's precious dry wit, will have her own space in this comic book too – a very special place because she is a very special young woman.

When Francis and I married in 1993, Anthony was not invited. I felt as though I hadn't been invited either, as after the ceremony, I sat on the kitchen floor of my new home and cried. I cried even more when I discovered a bunch of yellow roses stuffed behind the fridge. John, thirty-years old and my first husband, whom I had married at nineteen years of age, had attempted to reach me before the ceremony and I had not been told. The days of rather incestuous relationships and friendships, the stifling egos were incredibly linked to one pub in York City Centre. Richard the Third (or as we knew it 'The Grobs'). Had I taken hold of the golden hours that existed when Anthony and I were in the same place, at the same time, and ready – all of this might have been different. I gave birth to our son Michael and our daughter Lucy, 1986 and 1988. Our marriage ended in 1992, for many reasons – psychosis wasn't particularly helpful. John was one of the good guys.

How my river runs

I was thinking the other day, about the night I had a party at my home, in 1992. John and I had split up and the house was full of friends and family dancing like crazy folk to music that was way too loud. John had come to bring some of the children's things over and had inadvertently found himself in a tussle with my soon to be second husband, Francis. We had just got together and I was trying very hard to find some kind of solid ground outside of the soaring and the sinking inside of my head. I was yet to receive an accurate diagnosis and depression had a hand round my throat. Anthony turned up to the party and was also in a very dark place having not long lost his partner. I remember sitting on the living room floor, with Francis and a few friends. Out of nowhere, I smashed a large, heavy ash tray. It shattered. Without thinking at all, I brought down my right hand and pushed it into the broken glass. Francis gently took my hand and began to pull out the shards and larger pieces of glass from the heal of my hand and the palm. I was kneeling on the floor, my green tights torn to shreds, my green velvet hat hiding sliding mascara. Francis took my hand and said to me 'I'm going to marry you if I have to drag you to the altar'. 'OK' I thought. 'Good plan'. Its only when I look back on that night, I realize that three of my husbands were in my living room at the same time. Of course, at the time I was only married to John, and clearly not a bigamist. The following year I married Francis with less than two weeks between my divorce from John, and our wedding. I moved the children then five and six years old, into Francis's cottage in the village of Nestleton, high in the Yorkshire Wolds. I thought our life would be better there. This speedy act became the forerunner to some of the most colourful and bizarre experiences of my life. During the twelve years of our marriage – Francis, Michael, Lucy and I joined a cult, were baptized in a large tank in the middle of a cricket pitch, moved into a house previously owned by drug addicts with the intention of saving their souls. I gained a Bachelor's degree with honours in Counselling Studies, got a teaching diploma and became a Druid Priestess, with no absolutely NO sign of an exorcism. Flying high again, I was also made a Lifetime Fellow of the Millennium Association for my work with the arts and mental health. All these things before I knew what my brain was up to. The years to come would bring me all manner of treatments until the diagnosis of Bipolar Affective Disorder and Schizo-affective Disorder finally brought the right medication.

The tattered and dangerously balanced girl Francis had proposed to over a smashed ash tray, was the same reason he chose to walk away, twelve years later.

However, here I am in Hinckley Rail Station – waiting for Anthony who was waiting one minute away, one minute more. Again, I felt another lifetime pass through me.

As the train pulled in, I looked up and down the platform, franticly trying to recognize the face I knew so well. The long black spiralling hair and broad shoulders. The lavender coloured eyes, sweeping dark eye lashes and his lovable chunky nose. I even remembered the way his eyebrows reached a point in the middle. Beard or no beard? I had no clue as to what he looked like as he had successfully dodged all photographs of himself on Facebook.
I turned around, the platform too small to miss him and instantly saw my friend walk towards me. We hugged and kissed and held hands as we left the station, it was 1984 again.
This time felt different. The glances were side long and flirtatious – not the full face look of a best friend. As we got into a taxi to travel back to my home in Barwell, it almost felt like we were meeting for the first time. This time, however, the golden hour had touched us both at the same time.

Christmas Eve 1965 at around 4.20 pm, when the 100lb meteoroid hit the village, it broke up and scattered less than a mile from my house. Out of chaos we had found each other. Life had smashed at both of us but we managed to stay alive, despite attempts on both our parts to end a what we often saw as hopeless and crippling lives. I hurt with sadness when I thought of what we might have avoided if I had seen Anthony smile at me on the river and in the most special of hugs. Yet throughout the thirty years apart, we loved and lived with joy and for that I am grateful. I am grateful for John, Francis and Charles but most of all for

How my river runs

Michael and Lucy. I know that Anthony too has lived a life with genuine love and the joy of children and step children.

We sat and talked. Michael was due home from his care job around the Leicester villages. He was living with me at the time, in recovery from heroin addiction. We decided to walk into the village for a few drinks and settled on the largest pub in the village, empty apart from a couple of locals. We talked steadily for an hour or two. Then, I asked Anthony what he had expected from his visit with me. He had surreptitiously mentioned asking me a question and buying me white roses, during our telephone conversations. He looked at me and was very quiet. 'What is it'? I asked, 'Just say it'. So he did. 'Will you marry me'?
'Yes', I answered. And that was that. The barman bought us a drink.

The next few days felt strange and unreal but floodlit by happiness at a relationship long overdue. We bought a ruby oval ring surrounded by diamonds and set in white gold. It fit first time. I later placed it on my right hand, as Anthony's mother's ring was given to me to wear. Even that wasn't straight forward. Anthony's parents had both passed away in the previous six years and the ring was in the safe-keeping of Anthony's ex-wife Tessa. I had known Anthony's parents over thirty years ago when his mum had cooked me sausage and chips because wanted to look after me. I was rather lost, with a head full of noise and confidence shattered from my first sexual encounter, which I will share with you further on. Tessa has spent the last ten years in a relationship with Anthony's brother, which is a bit unusual as a family dynamic. It works though. Tessa's only child, Jane, immediately made me feel at home. At twenty-three years of age, Jane knew her own mind fiercely and her marriage to David, then fifty-nine years old was wonderful and they asked me to perform their hand-fasting ceremony in Tessa's back garden. I felt so blessed to have been brought into Anthony's family. Had we all met outside of the labels 'ex-wife' and 'ex-wife's daughter', we would still have become great friends. The day I met them, Anthony took me round to Tessa's house. It was the week after Anthony and I had got engaged. Walking up Tessa's path I was amazed to see ribbons and balloons taped to the front door, wishing us well on our engagement. Inside the house, Tessa had baked us a cake with two cats on the top. Everyone gave us gifts and I was taken aback by their care and genuine congratulations.

Performing the Hand fasting ceremony for Jane and David surrounded by roses, dried corn and lavender, the altar looked stunning. I asked Jane and David to bake a loaf of bread together, to honour the first harvest and the festival of Lughnasadh, we then broke the bread in the ceremony. A small group of guests had gathered including my own parents. Other than my sister's son, for whom I had created a naming ceremony, my parents had never seen my work as a Druid. Jane and David's ceremony was really something special as the family was captured in a situation that shouldn't have worked but did. I decorated the trees with flowers, and made a large bouquet with pink lilies and white roses. Jane wore my silver Elfin crown and we wove ivy through and around it. She looked absolutely incredible and the photographs taken with David and Jane's white Husky dog, Loki are some of the loveliest wedding photographs I think I have ever seen.

My intention is to pull the strands of my life together so that my stories will form a whole and make sense. I hope you don't mind jumping around with me a little.

After Anthony and I got engaged, the big questions started to arise. Anthony lived in a small flat (where he had lived for the previous ten years after splitting up with Tessa). He loved his flat and I enjoyed staying there with him, but there was no space for me to move in. I lived in Barwell, in a very large house. I had felt that I would never have the same kind of house back in York as I could never afford it. Charles had left me the house and I couldn't imagine Anthony moving in with me, although he was happy to. My only friends, Sarah and my university friend Rob were my life lines. My once fabulous neighbours had moved to the dark side out of concern for me and they were dubious about Anthony. All things considered, I decided to sell up and move home to

How my river runs

York. Moving home to be near my parents was also the main consideration. I put my house up for sale.

Two months later, the house hadn't sold but my neighbours on the other side (not the dark side) had given me an offer. A house over the road from my parents, in York by the river, and also my old stomping ground came up for sale. I knew the house well as the couple and their children had been exceptional friends (more like family) before Kath passed away a couple of years earlier. When I was in my late teens, Kath had been one of only three people to tell me that they were aware of my struggles and could see how hard things were for me back at home with my parents. It felt right to buy the house. So I accepted a much lower offer than the Barwell house was worth, wanting our happy neighbours to have it, and set about organizing the move. Our buyers had been through a great deal during the eight years that Charles and I had lived next door. The couple were really good to know and they were bikers, which had made me feel immediately at home. Unfortunately, our neighbour's husband also had Bipolar Affective disorder, and his medication was very unstable. On more than one occasion he could be seen leaping over the back fence running into the dark followed by policemen. The family had a large trampoline in their back garden, close to our fence. One day, Jez, shouted that he was going to bounce up and down on it, in an attempt at holding a conversation. Mania can be so many things that people love, intensely humorous and attractive. I felt for him, and understood his pain. Also that of his wife. In buying my house, their daughter and her young family could enjoy the two properties together, making a great place to live, for children and grandchildren alike.

Anthony and I decided to get married at York Register Office on June 24th, two days before my birthday, three months from our engagement. I could hardly believe that a year on from the terrible days, I would be marrying my lovely friend. The other brilliant thing was that everyone, friends and family alike were really happy about it. They had seen so much of my devastated thinking that the wedding came as a welcome relief. Also, nobody was surprised which made me

think again how things might have turned out, had it not been for that cold bottle of wine.
It was amazing to be amongst my friends and family again.

Paul the potter was a German sculptor, on a different internet dating site and weeks before Anthony appeared. Living in a cottage way out in the sticks, an hour from County Cork, Ireland, we also had several Skype sessions. Paul was twelve years older than me, with long grey hair and a bohemian looking room which I could see through his camera. We talked about me visiting him and he wanted to know what I liked for breakfast. I told him jam and bread so he proceeded to buy gourmet jam. It became obvious very quickly that this was expected to be a full-on visit. At the time however, it was around my forty-ninth birthday and I realised I was heading full pelt into something I didn't know was even safe. Yet I had done this with Charles, and I was used to throwing myself in at the deep end. I had hurtled into the unknown all my life. I bought the ticket and took instructions on how to reach the cottage. Paul's birthday was around the same time as mine. Knowing that he loved the Rolling Stones, I sent him a print of the Last Supper, with all the disciples as members of the Stones. In the picture were Hendrix and Dylan. A real mix of divine personalities. Paul recorded me a bunch of Stones CDs and posted them to me.

I had picked up my training in Shamanism and was travelling to Lancaster by train most weekends. My first visit to the lectures took place in the stark grounds of a large dark grammar school, close to where a great many executions had taken place. I initially felt a sense of unease, but this soon subsided when the studying began.

I had taken my tablet with me so I could talk with Paul but I didn't expect Charles to show up on my first Shamanic training session. Around thirty of us were sitting in a circle waiting for the lecturer to start speaking. It was noisy and good natured. Suddenly, the man sitting to my left who I didn't know, had never met and had only just arrived, looked at me and said 'Why have I got an albatross sitting in front of me?' Charles's first email to me, told me that he was searching for a lady albatross. We even placed an albatross in the centre of our wedding cake.

I did my first Shamanic journey that day. I paired up with the man who had so obviously received the albatross from Charles. When it was his turn to tune into my journey, David (as the fascinating chap was called) described the coast of Ireland, but plainly stated that he didn't see a way across there for me. I was a little annoyed as I was excited about the visit, but I also knew that Charles had spoken through David. The day before my visit to Cork, I booked a taxi from the airport to the cottage. It came in at around one hundred pounds. Paul was going to meet me at the top of the steep hill. It did occur to me that he could have met me at the airport and I kept thinking about what he had said a couple of days earlier 'The things I could do with you'. I found it difficult to pack my suitcase. I had only lost Charles ten months earlier and I just couldn't find a level place from which to think. I decided to ring the airport as I wasn't sure exactly what time I would arrive in Cork. It was very strange indeed. Instead of getting the airport I received a pre-recorded warning message about meeting strangers on the internet. I was dumb-struck. I immediately unpacked my case and messaged Paul to tell him I wouldn't be going. I felt a bit guilty about the jam but I also felt that Charles was trying to warn me. It turned out to be a massively great thing that I didn't go. At the time, the psychiatric Crisis Team were still visiting me every day after Charles's death. One of my nurses looked a little like me. She had red hair and wore long skirts with a lot of lacy stuff. I explained to her about my cancelled plans (I had kept the visit a secret from my doctor). She went a whiter shade of pale (yes, I liked that reference too) ... and asked to see a picture of Paul. It turned out that she was on the same dating website as me and was also chatting to the German jam wielding potter of Cork. In fact, he was messaging my nurse at the same time as talking to me! What a prick.

Eight years earlier in January 2006, I had tried to find a place where I belonged other than with Simon or Charles. I decided to try and find interesting, intellectual women who would take me into a place where I could feel valued and safe. The university I had studied at hosted a large lesbian literature event. I went along, completely unprepared. I felt truly like a fish out of water, wandering about and looking at the stalls with often racy covers and astonishing titles. Drawn by the talent, I attempted to sit through a couple of lectures all the while looking at the other women and wondering if they might be a good place to start. Surrounded by women, I felt stranded on an island where no-one could see me. I spelled out my name in rocks, kicked up the water around me and shouted to the people riding happily in their boats. I was invisible. I could not speak the language. Learning that a lesbian disco was to take place that evening, I decided to dress up and go, albeit alone. When I arrived at the main hall – a marvellously loud and large DJ named Mad Mandy was already in full swing. I scanned the room, feeling like I was in an alternative universe. Only five years earlier I had queued in this room to get my degree paperwork sorted out. Francis had waited for me outside. It was my turn to be on the outside. I jumped at the first puddle I saw, sitting on the edge of a lively group of around ten women. It was the loneliest place, and I was a tourist in what I had thought would be a safe land. A couple of people gave me the once over and one woman even commented on my boobs. I smiled not least because I didn't have a clue what to say. I could have laughed at my boobs being a reason for comment with a man, knowing he was nervous and a little inappropriate. A woman speaking to me like this was so out of my experience that I had no clue how to respond. I sat there, like the unpopular girl in school who nobody wants to talk to. Deciding to leave, I gathered my coat and the 'boob' lady touched my arm. 'Do you fancy coming to a barbeque tomorrow?' she smiled. I was thrilled to be included and I jumped at the chance. Sue was a small woman with short hair and a strong grin. I walked out of the hall and set off home, feeling a tinge of optimism.

The following day was Sunday and I waited by the church for Sue to pick me up in her car. I was still fumbling to understand the language and did not know how to engage with the circle of friends I was getting to know. I was on the outside. At the barbeque it was the same situation. The humour seemed aggressive and I found it strange and unfamiliar. I helped myself to gateaux feeling more and more isolated. This was so like being at school, ostracized and lacking in what it would take to be included. The afternoon ended in a game of scrabble and I was now so out of my depth that I wanted to run back to the Doll's House, albeit a place of isolation in itself. Cath, a slight woman with greying cropped hair offered to give me a lift. When we reached my house I invited her in for coffee .... There it was again... the ubiquitous cup. Cath and I sat on the sofa I had brought with me from the home I had left behind. She began to try and kiss me. I was so shocked, I'm not sure why – I had wanted to belong again. I attempted to respond as she tried to take things further. All of a sudden, every door within me slammed shut. With a bang. I knew in an instant that this was not my future. Every cell within me shrank away. This was the start of my sobbing. The quaking fear that shrouded my sanity. Stunned, Cath tried to calm me, apologizing. I held her hand and between the tears I explained that this was not her fault, it was my mistake. I would have tried anything at that point to feel of worth again. Of worth as a wife or a girlfriend, as a person. I could not restrain the overwhelming tide of insanity. I cannot even say emotion, because emotion is mostly sane. Just as it would be eight years down the road, I lost all ability to think clearly. Suddenly I picked up my phone and telephoned John. John's wife Clara answered and tried to calm me as I begged her to give me Charles's phone number. I had destroyed my ability to ring him but had given the number to John and Clara just in case I found myself in Coventry. As Cath stroked my arm, and brought me a mug of tea (not coffee) Clara began to tell me that I was loved and was not alone. After the two attempts at suicide, I think my friends were wary of my instability. After more attempts to reassure me, Clare gave me the number. I rang immediately. Dot answered. Barely able to speak I asked to talk with Charles. She called him to the phone. I attempted to reach him through the building hysteria. 'I am here with a woman and I want to come to Coventry', I screamed. This telephone call was to become iconic in our memory and even now I remember, cringing with terror.

From March 2014 to March 2015 I sailed and I sank. I took Lucy to Berlin where we visited an abandoned theme park on the outskirts of the city. How Lucy found it I will never know. When we arrived, it was shut to visitors and guarded by men in uniforms with large dogs. This didn't prevent my daughter however, as she found a bit of loose fencing and truly expected us to roll under it like secret agents. I declined the offer, much to Lucy's disappointment. I also took Michael to Iceland, which was also a strange trip. I booked the four-day break on a discount site and when we arrived, we were too far out of Reykjavík to walk and The Northern Lights were cancelled. We were given one tiny room, with a bathroom and toiled surrounded by clear glass. Not great when your son is twenty-eight years old and has a secret addiction. We did have fun though, whale watching and buying leather wrist bands.

I decided to clear out the house, but it felt physically painful to bag up Charles's stuff, the piles of papers and some clothing. There was no point in keeping it all though. I kept the things that were him. Janice came over and told me the news.

Some local children (more like young youths) had reached into the skip and stolen the bags containing Charles's papers and contact lenses and the like. The whole lot had been thrown in hedges and down the local lanes. I walked out the back into the next street. It had been raining that day and the back lane was really muddy. All I could see was identification cards, letters, work papers and personal details. The contact lenses had been opened and they were hanging in the bush like some kind of sick Christmas tree. I tried to pick everything up but the mud covered so much of it. A woman walked past with her dog and she asked me if I had been burgled. I replied that someone had stolen my dead husband's possessions and thrown then over the whole area. She didn't know what to say and I didn't know how to explain.

When June 2015 arrived, and my wedding to Anthony approached, I threw caution to the wind and began ordering wedding dresses. We chose not to send out invites (not least because there was only ten weeks between getting together and the wedding itself). We asked our friends and family informally. I had asked Michael to give me away, but three weeks before the wedding, he went into melt-down and I discovered the extent of his addiction to heroin. This is for a later chapter and not here with the wedding celebrations.

I was sadder than I can say not to have Michael give me away, but in his place, Lucy took over. I had asked Sarah to be my bridesmaid. By this time, she was seven months pregnant and looking every part the glorious woman. I remembered that day, how Charles had paid for Sarah and I to go to a spa whilst he was in hospital. We had been in hysterics because the treatment we had chosen was called 'pig in mud'. We sat in a tiled Moroccan booth, facing one another, knees practically touching. There was no mud in sight and as we waited a suspicious mist rose up from the floor inch by inch. When it reached our noses, suddenly, cold water poured down on Sarah from above. I snorted like a pig and then it happened to me too. 'I've been water boarded'! She shouted. Later that afternoon, Sarah was in her massage session when my phone rang. It was the hospital, Charles was failing and I can see Sarah now, running like Anika Rice through the corridor getting dressed as she went.
These things I remembered when she walked before me down the aisle and I turned to meet Anthony's gaze.

I settled on a vintage-style, full length blush lace dress. It was a stunning morning and everyone seemed to be smiling. Sarah and her family had brought me to York from Barwell the day before. I had been feeling really worn down, worried about Michael and a bit scared about my quick decision to marry Anthony, if I'm honest. I knew absolutely that it was what I wanted but I think I was just tired and sad. The day itself was fantastic however, and a real change of mood came with it. Sarah came over to my parent's house, which was a short walk from the town centre and the Register Office. I smiled as the Register Office was just a zebra crossing away from the psychiatric hospital where I spent my first admissions and consultations. I also knew that I would be back there in the not too distant future. Sarah and I got out of the car, lovingly decorated by my sister and her friend and we walked down the beautiful road to the Register Office. People waved from their cars and on the street. I began to feel properly happy, in the right place at the right time. All of a sudden, a blue suited figure ran towards me. Anthony's twenty-six-year-old son was waving his arms and grabbed hold of me really tightly. 'My new Mummy'! he shouted. 'I am really really happy'! It was the ultimate icing on the cake. I laughed at Josh and said to him 'Is he here yet'? 'He's already there', Josh grinned. 'He doesn't mess about'.

When Sarah, Lucy and I entered the room to 'How long will I love you?' by Ellie Goulding. How Long Will I Love You lyrics © Sony/ATV Music Publishing LLC

Anthony was smiling at me. His son Josh, was smiling too as his best man. I had written a poem for him. My last poem was for Charles and was read at his funeral. As we joined hands and grinned at each other, the moment was truly golden. I wasn't manic, I wasn't agitated, and the peace crept into my brain like the welcome return of a loved one in the night.
I wore a swan necklace and a swan bracelet.

Two days later we rode to my sister's house in Langthwaite, Arkengarthdale on Anthony's large motorbike. I held on to Anthony with our large rucksack on my back. My sister and her neighbour had created a honeymoon nest for us in the large conservatory overlooked only by the purple Daleside and assorted sheep. There were baskets of fruit and cake, Champaign, cards and streamers everywhere. Happy birthday banners and wedding congratulations hung from every window. My sister had baked most of the food herself and it truly was a moment from heaven.

How my river runs

Chapter Six
The River Source, Crescendo of the Voiceless Choir

I was born in 1966, York, to the sound of cheers. My Mother had a difficult pregnancy which concluded in the final month as a hospital stay. We were placenta Previa and I was blessed while still in my Mother's belly. As our Football World Cup played out, I was screaming my head off, literally.

My Mother is a self-made woman, who bought her own school in 1963. She made her way through early life by making people laugh. I recognize in myself the same desire to be of worth.
For much of my life, probably the first thirty-eight years, we chose not to speak of pain that was easiest left behind. When I began to study for my degree in Counselling Studies, I realised that many things had been compartmentalized. My mum said that this is how bad memories should stay, but I believe that all boxes begin to leak over time.

As a child, my Mother swam in the river. Around the bridge closest to our home, she would tell us tales of the 'big drop', where the river bed fell away and the currents were lethal. My sister and I were not allowed to swim in the river, but we did dabble our feet in the edge when summer made the water look clean.

Grandad owned a boat that one day broke down and needed to be towed to land by a friend with a much larger boat. Mum and the family were transferred to the friend's boat and to this day, Mum remembers Grandad's face when the tow broke.
She turned around to see Grandad standing stranded as they continued on without him. A day without power, yet my grandfather was powerful. Serving the whole of the war firstly on the big guns in the Royal Artillery, always in First Aid and then for the rest of it as a Medic. A big man with a gentle heart, full of a desire to be of worth also.

Helen Mary Barr

The Inevitable Flood

After Lammas it rained so much.
The first fruits hung and neared their drop.
I walked with my Father across the Ings. My Mother remained
And there she sings , obscured by steam and long gone things.
I slipped at the edges, the Ouse broke its banks,
Drowning the Kingcups and choking the drains.
The Harvest moon blushed as a heavy pink stain
An August round apple in new summer rain.
Provocative and unapologetic.
At night my heart shivered and stretched
Tall as the ache of the growing Eucalyptus tree,
 gangly and awkward etched
Darkly, outside my bedroom window.
The Ings were sinking in rivulets, crossing the land in black and glassy veins,
Blood and water invading the earth, changing
The shape of its body, all that remains
Are tall grasses.
In my red wellies, painful and tight, wishing for pretty showers,
 Not this cold water pushing at my shins,
I watched pale Cow Parsley flowers
Float upside down, like pond skaters on the surface.
Remembering Summer and gold butter bunches of childish smiles,
Kingcups for my Mother.
I could no longer see my face in their yellow glow,
 not in this dark mirror.
The first of her daughters to breathe
Underwater.
I felt this little girl leave, and her body was clammy and white
With petals falling on her frightened face.
Pouring unstoppable, the flood swept childish things clean away.
In horror I saw my pale figure drifting, my face turned towards the reddened moon.
With a shudder, I realized that my feet had become quite naked.

How my river runs

My earliest memory is riding on the back of my Mother's
scooter to 'Premier Commercial School' which sat neatly in
Stonegate, York, in the shadow of York Minster. I remember
being amongst the students who came to learn typewriting
and shorthand, and sitting with them at lunchtime as they
made their coffee and hot chocolate. I was brought up
listening to the sound of my mother teaching. Also, the
school in Stonegate was haunted. Every evening after class
had ended, the chairs would be placed neatly on top of the
desks. Even as a little child I was afraid the following
morning to arrive at the school only to find the light bulb
smashed and the chairs scattered across the floor. The
school was built in 1500 with an enormous tree going up
through the floors, and as with most places in York, it had a
strange history. My parents married in July 1963 and later
that Summer, Mum moved into the school along with her
brother Raymond who worked with her in a printing and
duplicating business on the top floor. Stonegate (one of the
most recognized streets in York) needed to be closed so that
a large crane could lift my uncle's printer in through the
window.

Footsteps could be heard coming up the numerous narrow
stairs to the school and frequently there would be nobody
there. My cousins Jo, Chris and I remember our days
together playing almost in touching distance of the Minster.

The second school my Mother moved to was even scarier.
The year my Sister Elizabeth (Liff) was born, 1970, my
Mother took premises on the banks of the river. Just outside
the school gate, river boats were moored for hiring and for
tourist rides. I still love to see the boats today, they are red
and pretty and make me feel safe when the river is angry
and rising. In our late teens and early twenties, Liff and I
worked for our Mother at the school.

In 1988 we had just begun to introduce computer lessons
and were in awe of the black screen and green text. My
sister and I had 'found' one another and become best
friends. At sixteen years old, Liff was the target of a violent
sexual attack. I was living in Warthill, a village not far from

York, with John and one-year-old Michael. We had no phone at the time and my parents would ring the phone box outside the house or contact a family in the village with an emergency. Warthill is a small place with only four Council houses, of which ours was one. The rest of the village belonged to wealthy families, directors from prominent Yorkshire companies. I think that the predominantly Christian community saw John, Michael and I as a family in need. It is true that we had virtually no money, no carpets and were unable to walk into York to get family support, but it was a strange and often humorous time. Sitting in front of the fire one evening, a sudden and frightening noise filled the room. Suddenly a vast cloud of soot rushed out from the fireplace and covered both John, Michael and myself. We sat looking at one another, realizing that we had forgotten to sweep the chimney.

Michael wasn't feeding properly, so the doctor visited us and asked to see me breast feeding him to get an idea of what was going wrong. The room was silent, almost biblical as the doctor and John watched Michael feeding. Out of nowhere, the cork from our demi-john of home brewed wine exploded and hit the ceiling. The doctor nearly jumped out of his skin as did John and I but Michael just carried on feeding quietly away.

When food ran low, John put on dark clothes and a black hat, then slipped into the night like a ninja to pick potatoes from a nearby field. We would then bake them or make ourselves crisps. My overriding memory however, is John, filling a metal bucket with burning coals from our living room fire, then running upstairs to try and put them into the bedroom fireplace. The smoke filled the house so much that we had to go out and reassure the neighbours that we weren't on fire. When we chose to try for another baby, people were understandably unsure. A couple of the village residents started leaving hampers on our doorstep. Home-made cakes, cheese and pickles along with nappies and other household shopping started to arrive. John understandably found this hard because he felt as though people thought he couldn't take care of his family, which he could and did. People mistakenly thought time and again that John and I had become pregnant with Michael accidentally. This couldn't be further from the truth. In our flat, the same one that Anthony and I were stopped short in our tracks, John and I decided to get married and we also chose to start trying for a baby. The day we got engaged, we sat at the front of York Minster and put on the ring. I had chosen the ring and it was a simple moonstone set in gold. It was true that we had very little, but the idea of starting a family was something I bought into completely. At nineteen years old, a new family of my own was the overwhelming choice. My relationship with my parents was at best complicated and I was driven to find worth wherever I could find it, especially in a family of my own making.

I was four months' pregnant with Lucy when the call came from our neighbour. She walked to our house and knocked on the door. I knew that something terrible must have happened.
I ran through the evening as it turned to dark and rang my Mother back from our neighbour's phone. When she answered she could barely speak, but I felt strong because for once I was on the saving end of the situation, whatever it was. I was prepared for anything, right at that point. My sister, who rarely socialized had been with her best friend and a couple of boys who were known to the group. Liff was in her first relationship at the time and saw the conversation as friendly, turning to music mostly. Liff is a wonderful singer and wanted to learn the guitar. She was talking to one of the group about this and he invited her back to his flat to talk about guitar lessons.

Mum and Dad already had the police waiting and an ambulance was soon called. Liff went to the hospital, her clothes bagged up and her mouth firmly shut. My Father's middle brother, a Detective Sergeant in the police force further down South advised that it would be more painful to prosecute the young man as Liff would be needed to give evidence in court. However, the police did visit the flat and told the boy that they knew exactly what he had done. The boy was left in no uncertain terms that he was a rapist and should leave.

As I listened to my Mother on the phone, an anger rose in me that I had not felt before, ever. I wanted to go immediately to my parent's house because I knew that my Sister needed me. However, the police did visit the flat and the boy was left in no uncertain terms that he was a rapist.

My Sister's attacker had caused water to rise from the deep and brought to the surface memories better left boxed. Except that boxes do leak, no matter what people say. The following day I caught the bus into York and went straight to my parent's house. I could see that my dad had been crying. This was confusing to me, because I did not associate my Father with such emotion. It was only decade's later when my husband died that I learned my Father's expression of sadness.

When my Father turned sixty-five, I was determined to engage with my parents on a positive emotional level. My sister and I hired a video camera and we made a film. The film was a strange piece that would have done well in a tiny fringe theatre. Between us, we acted out some of the memories from our childhood, not all of them good ones. Liff dressed up as Dad, in a mac and flat cap. I tried to lift up the TV to take it into my bedroom, then Liff, as Dad, tried to kick me and damage his foot. This was all very humorous as we filmed it but to be honest it was a little unnerving. A damaging event, replayed to the bursting of banks as we laughed at what had happened. In my early teens I attempted to borrow the portable TV and I had wanted to put it in my bedroom for the evening, nobody else wanted to use it. My Mother was in the shower and she refused to let me take the TV, shouting that I was not to touch it. I didn't understand why, particularly as my Father had said it was OK. I tried to lift the TV and my Father took a swing at me with his foot, hitting it hard against the wall and causing a lot of pain. In fact, we thought he had broken it.

Recently, my Mother told me a story. It was the day of her Mum's funeral. Grandmother's death was sudden, in fact she had been planning a holiday and bought lots of new clothes to take with her. Standing in the hall, the same hallway where my Father would damage his foot, my Mother answered the door to face a man, part of the funeral services, who had assaulted her years before. 'I've brought Mum home', he said.

I know that my childhood brain moved quickly from obsession to obsession and I know I was neither calm nor peaceful. Battered daily by thoughts and fears I could not control, I consumed anything that could possibly put a stick in my jaws. In fact, only recently my mother said to me, that had she and my Father known about my illness, my life would have been completely different. I struggle with this, but take it as some sort of acceptance. I was four years old when Liff was brought home from hospital for the first time. (I need to say at this point that we have only begun to call my Sister 'Liff' in recent years. Michael and Lucy could not say 'Elizabeth' so we began to use their version of the name). Mum tells me that the hour she left me at home to go into hospital and give birth to my sister, she stroked my hair whilst I was asleep. 'How could I ever love anyone else as much as I love you'? she remembered thinking. I felt the same when crouched on the floor, in labour with Lucy and handing over Michael to Mum. I looked at the face I recognized as my own and kissed his cheeks. I knew he would always be my first son, whatever happened that night.

In 1970 my sister arrived and was placed in a crib inside the bedroom that was to become mine. My new bedroom had been my Mother's room as she grew up. It was bright and sunny but I never felt as though it was my own.

I feel that in that moment, that my head was going to explode.

When I arrived in York from Warthill, with Michael strapped to me in a carrier, I looked at my Father's face, and his swollen eyes and then at my mother, who was stiff lipped and aggressive looking. Liff told me that our mum had walked past her in the hospital and was becoming increasingly hard to understand. I remembered my staggered road to adolescence as something that was difficult for us to deal with. My overwhelming fear of being to blame for something terrible meant that I felt that I was only acceptable as a child, a child who wrote poetry and did not have any interest in growing up. As an adolescent I felt of no worth at all and didn't know how to navigate the changing waters.

During the following days, Mum began to make odd comments which felt like clues as to the reason for her reaction. We had always known that she had been a victim of a sexual attack in her early teens, although the details were missing, and it was clear that this knowledge was to remain within her own mind, inside a box.

Compartmentalising into boxes may feel safe, but inevitably, the fluidity of pain leaks. It seemed that mum had been hit on a personal level by my sister's attack.

Mum had told us that as a young person, she played the class clown and didn't always fit in. What she didn't seem to realise was how much better she was than many people. She had made a beautiful career for herself, her humour was natural and didn't need to be a safety valve for acceptance. Mum is genuinely funny and naturally giving, she is also a woman ahead of her time, a woman who built a life that most women wouldn't know how to even start. The warm, funny self-made lady who wore pink or lilac in her hair to teach did not need to hide anything. Keeping pain private is one way to be, but it will always be a painful secret. We should never feel ashamed by what others have done to us. Just be yourself, and that is enough.

After a short while, Mum began to calm down a great deal and to grieve over what happened rather than hitting out at it with fists made by her own history. The one thing I couldn't add to the situation was my own voice. I had always felt flawed, much less than perfect. At sixteen years of age, I went out into the wilderness of the bike pub with my cousin Jo. Unable to cope with a family holiday to Scotland, I had remained at home and stayed with my Uncle, Aunt and two cousins, Jo and her brother Chris. My Uncle was my Mum's only brother and he had married the girl next door, literally, the house which adjoined our family home.

How my river runs

My journey into the bike pub that night was to bring me three husbands, two fiancés' and two children. It was where I thought I might feel some worth, given that such groups come together because they often don't fit in elsewhere. The truth was that I felt even less attractive and more lacking in acceptability than ever.

I crept into the pub, feeling sort of empowered by my foray and a world of imperfection. Jo pretty soon found her best mate, who at the time was in a relationship with Francis, who was to become my second husband ten years later.

The first couple of times I ventured forth, I was drawn to two boys, but one in particular. He had long blonde hair and dark eyes. It would be fair to say that I liked him straight off. He seemed deep. I had not had a real relationship with anyone. I had found crushes and the odd dalliance or two with boys I met at the local disco, but I had never ever felt attractive or desirable. I didn't know how to feel these things. Bullies find a way to damage you from the inside out, even if a fist is never raised. I had been bullied so much at school that I thought I would never be part of normal life as a young person. I had been spat on at the bus stop, pushed from bus seats on my way to school and kicked whilst waiting for class. Only Margaret, my school friend came to my rescue and also my Mother, who became a tigress on such occasions, contacting parents and writing letters to the school, some of which were read out in assembly. Everyone knew who was writing but I didn't mind because I was being protected. Again, my ability to keep a slight distance from the bullies and myself by talking about all things paranormal, scaring them, worked in my favour.

In the bike pub, just turned sixteen years old I watched the blond young man came over to talk to me with his mate. We talked but I had no clue how to hold a conversation with him as I did not seem to have any way of understanding what was happening.

During my teens, I would routinely try and escape from home, with exaggerated attempts at running away. The people living across the back to our garden, would telephone my Mother to say that I had the bedroom window open and was climbing out. The idea of running remains with me to this day as a blessed relief from my attempts at controlling the relentless noise inside my head. One afternoon, I ran out of the house, having been locked in by my parents to prevent me from meeting up with my friend, who was seen as a disruptive influence. Interestingly, my friend's mother thought the same about me, and so she was locked in her house also. My friend lived above the family bakery and we had begun to investigate the bike pub together, getting to know boys and smoking cannabis. As I ran that day, I felt a freedom surge throughout my body, I think I was running from myself. I leapt over the front wall and ran to my friend, whose parents were out but had locked the front door. Clambering round the back into the garden, I pushed an old climbing frame up to the back wall of the house. My friend opened the bedroom window and climbed onto the metal frame. We took with us a diary each, a Bible and cakes from the bakery. Eventually, we decided to knock on the door of the Samaritans, who had offices in the centre of town. The kind women let us in and allowed us to sleep on the floor in sleeping bags. However, it was their firm policy that they needed to contact those responsible for us. When one of the ladies rang my parents, my Mother answered. She was told that I was safe but not where I was, as this too was policy in case the person seeking help was in danger. I was sixteen years old also which I think made a difference. I understand what it is to despair for your child, probably more than most as Michael put me in some terrible situations as a result of his drug use. I think that I was also so hard to understand, screaming and filled with jumbled thoughts. Just like the baby who was sick on all her clothes, my parents didn't know what to do anymore. They were relieved that I was safe but angry at my behaviour, telling the woman that I should not be listened to as I was mentally unwell. It had all become too much for us to deal with and as a family we ought to have seen the signs, but we just didn't. Perhaps one day I will have insight into my past but for now, I am content to just accept it.

The following morning, I walked into a public toilet and washed my face. I still felt free, even though I'm not sure what from, but I also felt homesick. In spite of the tough times at home growing up, I always felt chronic homesickness. I arrived home to a barrage of anger and disbelief. The anger raged and I slid between my bed and the wall it was up against. I stayed there.

The following week, I went with Pix to his house. It was a massive culture shock. After the strict way my home life was run, to see such a laid-back house was like being on another planet. Pix's dad was a security guard and he was laying on the living room floor with no shirt on. His brother and heavily pregnant girlfriend were on the sofa eating toast. Pix's two-year-old daughter was running around and his mother was making mugs of tea for everybody. The whole family were watching tea-time game shows. I sat down with Pix's brother and felt as though I couldn't move. I didn't know how to function in this environment. Part of me relished the relaxed house hold but a lot of me was terrified. I couldn't share what I was doing with my parents because I knew they would stop me from exploring this new world. I ought to have stopped exploring, but it's hard not to search for a way out when you are lost.

A few times, I just needed to run as fast as I could. I began to spend more time at the bike pub but my hair was wrong, it was short in the 'New Romantic' style. My only good friend, Margaret, whom I met at school when we were eleven years old had encouraged me to join her on stage at the local disco. Aged fifteen and dressed as Toyah, wearing long black gloves with two fingers cut out so I could eat chips, Margaret and I decided to get engaged and run away together. Our friendship remained firm for the rest of our lives, through our husbands, our pregnancies and miscarriages until her death from cervical cancer in 2002. Margaret had been my protector, my savior, the only one to encourage me in my off-the-wall behavior. When the bullies set in, she stood ground for me. I had grown up with a number of other friends but didn't ever feel that I belonged. I was standing in the front room at home, eleven year's old, when I saw a group of girls run up the path and post something through the letter box. My name was on the envelope and when I opened it, a tiny seed had been taped to the inside, with the words 'this is your brain' scrawled next to it. This pretty much sums up the way I saw myself amongst the local group of girls. Of course years later, I see a couple of them differently. They have even become friends, but for that to happen, I needed to accept myself and stop being afraid. The bike pub was my freedom, my chance to belong with others who were also on the edge of society.

My clothes didn't work either. I was a square peg in a dark hole. In an attempt at fitting in, I had become a student at the local sixth form college. When I had begun secondary school, after failing my eleven-plus, my Mother was bitterly disappointed. I didn't realize that her outburst was born of a suppressed need for me to succeed. My mum had worked hard to find her sense of worth and she wanted the same for me. I didn't understand this back then but now, as the boxes begin to leak, I understand. By the time I left school, I was sleeping at Pix's house or on the floor of bikers from the pub. I had very low grades, couldn't sleep and wanted nothing more to run away. I would return home for clean clothes and food. I saw the pain this caused Mum but my emotions were strangled and I couldn't communicate how painful it was to be the one breaking the home where my childhood self still existed. The doctor had referred me for counselling at the Family Centre where we were encouraged to go as a family. My Mother used her teaching associations to get me the place studying A levels. In the end, I couldn't cope with anything other than art, and every lesson I took was geared to this. As I saw more of Pix even though we barely spoke, I became more and more withdrawn. After the first term at Sixth Form I was taken to one side by the Head Mistress and asked if I were taking drugs. My face was pale with dark circles under my eyes. I had started to wear a dress belonging to my mother, and wrapped ribbon around my ankles thinking that it would look like sandals from Ancient Greece.

I couldn't seem to express myself well. Whoever I was lived deep inside my brain and only became real when the darkness drowned me or the mania took me into the sky, only to rain down into the river again. My secondary school leaving disco (which wasn't fancy dress) had come and gone, with my appearance as David Bowie from the music video 'Ashes to Ashes'. I wore knickerbockers in green and blue check, with a matching top and clown's collar. I had a pale blue beret on my head and lightening stripes drawn on my face, like Steve Strange in 'Fade to Grey' by Visage. The response I got was utter bewilderment. I wasn't picked on that night, because nobody knew how to deal with me. This was the first time that I had felt any sort of personal power. Even Margaret thought I had lost the plot. The evening culminated in my first ever childish grope, with a boy from another school, down in the deserted playground of my old primary school. I look back at the girl in the clown suit and how confused she was. What should have been a rite of passage left me feeling evil. A couple of years earlier I had gone on a school trip to Edinburgh for a few days. On the third night, giggling, my room-mate and I invited a couple of our fellow classmates, boys, into our room. The lads were really nice and didn't deserve the way I behaved. We split into two couples for a harmless snogging session and all was innocent fun until I was grabbed by terror. I took hold of my boy's curly hair, attempting to bang his head onto the wall. My friend looked at me incredulous as I ordered the boys out of the room, dragging the sheets onto the floor to search for 'stains'. All we had done was hug one another, fully clothed on top of the bed. I have no idea what stains I could have been looking for on the mattress or on the sheets and I didn't know then either. I was inexplicably compelled to search for the evidence. I quickly became hysterical and refused to sleep in my bed as it was dirty.

The following morning I convinced my friend that we should own up to having boys in our room. She went along with me but had no clue what I was doing or why I was doing it. After 'confessing' my crime to the teacher, my friend and I were met with a worried lecture on contraception. I can see now how ridiculous my behaviour was but equally more frighteningly, how out of control with paranoia I was. There was no reason for my behaviour other than a deep-seated fear of being wrong, or guilty.

Helen Mary Barr

I fought a duel for my poetry before I was nine years old.
Challenged by another girl also called Helen and her gang,
who thought her to be the world's greatest bard. A few
classmates got behind me (a completely new experience)
and challenged her work with mine. I don't think I will ever
stop laughing at the girl who normally bullied me, as she
turned and spat two lines from my Christmas poem with
such an expression that the other Helen might just combust
where she stood. The event calmed and Helen left the room
with several aggressive glances. I turned to follow and was
met full on in the right eye by Helen's fist. I suffered for my
art that day, but I loved every minute of it. Interestingly, the
first poem that was published, appearing in a book about my
primary school. I had written it for the school on leaving,
aged eleven years old.

The years spent at Secondary School, leading up to my
appearance as a clown at the school disco were marked for
me by rising waters. Fearful is the best word I can use to
describe them. Family holidays that were fun and bright
came and went, Christmas Days I remember as happy also,
but still I existed in another place. On a rock, in the middle of
the river without knowing how to swim, finding no response
that made any sense, blinking in the twilight.

I began to spend more and more time detached from home
life. I walked out of my studies in Sixth Form much to the
anger of my art teacher. Her parting comment to me hit hard
'Your Mother will be disgusted', I already knew that. My
friend Jacs came to rescue me with a motorcycle helmet and
the two of us walked out of the gate, climbed on the back of
two motorbikes and rode away with lads from the pub.

Pix's bedroom had no wallpaper on the walls and he had
written song lyrics all over them. I was fascinated by the
freedom he had to do so. I had taken a white winsiette night
dress belonging to my Cumbrian grandmother and I wore it,
thinking it appropriate. To this day the touch of winsiette fills
me with an overwhelming sense of dread and sadness. No
love. Keep quiet. Pix's parents were downstairs but he didn't
seem to care. My one happy memory is that Pix croggied me
home on the front of his bicycle. However the following

How my river runs

morning, sunshine spilled into my bedroom but it burnt the walls like acid. I had done a terrible thing. The river was in flood, not so as a tourist might notice but it was cutting its way through the bank all the same. The many geese living at the water's edge were pushed further into the trees by the feet of people moving in hurried formation. The birds remained by the water, holding on to their patch of civilization despite the increasing feet all around them.

I was in the bike pub, it was Friday and extremely busy. Pix and his friend Keith were in the main room and 'Radar Love' by Golden Earing filtered through the noise from the juke box.
I attempted to fit in, I really did. The idea of having a boyfriend was so alien to me that even standing next to a boy who recognized me as a friend let alone a girlfriend, was like a massive culture shock. Now that I had moved through the boundary of virginity I thought I had earned the right to be in the group. I can look back now and wish desperately that I had not done this and waited for Anthony, but I was driven by a need to belong and I thought that this was the right way to do things.

That night, just a few weeks after my sixteenth birthday, Pix suggested we climb up the ladder round the back of the pub onto a temporary building site. I thought this was a good idea, even romantic. I don't remember much about how it started. I thought that this was what happened between couples, a normal thing. I do remember screaming and I recall the snide voice from behind me, belittling and degrading. The sky was black and I think the time was around ten-thirty. Still believing that this was what happened in a relationship, I began to follow Pix back down the steps only to be met at the top by three of his friends who were sniggering. Something in me knew that they had witnessed what had happened, as it was clear that they had been in eyeshot. It also became clear that the rules of first love had been destroyed, drowned and violated. I could never go home again.

As we walked back into the car park, I suggested to Pix (still confused about what had happened) that we sit in his car and talk, thinking that now came the cuddles and kisses. I was in a lot of pain and my body had begun to feel separate from me. My Mother's voice filled my mind and I realised that I would have to keep what had happened a secret. I didn't understand that what had happened to me was abusive and utterly wrong, I just thought it was my fault as I was in a relationship and could have expected that this would happen. The rising tide I have been drenched in all my life, causes me confess my 'sins', to my mother. This has never been asked of me by anyone, but the voice within my thinking forces me to do this in order to find absolution. I knew that I never could not seek absolution, because I believed I would die and that my mother would die also.

The overriding memory of my years before anti-psychotic medication involve making lists and lists of anything I might be even remotely responsible for. Or to blame for in any way.
Pix had no interest in sitting in the car (something I had seen on the film Greece, with John Travolta) he wanted only to get back in the pub. I walked slowly behind the four of them and instead of going in, I sat on a bench overlooking the part of the river with shops and hotels on either side. Only further up to my left on the opposite side, the little hire boats were moored and the chimneys on the building Mum's school sat rising up from the bank. As I sat in the dark the colours leapt out of the night, reflected across the water. They were distorted and barely recognizable as the familiar busy street, or the school. Suddenly, seemingly out of nowhere a woman appeared. She had an Australian accent and was fairly small. I think she was middle aged and dressed in ordinary clothes. She was alone and sat down beside me. Turning to me, she asked me if I was alright. For some reason, I told her how lost I felt and she told me not to worry. She said she was a tourist, but looking back, I don't know what a lone Australian tourist would be doing walking by the river alone at night. I asked her if she would like to come into the pub for last orders, she thanked me profusely but told me it was time that she went. The lady spoke to me in a way that didn't criticize or belittle. I walked back into the pub. Pix had been

How my river runs

drinking a lot and he had in his hand a letter I had written to him. I have always written letters when I need to talk, something Michael began to do from an early age. He was reading what I had written out loud to the pub, which was in chaos anyway. Keith, the friend who was with Pix when I first met him, was telling him to stop. I tried to grab the letter, and I realised I was being bullied again. Losing interest, as bullies do, Pix dropped the letter. His only interest in me became the likelihood that I might be given a flat by Social Services as a social worker had been assigned to our family albeit for one visit.

Chameleon Speaker

She drinks her cold crap coffee down and hugs her knees in tight.
The jagged memories stab her brain with slivers of last night.
Avoiding mirrors, last night's face
Is streaked across this empty place
A painful sigh is sucked inside
It burns her as she tries to hide.

She looked into his honest face and liked the things he said.
Yet what he spoke was twisted and put lies inside her head.
Why is it then that what I see
Is never all it seems to be?
When pictures fade, melt and mutate
Make mockery and turn to hate.

The rules were changing constantly and nowhere could she stand.
Each moment drained her confidence her world was shifting sand.
The girl I was has gone away
I'd give my life for her, today.
Her life quite quickly fell apart
And somewhere she misplaced her heart.

Who are my friends who stand with me and what is real and true?
True and real is what I thought I saw and heard in you.
Tongues twisted, flapping, tripping thought.
Chameleon speaker sold and bought.
When all I need is simple trust
Still all around me turns to dust.

'Now hold that thought', she heard him cry so hold it tight she did.
But in her hands the thought turned snake and from her grip it slid.
Now empty handed, lost again
She hugged her knees against the pain
And wondering just what she'd gained
She vowed that she would still be sane.

After the happening on the roof round the back of the pub, I was walking through town on my own. It was Saturday and I recall wearing my Father's rain mac. It must have seemed like the right statement to make. At the bus stop there stood a girl I went to school with. I told her what had happened, thinking that she would think me one of the in-crowd now. She simply looked at me as if I had gone completely mad. I realised that afternoon, that I had no way of knowing what was acceptable behaviour. Even though I had been violated, I did not complain because I needed desperately to be accepted. This acceptance was only smoke and mirrors however and I felt more worthless than ever before. In the weeks to come I did not see Pix, in fact he made it quite clear that he had no time for me. When we did coincide with each other, he referred to me as 'ugly'… 'here comes ugly', and he delighted in telling everyone that he had taught me everything I knew.

Water ceased to flow around me that night on the roof and I began to scoop it up with my hands. I don't believe it is possible to store water in boxes, it should either be ice or steam. Either way it escapes.

Other than the girl at the bus stop, and Charles (who chose to not hear me) also my sister, the only person I have ever told about the roof-top violation has been Anthony. Close to me in so many ways, he saw the girl I was then as well as the wife I am to him now. He was enraged and immediately wanted to seek revenge on my behalf. His anger unlocked an anger of my own and for weeks after I told him I began to feel the repercussions for the first time of what had happened to me. I am now at peace with the child on the roof and in my mind, I climb the steps with a single daffodil, the flower of spring.

I see my relationship with my mother and sister, also my daughter as a tree. A tree underneath which we can sit and plant acorns. Poisoned branches can be taken away and roots will find the water they need along with geese to chatter upon it. When my art and poetry were exhibited in 2013, they consisted of a large tree, a female Christ figure crucified, arms outstretched forming the horizon. 'Perfection is a horizon that is never underfoot'. This is so, but we can plant trees and we can feed the geese. My sister held her pain deep within her roots, but gradually she became free. The joy of life and healing rose up within her and she opened her mouth to release the most exquisite of songs. Pain brings new growth and if we allow the cycle to run unhindered, life's waters give birth and we create a new song. Our life is no longer about that which hurt us, it is ours, in spite of the pain and we own it. All of it. Every wave and every undertow.

I moved into a flat with my friend Jacs and will always remember the large numbers of bikers we managed to squash into the small living room. We didn't have a TV but we did have a microwave. Bearing in mind that this was 1982, a microwave could be a lot of fun. We sat around watching sprouts dance and metal tea-pots spark.

After a few months, my friends and I moved into a shared house. Our landlords, Italians, lived opposite. The house was large and again, filled with many, many bikers. I hooked up with my first proper boyfriend. He was tall with long dark hair and he treated me with lots of love and kindness. By the time we were all evicted the eviction list contained at least twenty names which is great going considering that only six of us were tenants.

My boyfriend and I were given a council flat and we got a dog who continually ran away. The lady living downstairs from us called the police because she heard me screaming and thumping around in our flat above her. Rightly, she assumed that I was being beaten up, but wrongly, because it was me myself and I, thrashing around on the bedroom carpet in my sleep, throwing my body around the room and screaming for all to hear.

We were then offered a direct swap with a woman and son who lived further up the road. They wanted to move into our flat and they offered us their three-bedroomed house. I was just turning eighteen. On the day of the swap I gave my flat keys to the incoming woman and son, but on returning home from my morning at the family school I found all my possessions lying on the grass outside the houses. Paperwork and slippers flapped in the wind. I was aghast. My boyfriend couldn't make it home so I ordered the people moving into our flat to take our things to the house. In a way, writing this autobiography has felt a little like that day, watching my private things blowing around for all to see, unhindered and unstopped. Worse, because my family's slippers are being blown about the front of our house. I will gather them up and put them neatly in pairs where they belong.

Now living in the house, we discovered that the son living in our flat hated us for the house move. He embarked on a rampage of mashed potato and soft plum throwing making our windows very hard to clean. One day a young man with gorgeous long dark curls and lavender eyes turned up to visit with his friend. Anthony smiled at me and we were friends forever. Leaving my boyfriend for Anthony's friend Paul, I soon moved back to the small flat I had started out in. This too filled with bikers, pot and beer. Anthony and I wandered around together, visiting quiet places to talk and to our parent's houses for tea. Very often people presumed we were together but the truth was that I was in a relationship with Paul. Anthony was so safe and it felt wrong to push things into what I felt would be a precarious situation. I didn't want to lose him. When John came along to the flat with his laughter and his owl impressions, I was drawn to the idea of starting a family with him. So I did.

As a young mother of two, with a husband who loved me and who I loved in return, but was more like a best friend, life continued to be slightly off the wall. John bought a duckling home and we filled an old bath with water in the garden. Chester the duck laid eggs and the children collected them, Chester snapping at their heels. We attempted to add another little duckling, who had other ideas of home and did a runner out through the hedge and across the hockey field. Unfortunately, the yellow and brown speedy ball of fluff was followed in hot pursuit by Lucy, completely naked apart from a bright necklace. My moods were affected badly by hormonal shifts and I now recognize the disordered thinking and bipolar tendencies in lots of my actions. One warm spring day in 1990, I was particularly agitated and no doubt driving John crazy. The previous day I had decided to scrape all the polystyrene tiles from the living room ceiling and the whole room looked like a snow drift. I wanted to iron some clothes but couldn't seem to get past unravelling the iron cord. John made me a coffee and I began to feel much calmer. So calm in fact that I took my ironing board outside into the back garden, fixed the iron to an extension wire and began pressing shirts and shorts in the fresh air, happy as a lark. I really enjoyed my coffee so asked John for another one, which he happily brought to me, singing a selection of my favourite songs as he set it down on the garden wall. I emptied the entire basket of clothes and only then caught sight of John laughing through the kitchen window. BANG COFFEE!! I shouted. My husband had made me coffee laced with just enough cannabis to calm the edges. Now I wouldn't recommend this as a way to deal with agitation, especially not these days but back then, if he could have done, it would have been just what the doctor ordered.

Helen Mary Barr

How my river runs

Chapter Seven
Exorcism at the Coffee Club

Last Saturday, Anthony and I went to a psychic healing event in Harrogate. I needed to research the Tarot Readers that would be there. My own Tarot reading skills were coming back to life and I had decided to pull together my seven years of study in counselling, arts and humanities and teaching. My skills as a Tarot Reader and Divination Counsellor however, were where I had decided to stake my claim. So many years, wanting to practice the art of divination and so many years putting it off.

That night when we got home, I played Anthony the CD recording of the reading I had been given. The information was astounding and eerily accurate. The Reader spoke about my need to get back into my 'wig-wham'. I smiled at this as I remembered the little red pop up tent I had put up in the front bedroom in Barwell. Charles had just accepted the tent in the house, knowing better than to try and explain what I was doing lying in it, surrounded by cushions, cats and fairy lights. The neighbours had really laughed and I had laughed too, at their inability to just ask me what it was all about.

I was upstairs fiddling with the computer (probably this book) and Anthony called me downstairs. I didn't know whether to laugh, cry or hug my wonderful husband. A very large tent filled the dining room, and I do mean 'filled'. It was almost impossible to walk past it to get to the kitchen and it was stuffed with pillows and a duvet. We put out the lights, I crawled into the tent and Anthony found the CD recording of 'Angelic Wisdom' we had bought at the fair. CD placed in the stereo, he flung himself into the tent so we could lie in our wig-wham and listen to the celestial messages. That's when it started. The attack of the zombie cats. We have seven cats and most of them were now hurling themselves into the tent around our heads, sticking their claws through the material and making it impossible to lie down. We tried very hard to listen to the angelic wisdom but sadly, it was not to be. I don't think I have laughed so much in years, literally.

The experience made me think about how different life had been in the late 1980's and early 1990's. How degraded and belittled I had felt as my life with Tarot began to take flight. Lucy, Michael and myself (then aged five and six years old) had not long moved to Nestleton. My marriage to their Father John was over and now Autumn 1992, Francis and I planned a March wedding for 1993. After a loud and life changing party the previous April in Francis's Nestleton cottage, it felt strange to be packing up, children and all, to move there and make a new family. Looking back at this now, I see once again the hallmark of mania, but at the time, a new life in a village with a pond and one bus a day into the nearest town felt wonderful. John was always a lovely man (and we are good friends to this day) but I felt an old recognisable need to escape and reshape everything. I wanted the children to have a special life with a village school and with dale sides to slide down on coal sacks in the snow. We got all of this, but we also got a whole shower of s**t as well.

Heady feelings of overwhelming responsibility manifested daily. From this day now, I can look back at some of my fears and almost smile. This helps when I am unable to get up and meet the day. One such summer picnic gives me a fine example of this. Michael, Lucy, our great friend Liza and I, having not long being relocated to the village walked across the nearby fields carrying bags of food. Also a pack of cigarettes. After sitting for a while, we packed up and went back to the cottage. The following day, Liza, who stayed with us for a few days, the children and I walked to the nearest village. As we passed by the field we had picnicked in the day before, I was struck dumb in terror, because it was burned to the ground and smoking. Now I do know that smoking in a field is wrong, even though said cigarettes were put out into a drinks can, but even knowing this I was convinced I had burned down the farmer's field. Thoughts began to tumble, over and over. I had cost the farmer his yearly income and would certainly have to leave Nestleton. This fear did not even begin to subside until Francis explained the process of burning the fields by the farmers. Even then, I couldn't be completely sure that I hadn't caused it.

How my river runs

Through our cottage letterbox, one really gorgeous sparkling October morning, came a leaflet. 'The Rambler'. It seemed that a lady, Sally, living just round the corner opposite the pond edited the local booklet. In it, were tips and jokes and most importantly to me, adverts for services such as the garage, mobile library and other village type stuff. Just what I wanted, village items.

For the last couple of years in York, I had had some success as a self-taught Tarot Reader. Some really scary stuff had come along with it, stuff which terrifies some of my friends to this day, but more of that later on. It seemed like a fantastic idea to advertise my skills, along with a proof reading and typing service. (Life was much simpler then, and a typewriter was my favourite piece of hardware, having been brought up around office technology at my Mother's school since 1966, the year I was born). So, I telephoned Sally and asked her to place an advertisement for me in 'The Rambler'. Within the hour, Sally rang me back and asked if she could come round for a chat. Sally was a genuinely honest and lovely lady. She was to become a vibrant component of our weird village world and I could never have guessed how things would turn out for my naïve little family. We sat down in the kitchen of our cottage, which was wonderful amongst the shivers and the wet leaves. I had brought my wood burning stove with me from York (it had been a wedding present from John's Mother actually and I did feel guilty, when I fired it up and felt even more rural). 'So', Sally started. 'The typing service looks great; I can see that being really useful. But the Tarot Reading', she slowly shook her head, 'the Tarot Reading would not be so useful'. I felt a little bemused and knocked down by her response, to what had been a good little side line in York. 'My husband Andrew is the Lay Preacher here in the village, and many of the villagers, as practicing Christians would object to the Tarot'.
I must admit, I did feel a little like I'd been singled out as a Devil worshiper. 'OK, then', I agreed, I won't advertise'. A little annoyed I decided to keep my Reading a secret and to bring it out in York or when friends visited. 'Actually', Sally went on – 'I wondered if you might like to come to a Coffee

Club book meeting in Driffield'? Now that, is right up my street I thought. 'I would love to go', I bounced. Michael would be at school, but Lucy could accompany me and a day out was just what I wanted. A village day out with my new village friend. The night before our Coffee Club bookstall, Sally telephoned. She sounded apologetic. 'I am so sorry, but I can't make it' she said, genuinely sorry, 'but I have a couple who would love to take you with them, Peter and Jane, the best part is that they are the visiting speakers'. Curious as to what they could be speaking about, when I thought this meeting was just to buy books, I agreed to be picked up the following morning, nine o'clock by the pond.

As I stood by the crisp water with its cold ducks, I waited with Lucy for a car I didn't recognize and people I didn't know. (This would form the pattern for the next twenty-four years of highs and lows, adventures and nightmares). I loved the pond. The landlord of the village pub would take the duck eggs every year to nurture them. When hatched, he returned the ducklings to the pond. Every day, the ducklings, following the parent ducks in a line across the road to the garden behind the pub and back again at night. The landlord could often be seen standing in the busy road with a sign to stop the traffic.

As the blue estate car circled the pond slowly, I guessed that Peter and Jane were inside. A rear door opened for us and we set off for Driffield. The conversation was very slow and I did try to ask a few questions about the talk but with little response.

In what seemed like only a few minutes, the car stopped and Lucy was led into a crèche of some sort. Now I can understand you thinking how stupid this was, to let my five-year-old daughter go into what essentially was the lounge in a hotel, with strangers, but I think my reasoning was that she must be safe as I knew where Sally lived and she had endorsed the trip. I got back into the car and we travelled for another ten minutes. Arriving at a different hotel, I was ushered inside. There were a few books scattered around, I will give them that – but the main focus was the stage and the large seating area for the audience. I began to feel a little bit out of my depth to be honest. Around thirty people took the seats and I was encouraged to sit in the front row. Peter and Jane began to talk.

At first my overriding impression was that they seemed utterly miserable. Jane talked about her time spent with a group of bikers. Of course, this immediately caught my attention, as virtually every friend I had was a biker; three of my four husbands in fact and even Charles lived much of his life in a world of bikers. As I listened however, I realised that Jane was describing her former years as being 'of the Devil'. I was utterly shocked. It was the first time I had ever heard anything like this (little did I know what was to come in the next twelve years)! Peter then picked up the story and became very animated when he described how terrible the years were for Jane as she drank and smoked a little cannabis. The tone continued to be dire and formidable. Finally, the discussion (which wasn't a discussion, but an offensive lecture – to me, anyway), melted into the saving of Jane by an Almighty God who cleansed her from all her biker sins. I literally couldn't take my eyes from the stage. My mouth open, I began to feel a little unsafe but in need of cleansing.

Only minutes after the talk, both Peter and Jane were seated either side of me. The two women who had flanked my seat, enthusiastically and swiftly moved in a rather orchestrated movement. Jane put her hand on my head, 'I can feel your darkness', she pushed, in a low and unpleasant voice. 'You have been where I have been, and Christ is bringing you into the light'. I began to feel rather panicked, but this ascended into a quiet hysteria when Peter asked if he could put his hand on my stomach. Placing his hands there, as I will tell you later, triggered an even more shrill response. This strange man pressing his hand below my belly button – even if he did ask (just), found me dreadfully upset.

This is when things began to get weird (the start of weird)! Peter began shrieking in what sounded like a Middle Eastern language, and his voice got louder and louder. Jane then joined in, in English 'You cannot have this child of God' she screamed, in a way that only the theatrical can accomplish. Jane pushed down hard on my head, John pushed into my tummy and I was shocked into silence. They continued, the room still filled with people, some of them joining in with the Arabic style chanting. 'You are free'. Jane announced. I replied, with exactly what they wanted to hear 'I feel like a massive weight has been lifted'. I don't even know why I said it. Over the coming years I would begin to learn why I was so compliant, but right then and there, I didn't have a clue. I was fresh meat, and far more attractive than Christians already saved.

'We were here for you today', Peter said. 'You can now burn your Tarot cards'.
It was then that I realised I had been set up.
I turned around and almost dropped the coffee I had been given (the only true element of the promised outing), to find Lucy, sitting behind me, drinking fresh orange juice from a rather adult glass. She had witnessed it all. This was the first time that one or both of my children would see me being exorcised. The following exorcism involved a vat of vegetable oil, so at least there was more entertainment value. This was the beginning.

I would welcome, years later, Christian members from a respectable worship group into my home where I allowed them to fill bin bags full with my wonderful books – expensive hardback covers torn to shreds in a fit of religious fervour. Even the painting I had taken great pains to create was slashed and destroyed. Searching for peace, I was led to believe that my psychiatric illness was the devil itself, along with all my tablets and I should free myself from everything prescribed by the doctor. Judge for yourselves my friends.

Our cottage was opposite the village pub (now brought down to the ground and replaced with houses). We visited the pub most days as it was more of a second home. If we needed to borrow some sugar or an onion, we would pop over. Although the village was small, the road between our cottage and the pub was the main road from York to the coast. The empty grain wagons thundered along. Dangerous for children and also pets. Fortunately, our cat lived but it was touch and go.

When our March wedding happened, Sally and some other members of the village decorated a wheel barrow with a white sheet and ribbons as a surprise. My dress was made from forest green silk and my bridesmaids, (Liff and the neighbour's daughter) wore gold. My sister had the same dress as me, just a little plainer. Francis put myself, Lucy and Michael into the wheelbarrow, pushing us from the Norman church, over the main road and to the pub, where our reception was taking place. I don't think I will ever forget Francis trying to get out into the road, with assorted wedding guests, between speeding grain wagons and into the pub. Sally and the neighbours had made a buffet for us. They had used green food colouring as much as possible. Francis hadn't written a speech and there was no top table. I ended up sitting alone at the bar. Francis's best man who was also his boss at the printing company put together a plate of food for me. He and my dad made a speech. Dad said that he had felt honoured to walk me down the aisle. Basil composed a wedding march especially for us and it is these things that I remember with love.

It was the first time I had met Francis's family properly. Both his sisters and brother all arrived with their families and stayed in Bed and Breakfast houses throughout the village. I have fond memories of this and it is probably one of the few times I felt that I had moved into a village. (Apart from our first Christmas, when it snowed on Christmas Day and we picked up a twelve feet tall Christmas Tree). After the difficulties born from previous years, it made me smile when Francis said to me 'Believe it, it's real'. At that point I think it was. I was happy.

The wedding reception was very strange. Francis's Mum had brought a brilliant set of Thunderbirds toys. Michael decided it would be a good idea to push them all down the pockets of the pool table. The pool table had to be dismantled. He then got together with one of the other boys and they finished any leftover drinks that they could find. At six years' old we had to call both him and his friend down from the neighbour's roof. No problems thank goodness. Margaret sang and our friend Basil played for her. (In 2016, Basil would go on to play for Lucy's wedding also.

It was a very amusing sight to witness a number of long haired fairly tough bikers dancing to the theme tune from the cartoon 'Rhubarb and Custard'. I didn't feel completely at ease, as the guests flooded in for an evening in the pub. My parents left for a meal taking the children with them. It felt as though I was in a soundproof black case and nobody could see or hear me, but I could see blurred images and hear muffled sounds. I also realised that I hadn't sorted out anything to wear at night, which sounds odd I know. It wasn't that I hadn't thought about it, I had investigated an Egyptian costume, my favourite black velvet dress (with holes in the underarms, so no good) and that was it. I ended up borrowing my friend's dress that she had worn during the day and hanging a crystal round my neck. My brain had then shut down. The ideas and thoughts in my head had become so loud that I could barely think. I also missed Anthony because he would have understood.

In the eighteen months we lived in Nestleton, we hosted some great parties. It really did feel strange because I had been to parties at the cottage in the past. Several times, both Anthony and John had been there too and once again the otherworld experience of the connections we all shared raised its head. I distinctly remember Anthony making me a jacket potato in Francis's microwave the night Francis and I looked at one another as more than friends, for the first time. John had stayed at home with Michael and Lucy. We did nothing but argue and I just wanted to get out. It broke my heart too as I knew that I was fracturing our family. I had honestly wanted my marriage with John to be a lasting one. I still loved him but there was too much missing and he didn't seem to be there as my husband in the way that I wanted him to.

Now, married to Francis, I was there in the cottage again and having a New Year's Eve party. The whole village seemed to be involved. Sally cooked a curry, and the rest of us had also cooked or baked something. It was incredibly icy walking from the cottage to the pond. I had also invited lots of friends from York. My best friend Margaret had come and it was amazing to have some special time with her. Sixteen years and low self-esteem brought many different experiences into my life. Margaret had been my only ally against bullies at our secondary school. Children can sniff out a person of difference and usually kind people will bare their teeth out of fear of the unknown. I found that the best way to keep the bullies away from me, or at the very least unsure about me, was to read their palms and tell them about the spells I could cast. I even resorted to bringing a mirror into school with me, daring the other children to look into it and recite the Lord's Prayer backwards. This, I told them, would summon the devil. If they dared. This was when Margaret wasn't available.

Both Michael and Lucy were bullied at their new village school. Every morning I would take them to the pond where a small bus would pick them up, moving on to pick up other children from farms and remote areas, arriving at the smart school well on the way towards Driffield. One day I realised that both school bags had been kicked. When I went to the pond to pick them up, Lucy arrived partially trapped in the bus door as she tried to get off. I was so angry that I wanted to drown all the other children in the pond. I seethed and seethed. The following morning, when the bus arrived, I ignored the bus driver and got onto the bus myself. I stood at the front and proceeded to shout at every single child, so that they were completely aware that I knew they were bullies. Then I stayed on the bus for a while, getting off further on the trip. The idea of village life is very tempting, especially for children, but my experience has shown me that villages can be inward staring and they are a hothouse for anger and nastiness. Everybody knows everybody else's business. Obviously this isn't true of all villages, my sister Liff now lives in a gorgeous village but they work in a town and know how to stand up for themselves (most of the time).

First it was earthquakes, then floods.

I rang several of my friends on a daily basis to asked them how an earthquake might affect our village. I had begun to study some of the stranger conspiracy theories, New Age literature talking about flooding and changes in geographic structure. Everything I did worried me and seemed to be a waste of time. If I painted a wall in the cottage, it felt un-necessary because I believed that the cottage was going to be swept away and destroyed. Drowned by a tidal wave.

On moving to Barwell with Charles in 2007, the village's logo showing meteoroids hitting the earth gave rise to my 'magical thinking', demonstrating the unseen links between everything in my life. I will always struggle in the knowledge that my thoughts could easily be paranoid, or genuinely mystical. As a Shamanic Therapist, I try to ride both seas.

It didn't matter to me that Nestleton was high up in the Yorkshire Wolds. I believed we were doomed. This, pushed me further into the arms of the Evangelical church. I desperately needed to hold on to something that would save me. Looking back, I can clearly see the waves of paranoia literally flooding my brain but I didn't realize that I was mentally ill. I thought I was a prophet.

Sally placed a fun joke in the Rambler, aimed at me but not meaning to be hurtful. She drew a picture of Noah standing next to his ark in a modern (our village) setting. A person (myself) was walking past and asking Noah 'Is there something you aren't telling me'?
Soon after, Francis was made redundant and we found it hard to meet the mortgage payments. We decided to leave the cottage empty but up for sale. After looking for a rented property on the East Coast, we found a bungalow in a small village outside Hornsea.
My ideas of rural living and happy villagers had been sunk along with my ark of a brain. However, I did leave a lasting legacy, cheekily published by Sally in the Rambler.

'Second hand, nearly new cauldron, witch's wand, hat and spell book.

Cat not for sale.

Thanks must go to the previous Parish Council who opted out of the ducking stool program.
Sale due to relocation'.

On leaving Nestleton, Francis and I stayed good friends with Sally and Andrew and I began to enjoy their particular brand of Christianity which revolved around Celtic teaching and stayed clear of screaming and vegetable oil.

This small respite however, proved to be the only break our family would experience from speaking in tongues, cults and demons. The fun was only just beginning.

Helen Mary Barr

How my river runs

Chapter Eight
Walking on Water

Francis, Michael Lucy and I travelled to the village of Whitly in our beaten up old Skoda. However, the starter motor had broken and we were unable to stop before our destination. Sally and Andrew were driving in front of us and they pulled into a pub car park, thinking we could all stop for a rest. However, as they got out of their car and waved at us, we went sailing by, waving at them shouting 'We can't stop'!

I laugh when I think of this because it was the forerunner to the next few years when we really couldn't stop and we waved goodbye to our friends and their Celtic Christian ways. We were headed for more complicated and more sinister waters.

Michael, then eight years old, had initially refused to get into the car, embarrassed that it was a Skoda. We had convinced him that it was really a racing car because it had bucket seats.

Things became more bizarre when we pulled into the drive of the bungalow we were planning to rent. Immediately a flustered woman in her early forties came rushing out carrying a large cool bag (or so it appeared). Attempting to open the boot and give us the box, we leapt out, confused. Our new neighbour, Paula, realizing her mistake began to apologize over and over again. I couldn't stop laughing when I realised that Paula had thought we were the meals on wheels' people. Paula and her husband Keifer, a little older with dark thinning hair which blew about in his very physical conversation invited us in for coffee and we learned pretty quickly that they were devout Christians, of the Evangelical kind.

The main door to our bungalow faced Paula and Keifer's door, which didn't lead to much privacy for either of us. Particularly as I was to become a God obsessed nut job, needing Keifer to bless every piece of mail I posted and every piece of mail that entered our house. Mind you, I don't think Keifer thought too much of it. The week the four of us moved in to the bungalow, he insisted on coming round to cast out demons from every electrical appliance in the house. He also asked us to destroy a pottery ornament of a Viking as he believed that an evil spirit might live inside of it. Francis duly placed the Viking into a plastic bag and smashed it to bits with a hammer. I was quite pleased as it had been a gift from a previous fiancé.

The bungalow had two bedrooms and the largest one we gave to the children. It was a nice house; ten minute's walk from the sea. The coast however had horrendous erosion and fell into the sea roughly six feet every year. The tides were also lethal and snatched one of Lucy's sandals straight from her foot.

We soon discovered that Paula and Keifer's church had three village sites to it and that we had arrived on the run up to the third church being opened in the village hall. Paula and Keifer were to head up the church, with Keifer as Pastor and Paula as head of the worship group.

My exposure to the Evangelical Charismatic movement sprang only from my ill-fated coffee club meeting with Peter and Jane. It became obvious that Francis and I were to be a part of the church. Francis was more used to the movement as both his parents were Evangelical Christians. I however, had taken to hiding on the floor in Nestleton every time Peter and Jane called to see me. I didn't know it at the time, but I was ripe for the Evangelical lifestyle. Chemicals rushing to the point of mania in my brain, fed my desire for extraordinary experiences and in fact assisted my life as part of the church. The low periods falling straight from the back of mania, also made me desperate for healing and prayer. However, I need to say right now, that I do not believe my illness causes every spiritual experience. Over the years I have travelled and journeyed through lots of incredible manifestations, in Druidry and Shamanism. It doesn't take much to look at indigenous tribes and see that ecstatic connection with many worlds, upper worlds and lower, fuels visions and healing, without question.

How my river runs

Charismatic Christianity, one would think, could utilize the same power. Not really. It despises the work I do and considers it demonic. There are exceptions to this, obviously. If I turned up to an Evangelical meeting, picked up my drum to create a healing journey with the intention of bringing back information to help a client, I would find myself exorcised, again.

It was a really arduous day, moving into Whitly but at the end of it, Paula made us all tea and we fell on our matrass and slept. The following day we set about screwing together our beds and arranging the furniture. It was Easter Friday and Paula and Keifer were busy all day preparing sermons and worship music. I really liked the large living room as it had big bay windows and a neat front garden. Keifer soon began checking our room every time he walked past the house on his way to the 'Headlands' council estate. He had a mission. It had been given to him by God and I was fascinated by it. Keifer believed that God had charged him with the task of converting the whole village to Christianity. Paula and he had both given up work and devoted every single day supporting the many villagers, taking food, prescriptions and particularly a gardening service, all free of charge. It wasn't long before it was apparent that God had spoken to Keifer about Francis. Within a month he was out every day, mowing lawns and reading the Bible with residents. God had also spoken about me and it seemed that my role was to help run the Sunday school and also the after-school club. I didn't mind this at all as it meant that I got to play with collage and glitter. Our conversion began to accelerate, mainly, I think, because I still longed for the happy village experience and I wanted it most of all for Michael and Lucy. Having a Pastor and his wife on tap however, also fed into my desperate need for peace and stability. I constantly asked for prayer and I was never turned away. Things were sometimes awkward, when Paula and Keifer had invited another family over for Sunday lunch, after the service. Because our gardens had no fence and were adjoining, the children didn't understand why sometimes they needed to stay on our side. I have fond memories of the year we spent in Whitly and both Michael and Lucy loved playing with new friends who lived on farms. Lucy would sing into the tall hollyhock flowers, pretending they were her microphone and Michael sped around on his bike and skateboard. All of the farming families belonged to the church and I was thrilled to finally know that my children were enjoying the countryside safely. One farm in particular, owned by a family where the husband was a church elder and the wife was a worship leader with Paula, farmed a field known as the 'sea field'. As part of the coastal erosion the field had dropped to a plateau but was still useable land. Both Grandparents of the family belonged to the second branch of the church, where they were church leaders and the Pastor.

Sometimes it felt a little claustrophobic. Just about everything I had experienced throughout my past was fair game for being 'prayed out'. One event after another involved hands being laid upon me so that the devil's work could be removed. Not exorcism so to speak, but a more restrained removal without oil (with the strange language). I listened to church members of all ages give their 'testimonies' as to how God had saved them and I was struck by how similar the experiences were. Now, I believe that there is a unique communication and a communion with God, for every single person on the planet, both living in the physical and passed over. Including those not yet born. Every person is individual and so is their experience of God. Although I found a lot of comfort in the strange village we were living in, I began to feel that I could not share who I really was because I would need prayer. Even when Margaret and her partner Dylan arrived for a surprise visit, I left them having coffee in the sitting room and ran next door to Paula and Keifer for prayer against homosexual thoughts. It didn't occur to me that my old friend and I had supported one another and truly loved each other – all I saw was evil. How wrong I was. How utterly wrong.

Francis bumbled happily along with our situation although he was working on a voluntary basis now, for no money. One day we found an envelope through the door with ten pounds in it and an anonymous instruction to go out for lunch. Mysteriously, Paula arrived the following day to tell me she had felt called to babysit for the afternoon. Francis and I walked to the pub on top of the cliff. There was nothing between it and the sea apart from approximately two hundred yards. As we sat there eating pie and chips, the realization that the pub would fall into the sea in the not too distant future gave an eerie atmosphere of apocalyptic vision. Not long after this I began to wake up terrified of asteroids hitting the earth. The image would not leave me and I began to stop thinking about anything other than imminent destruction. The old paranoia started to seep into my veins. Destruction. One step further than the tidal wave of Nestleton. All consuming.

Not long after we moved into the bungalow, Keifer decided to show us his special HQ. In the back bedroom, a small sized room the same as Francis and mine's bedroom, Keifer had blank paper covering every wall. The names of every person in the village who had been converted to Christ under Keifer's mission were written from ceiling to floor. Names and names and lists of names. Keifer had written the letter 'C' beside those people he had converted to Christ, and the extra special 'CC' denoted a committed Christian, someone who had invited Jesus into their hearts and handed their life over to him. I was slightly amazed, mainly because of the sheer dedication but there was also something about it that worried me a little.
However, I do believe in synchronicity and events following on from our life in Whitly would back this up, without a doubt.

Our life in the village was utterly consumed by Christianity. The first Sunday that we attended the new branch of the church, where Keifer was Pastor, I could not believe my eyes, or ears. The congregation in the church hall was around forty people strong, all of whom were known to Paula and Keifer, all except for a couple around the same age as Francis and I and their three children. They had recently moved from York into the village, having left their church behind and followed what they believed was God's calling. Helen and Mitch were lovely but even more entrenched in the Charismatic expression of Christianity than the rest of the church seemed to be. Now, Francis and I had not brought a television with us but had decided to have a coin operated one, something I had never seen before. This was not acceptable however and seen as a dangerous object, to Mitch. As was reading any other book than The Bible. Our relationship with Helen and Mitch was to become the stuff of legend for me, as I blame our demise from the Evangelical Movement on our relationship with them. I thank them for this, absolutely. This will all become clear.

I did laugh so much at Paula and Keifer (in a gentle way) as they did have a TV. They loved to watch James Bond films, which they had either taped or bought as video tapes. They were unable to watch the films as a whole however as parts of them were deemed to be of the devil. My particular favourite of their taped films, was 'Live and Let Die'. The film existed now for them to watch in the highly edited version, with every voodoo scene cut out. Unfortunately, this didn't leave much. They enjoyed it all the same.

Another of Paula and Keifer's lovely ways involved putting a curtain across their front door if they didn't want to be disturbed by visitors. It was brilliant to think of the two of them having their private time, the curtain closed to the rest of the world.

Mitch and Helen often mentioned some quite strange beliefs. Helen had become involved with a rather aggressive and difficult to understand woman who lived in the village with her husband and two children. The two of them were almost impossible to make sense out of, and I tried, on many occasions. Already having a son in his early teens, Mitch believed that every book in the world except for the Bible was wrong and not to be trusted. He had chosen however in his wisdom, Helen, as his wife. Helen also had a son in his teens and a daughter. She was pregnant with Mitch's child. For the life of me I couldn't understand the way Mitch spoke, particularly about his calling to marry Helen as he could be quite derogatory. The things he said would have made me so angry that I wouldn't have had anything to do with him. Annie, the woman who had tried to befriend us, and had succeeded in enveloping Helen (already filled with extreme beliefs) made me incredibly angry also. After inviting

How my river runs

Francis, myself and the children for tea, she literally filled a large wooden dining table with homemade food. Her calling, she explained was to feed people. There was no way on earth (or in heaven) that we could have eaten all the food she put out. This made Annie angry and she began making us feel ungrateful. Michael and Lucy were playing in the garden and Annie began to speak nastily also about how our children were damaging her flowers. I found myself feeling very uncomfortable.

Annie's husband was much smaller in height and stature to Annie. A church member had sneakily joked with me that he was more than six feet tall before he had married Annie. Annie herself, explained to us how God had told her she was to be married and to get ready. She had never had a partner and was full of pride at her virgin status. Before even knowing the man God had chosen for her, Annie chose her wedding cake and bought her dress. God then showed her who her husband was. They were married. However, Annie also explained to Francis and myself, that she had been sexually abused by an elder from one of the other churches, whilst staying with the family as a lodger. I tried very hard to listen to her story, but with my own past I couldn't relate to what she said. She explained to us that the man would watch her in the bath through a hole in the ceiling. There seemed to be a large amount of animosity and I found her hard to listen to. She appeared to be full of venom. All the same, I thanked God for a new friendship but explained to Paula what Annie had told me. Paula made the decision to tell the Pastors of the other two churches as Annie, it seemed had made a habit of telling her story to newcomers. The accusation had been looked into many times. The Pastors of all three churches offered to give us counselling but in the end, we settled for a good old laying on of hands.

I have met and spoken with people of all spiritual persuasion but to be honest, I find Charismatic Evangelical Christians are by far the most extreme.

I learned to speak the strange Middle Eastern sounding language in Whitly, right there in my neighbour's bungalow. The language, referred to as 'speaking in tongues was a fascinating experience. It didn't seem possible to just launch into free-flowing guttural noises that had no meaning to me whatsoever. Keifer suggested that I begin by repeating the phrase 'She came on a Honda', and to say the words more and more quickly. This did give rise to some naturally occurring random noises but I didn't like the idea of artificially creating the gift. I heard quite a few people speak in tongues during the meetings and I have to admit that it had now caught my interest. Keifer would speak more and more loudly, often for more than ten minutes and then somebody else would interpret the message. I began to find that I was able to guess the message to myself, before hearing it from other church members. Now I know as well as anyone, (especially after my years of training at university) that it is very easy to trick the mind using incredibly subtle and crafted suggestion. I love and admire Derren Brown and all that he has taught me in his amazing work. But. I know it's a big but, there really is something special about speaking in tongues. Apparently the gift of tongues and the interpretation, also prophecy are gifts given by the Holy Spirit at Pentecost. I have now moved so far away from Evangelical Christianity that if their truth is correct I can only rely on my past with God to save me from a future hell. (He hasn't saved me from it so far, I've had to take it by the throat and shake it till it died in my fist). However, I have felt the power of speaking in tongues and I believe it is a transferable skill. I use it now in my ceremonial preparation and my healing work. Prophecy too, is a large part of the way I work with clients and the subtleties involved with their council. Of course the Charismatic folk would have us believe that this is a counterfeit gift, mirrored for evil ends by the Devil. I don't believe in the Devil. I believe in the absence of light and the absence of goodness, but we create our own demons in this world. The Devil should be left in the Middle Ages, where he came from, as a weapon to control the good Christian people.

Some of the most painful and upsetting things have been said to me during a Church meeting or a service. When visiting Annie, for a vat of coffee and a factory full of biscuits, Francis and I were surprised by the level of nastiness that masquerades as Christian honesty. You will remember that

How my river runs

Annie the virgin was given a man to marry by God. As we sat in Annie's living room, listening to her stories of devastating abuse, we came to the subject of Francis and I having a baby of our own. This was something we both wanted and were in the process of discussing with the IVF clinic in Hull.

'Well', Annie grunted, 'God needs to clear your tubes out, because you have had lots of men'. My boys are both blessed by God in their conception because I was a virgin. I choked on my millionth custard cream. I honestly cannot believe the way I responded to the nonsense leaving that woman's mouth. 'I haven't, have I'? I looked at Francis. He was as bemused as I was. I even began taking account of my previous relationships. The larger than life, rather ignorant woman just sat there and smiled. 'Well', I replied 'We can't all bear sons of God'.

Francis and I were invited to a baptism. Our baptism. Next to the church hall was a large cricket pitch. On the cricket pitch a large blue tank had been erected with steps leading up to it. I was immediately struck by the idea of washing away sins and coming up clean and Francis was happy that his Mother would come for the occasion. I found it very difficult to be around them and I could not pitch myself into the animated conversations. The more intimidated I felt, the quieter I became. Even to the point of staying in the bedroom when visiting their home in Wales. A large family gathering took place in the Scottish Highlands. All manner of family games and activities took place. Michael and Lucy ran about the grounds of the hunting lodge, toasting marshmallows and playing hide and seek. The more the weekend went on, the more unbearable I found it. It seemed to me that this bright little gathering was way out of my league. I simply wasn't good enough. This made me keep my mouth shut even more and spend hours crying so much that my eye lids were swollen to the point of disfigurement. I slept during the day whilst the fun exploded all around me and I was certain that the family viewed me as a waste of space. I tried to jump into the empty spaces around the dinner table, infrequent as they were, I was unable to hold my own in any of the conversations. It seemed that I was being forced underwater by the might of Francis's clan as they splashed around above me in perfect formation. They never did meet me properly. Francis's parents were keen Charismatic Evangelicals. I witnessed the might of the evangelical church when we all stayed at a summer camp down South, along with Michael and Lucy. Watching my in-laws pray out evil spirits put things into perspective. I was on home territory and could hold my own around demons and angels alike.

 So it was agreed. My parents would come to Whitly for the baptism, and Francis's Mother would also come. His Father was unable to make it.
The day arrived and the tank was filled. A number of us from all three churches were due to be baptized as well as the young grandson (approximately nine years old) from the leaders of the second church. Francis was first to enter the water which came up to his chest. Keifer and the grandfather of the young boy lay Francis back, quickly into the water. They then brought him back up having been submerged completely. Francis looked really happy and so despite being nervous, I too went under the water. As I came up, I began to laugh hysterically and everyone laughed with me, also the music and singing started. Light-headed and filled with mania, it was assumed that I had actually been filled with the Holy Spirit. The leader's grandson was next. He had chosen to wear black shorts and a black t-shirt. After his baptism, he got changed into white shorts and t-shirt. To this day I remember that child who had apparently chosen to do this. I wonder how a nine-year-old boy could ever think of himself as having been sinful. I understand that this is a philosophical state and a baptism from the natural state of man, as sinful. How can a child fully understand this? How can he think of himself as having been fundamentally separate from God and born from sin?

After the dunking, we all gathered in the church hall for tea. A small service was held and a word from God was given to me by Paula. She told me, publicly, that God had given me a flower, for my baptism. My Mum, not a Charismatic Christian and rarely a commentator on spiritual matters (although open to the idea) decided to stand up and tell the congregation that I was a special flower to my family. It was a beautiful thing to do. I was then asked to speak to the congregation (as we all were) and I found myself apologizing for the things I had done. I became flustered and upset. Paula stepped in and helped me. I can see her face now, nodding thoughtfully as she always did when listening to God, or supporting someone. Paula was an angel and probably still is.

The next memory that still particularly bites to this day, comes from a Sunday morning service. The room was very full that day and Keifer was in full swing. He spoke in tongues for quite a while and then began to shout the interpretation himself. I know that Paula was moved by what he said, but with his usual Keifer exuberance, he shouted a long thank you that Paula had kept herself 'clean' for their marriage and that her virginity was priceless. Now I can forgive Keifer, because he found his God rather dramatically after a period of alcoholic psychosis. He swears that he is healed from alcoholism and is able to drink a couple of cans of larger at the weekend. I love both Paula and Keifer and I believe that they believe this is true. I am not in a place to judge the truth of this as my life now involves taking many leaps of faith. Paula had waited for the man she believed God had in mind for her and for me, this is a beautiful thing. Paula is a beautiful woman and one of the most genuine and compassionate people I have ever known. She supported me by calling me in to her home because she happened to be up at three in the morning and saw me running out of the drive towards the sea. Whisked up by a mania that made me outspoken and outrageous, demanding to use her telephone to ring my parents, I had drunk far more than I should have. Lucy had found my behaviour fascinating as I showed her the stretch marks on my belly, that I gained when carrying her. She began telling everyone 'My mummy has scratches on her belly because she loved me so much.' I ran about the street laughing and shouting. Once the children were in bed I dropped so quickly it was physically painful. I began taking hot baths throughout the night because my muscles were in so much pain and I couldn't keep still. A run to the disappearing coastline was the only thing on my mind. As I ran, Paula called me. I sat with her, just the two of us and she made me warm milk and prayed for me. I had dug at my wrist with a knife, causing a small amount of bleeding. She wrapped a bandage around and we sat, watching the morning filter into the gloom. Keifer and Paula were and I imagine still are, the real deal. They blessed my family and are in no way responsible for the carnage that followed. Within a couple of months, we left the church and the village. Paula and Keifer had decided to sell their house, move into a camper van and go on the road with their message. Wonderful people who put all they had behind their vision. Before they left they asked Francis and I if we would take over the young people's mission. We declined, feeling the need to get back to York. When we did eventually arrive back in York, homeless, the synchronicity between ourselves and Helen and Mitch hit unbelievable proportions. Probably the strangest tale I have yet to write here. However, before we left the village in

Whitly, our finest and most colourful hour was yet to come.

Chapter Nine
The Army and the Mansion

I was sitting next door with Paula and I flicked idly through her magazines. Out of nowhere I became fascinated, entranced almost by a colourful magazine full of people I instantly related to. There was bright coloured hair, crazy dancing and young people, also older ones stretching their arms almost trance like into the air. Everyone appeared to be in similar clothes, military uniforms. The men wore blue red and green camouflage style jackets and trousers, the women more subdued non military style clothes. Lots of people wore bright orange crosses and there were photographs of double decker buses and minivans, each as bright as the hair and shoes. Reading through the magazine I learned that the organization printing the magazine was 'The Jesus Church'.

Straight onto it, in my radar search for enlightenment I sent in a letter to the magazine. Paula couldn't really advise me as she had only picked up the magazine recently. I wrote to The Jesus Church' about my family and our search for a spiritual home. I explained that we had lost our home in Nestleton and lost our income due to redundancy, but had ended up in a village by the sea following The Lord's word and were creating a mission.

Paula gave me the magazine, and I put my name on the mailing list. When the next issue came out, a reply had been printed to my letter, thanking me and expressing the hope that we might meet at some point.

A couple of weeks later, I was helping Paula do a full village leaflet drop, telling people about a visiting speaker. The streets were really quiet. Whitly is a very quiet place. It has only a couple of small shops and one of those was for servicing lawnmowers. (Which I only just realised is quite amusing given Keifer's lawn mowing mission). We had a shopping trolley each and were idly chatting whilst we put our leaflets through each door.

Out of the corner of my eye, I saw it. Paula saw it too. We stopped and just stared at one another. As we stood in the middle of a long row of terraced houses, we saw it again, passing the end of the street. Riding around us, in the quiet, uneventful streets, was a minivan, painted every colour of the rainbow, with 'Jesus Church' in large letters across the sides.

Without saying anything, the pair of us picked up our trollies and ran. As we reached home, it was too late to warn either Francis or Keifer. The van was right across the drive and the soldiers had walked into our living room without even knocking. It felt like mania had come home in a million people. The Jesus Church, as it existed in 1995 was very different to how it appears today. Dig beneath the surface (which I haven't and won't) it might still be the same. I hope not. That is not to say of course, that there was nothing good to be found there. It was however quite simply the most confusing and yes I will use the word cult, and also the word abusive organization I have ever had the misfortune to become entangled with. There is much documented evidence regarding the ways of the Jesus Church and I don't intend to give you an essay on the subject. What I will do, is to tell you what happened to us, as a family. I will try and give you a picture of what it feels like to have a desperate need for acceptance and belonging, and then have that need fed upon by twisted sharks who sadly do actually believe that what they do is right. After the army had invaded our house for a few hours and whipped us up into a frenzy of meteoric proportions, we arranged to begin our journey with them at one of the houses they owned in Sheffield. Mitch, the man who went on to make me question everything I think about God, gave Francis, Michael, Lucy and I a lift to the bus station. Looking like a small family group that belonged to a cult; me in my Mexican cloak with platts, Francis in his black and red Clint Eastwood hat and the children in their bright coats and dungarees, we were met at Meadow Hall. The exuberant people took us to the tall terraced house owned by the church and we were given the attic room to sleep in. This was clean and comfortable with a little card by one of the beds welcoming us. The kitchen was communal and it did seem as though everyone in the house belonged to one family. I don't have much recollection of the Sheffield house as we only stayed for one night. My strongest memory is of the loud sessions of speaking in tongues, where both children and adults alike participated. Had I not witnessed this strange phenomenon previously I would have been genuinely scared. The food was nice, and on the whole I think we were all excited by the journey to come. I truly hope that such experiences were positive in the lives of my children. I tried always to keep them safe and to make every day an adventure. There is no getting away from the fact, though, that this was a dangerous and unstable environment. The idea was, that we would travel the following day to one of the houses in Northampton and from there we would attend the Jesus Church gathering at Wembley in London.

We travelled by minibus to the large mansion, with gates and fences painted brightly and large, beautiful grounds. After being shown the large communal living area and kitchens, we met some of the families already living there. It struck me that the families we saw, appeared to be restricted by the choices available to them. A single mother asked one of the elders, a middle-aged man, if she might have some money to buy school photographs. She wanted to send some to her family. I didn't hear the whole of the conversation but it was blatantly obvious that the idea of contact with family came with great reservation and without support. Michael became friends with the young boy, James, and this made me think that joining the organization could be good for us.

We were given a small room with three beds in it and a small adjoining room with a kettle. Despite the frugal and unpleasant accommodation, something was pulling me to look further at making a commitment to the church. Francis experienced the same pull, but for him, the more elevated status of men over women and the sense of belonging to a group again, were the attraction. He explained to me that it reminded him of being in a group of bikers. Being around male friends. This I understood, because the temptation to belong to a group of like-minded individuals overrode the warning signals in my own psyche. I didn't realize it at the time, but I was vulnerable and open fodder for such an organization.

Standing in the very large living room, beautifully lit from the massive bay window overlooking the grounds I suddenly noticed Lucy. At seven years old, she was feisty and sure of herself, carrying in her stride all the confidence I had not yet begun to muster. She was marching across the grass pushing a toy doll's pram and to either side and behind, followed a little group of girls all a similar age. The scene made me laugh, she looked like a warrior. How could a girl be a warrior in a place where men were placed above them? I looked at the men in the church and began to realize that they were the leaders, the decision makers, the elevated ones. As we were shown more of the Jesus Church I also noticed that it wasn't just a sense of belonging that I was drawn to, it was the high-energy craziness wrapped around every worship session. The sessions happened every day, multiple times. We were driven to different houses all owned by the church and each one inhabited by a group of people, very often with profound difficulties. I also noticed that the focus very often settled upon young men with drug problems. The loud and animated prayer sessions slammed healing into the person receiving the prayer. Tongues screamed out from all around, resulting in violent uncontrollable shaking, and often, the passing out of the person being prayed for. I had seen people collapse seemingly in a trance, at the community church in Whitly. Loving the sensation of letting go, I too had allowed myself to be prayed for in that place, welcoming the sensation that God was healing me from the inside out. This was a different kettle of fish however. The collapse, the slaying in the spirit was more often than not violent and more intrusive than I had ever before witnessed. I felt myself crave the forceful body slam of the Holy Spirit, because the act recognized my latent energy burning up from my mind and soul. The power of my illness. Yet, I also know that within my rising to heaven and descending into hell, there are energies at work coming straight from the Creator. What part of my experience comes from misfiring chemicals, and which part is a spiritual revelation? I believe now that both of these things are true.

How my river runs

Bipolar Affective Disorder and Schizoaffective Disorder are the names by which my mind recognizes its inability to cope with the pouring in and the rushing out of energy. Spiritual rapture is revelation and experience of the creative force known as the Awen in Druidry, riding the powerful waves of inspiration and creativity, an ecstatic experience of God. It is no wonder then, that many creative people are diagnosed with Bipolar Affective Disorder. With a diagnosis that is recognized as Type One, meaning that my mania is profound and appears multiple times, I have often been angry at the many celebrities 'coming out' as Bipolar. I see now however why this is. The illness demands that we find a way to navigate the sinking and soaring, particularly the agitated third 'mixed state'. With the ability to see higher and with more depth than is usual, converting the powerful energy into creativity results in an artistic response. Art literally does heal the soul. I have only to draw your attention to the many artists, writers, actors and film makers, all of whom tread the fine line between creativity and insanity. The sadness at being alone with such pain can be lifted when we find that we belong. Between the unstifled scream for peace and the new friends who offered us a place to feel of worth, the choice to join the Jesus Church began to look more and more attractive.

Lucy brought me to my senses. After a few days, Francis was whisked off for hours at a time to look at the businesses owned by the church. After his redundancy, Francis had not found other work. He was shown the church garage, where the many buses, vans and cars were serviced. We began to realize that the church was in fact self-sufficient. Everything was provided in house. Food was brought to each house and the mansion, when a list was submitted of the shopping required. (This being a long time before internet shopping became the norm). Food was bought in bulk and the bakeries were run by women. I was shown one of the bakeries and watched the women bake bread and cakes for all the members. At the evening meal, one of the elders (a man) said he thought I would make a good 'old testament wife'. I began to feel my call to join the church diminish.

Michael, Lucy, Francis and I were invited to tea by an elderly couple. They lived in a very ordinary looking two bedroomed house on a nearby estate. The church, it seemed owned a lot of houses. The meal consisted of one sausage and a spoonful of beans each. As we prayed thanks for the meal, I caught Lucy's eye. Astute as always she was glaring at me as if I had gone completely mad. That stare burned into my brain and I threw an anchor into the safe world. It was explained to us that on committing to the church, a period of grace would be given. After that, if we still decided we wanted to join, we would be expected to give up our worldly possessions. Both Francis and I began to feel a little uneasy. We were being shown everything that we thought we needed but in truth, we were being reeled in.

A night or two after the strange meal, I was walking on the amazing original flagstones when a woman rushed up to me, holding her finger to her mouth and telling me to be quiet. I looked at her, confused, but she gestured upwards. I followed her gaze and there was Lucy, balancing on the wrong side of the bannister, dangling three floors up over the stone floor. My heart was in my mouth. I gingerly walked up the incredible staircase, whispering to Lucy that she must hold on and stop dancing about. Had she fallen, Lucy would without doubt have been killed. Known for her expertise as an escape artist, I was petrified as she seemed to know no fear. Reaching her, I swiftly reached over the bannister and pulled her back to the right side. I think it was then that the real, heavy doubt began to seep in.

As the Jesus Church Conference at Wembley approached, Francis and I were reticent. We decided to go because deep inside I think we both hoped it would be wonderful and all our doubts about the church would disappear. When the day arrived, we clambered on to a coach and each of us was given a packed lunch for our breakfast as it was a very early start. Michael and Lucy seemed excited at the trip. I don't think they knew what it was all about but to them, this was a new and exciting experience. The night before, after a busy worship group we were taken to a small house with four tenants. Here we were expected to take part in a prayer meeting. Michael and Lucy were with us and it was already late when we arrived at the house. Lucy asked to use the toilet, she was shown where it was and we sat down to lay hands on a young man with drug and alcohol problems. Suddenly, Lucy appeared at the door, tights in hand and asked 'Which is my room'? I felt absolutely gutted. My seven-year-old daughter had so quickly become adjusted to moving around this strange lifestyle, that she wanted to know where she would sleep. At that moment I felt as though I had completely let my children down. Taking them from house to house, moving from York to Nestleton then on to Whitly, searching for a way to find safety. Even moving husbands, from John to Francis. I know that every step I made was carried out with the intention of finding a better life, but I never did find it. I tried to, but I didn't. I always put my children at the front of my decisions but it was Lucy, here in this terrible place that was calling me to stop and think.

Arriving at Wembley took all of us by surprise. The long lines of bright coloured Jesus Church double decker buses and the swarms of people wearing their uniform. Men had the brightest and most interesting military style trousers and jackets and the women, plainer skirts and ordinary coats. We filed into the auditorium and soon, the extravaganza started. I have heard that a successful way to break down resistance in those who need to be assimilated is to make them stand for hours at a time. For almost twelve hours we sat in the same seat and stood for much of that time. Speaker after speaker challenged us to be more faithful, less selfish, on fire for God. On and on and on. The large cinema screen on the wall behind the speaker flashed images on and off, simple messages interspersed with shocking viewing, childbirth, starving African babies, on and on and on. Lasers shot across the roof and the stage. During this time, church members dressed in florescent clothing danced down the aisles carrying portable baptismal water. Bright butterflies and other childish, fantasy images were interwoven between the singing and the seats. Trumpets sounded throughout the auditorium. The hands-on healing and prayer continued without any sign of stopping. People dropped like flies, out of exhaustion but also by the hand of God who slayed them left right and centre. Lucy and Michael were so whipped up that I couldn't control them or keep them safe. They ran off into the crowd and I was told to believe that they would be safe.

All of us wore fluorescent orange crosses round our necks. Michael loved his and I kept them up until recently when I threw them away with all the other rubbish from the past. Michael had also wanted a walking dinosaur which we bought him from the service station on the journey down to London. He just wanted to have fun. This wasn't fun.

Again, I saw the young men as they lined up on the stage and the pastor who had started the movement placed his hand on the head of each 'soldier'. One by one they fell down into the waiting arms of someone primed to catch.

We were invited to the spiritual home of the Jesus Church, the small Baptist chapel where the pastor began his mission. A genuinely kind woman in her early forties, who had left many people dear to her in her quest for God, shared the story of her own baptism with me. She had joined the church with a very low opinion of herself for a number of reasons, mostly, I gathered, due to the wounds inflicted on her both physically and mentally in an abusive marriage. Linda told me that when she met some church members bearing witness to their faith during a street mission, they had prayed for her. She had then felt a call from Jesus to leave the life she had been living (Linda had already left her husband and was staying in a rented bedsit away from her family). She had been overcome with guilt about the decision to leave her husband and her devout Catholic family were not supportive of her decision. The street mission welcomed Linda that day and she began to take part more and more in the life of the church. When asked if she felt ready for baptism into the fellowship, Linda decided she had found her new family. The day she walked into the baptismal waters, the pool I now looked at before me, with just enough water for two and which sank into the floor of the chapel, she rose up feeling righteous and no longer damned. I could feel the spark of new life in everything Linda said to me. Being reborn from the waters is a ritual I relate to with a profoundly sacred mind. I see the similarities and the lack of difference between the restorative creative energy of Druidry and this raw, powerful Christ centred energy.

Linda told me with a beautiful grace, how it was snowing the night she was baptized. She believed that when she left the baptismal, she was physically whole as a woman, with her virginity restored. I realised that this was important to Linda, for her particular healing to take place, but again, I found the emphasis on sexual history and virginity a primitive hindrance rather than insightful spirit-led practice.

When Linda went outside into the snow, she found it to be virgin snow. Taking an old jam jar from inside the chapel, where a candle had been burning, she scooped the virgin snow into it. As soon as she got home to the house she shared with other members of the fellowship, she put the jam jar into the freezer to preserve it.

Linda's story affected me deeply. The idea that virginity can somehow be frozen and within the melting comes a great loss. Women are affected daily by abusive husbands. I have known and worked with many who must relearn to value themselves as precious, without the need to turn themselves back into children. For me, the value in purity only exists as long as a woman feels herself to be powerful and free. We rarely make love for the first time covered in the white wings of spirit and guided through by the arms of sacred ritual. For myself at least, making love meant nothing to me, I had no idea what it was or how I would find it. Most of us stumble through what is a traumatic and painful experience, learning about ourselves as the journey moves on. I believe that every minute in the life of our body must be seen as sacred. We must honour ourselves for everything we love, experience and endure. The power in the feminine is that we are strong, and not of worth only if we have managed to preserve a jam jar of virgin snow.

I am not saying that I don't believe in the spiritual power we experienced in the Jesus Church. I do believe in the power of the Holy Spirit but I know this force by many different names. As a Shaman I work with the same energies but in a more controlled and less haphazard way. I know myself to be the bridge between energy and client, allowing healing to cross and reach the source of pain. I would be called a heretic and a witch by the Jesus Church. I would be branded as a devil worshipper. I would brand them as confused, ignorant and not in the least informed about what I do despite the knowledge that we work from the same source. I know angels to be a genuine force for good, and I know that there are myriad worlds, and that these worlds can be walked and guides can be communed with.

As part of my Shamanic work, I open myself up to a few differing spirit beings. The first ally to come and meet me in both symbolic form and during a Shamanic Journey was the swan. My swan appeared just before Charles was diagnosed and it comes to me in all kinds of ways to this day. The swan is my first 'Power Animal' and I am able to take from the essence that comes with it and also offer healing with the energy too. The second Power Animal to come into my life, is the elk. I saw the elk standing at a distance, sideways on and looking full face at me. For a long time, I could not feel the essence of the elk, because I had interpreted the energy as a stag. Once I had found the animal's power, I was able to unlock all the symbolic meaning evoked by the animal. My elk grounds my thinking and I feel the presence of winter, also the element of earth. Another Power Animal I work with, is the humming bird. I feel that the energy of the bird is rather like the manic mind. Thoughts are so pressured, rushing in and out before they can be heard not unlike the humming bird's wings. They beat so fast that they appear still. I work with the energy of the humming bird when exploring the element of air, thought and inspiration. A whale has also come to me in my meditations. The whale bids me to climb in its back and it navigates the waters and the sea for me. Water is the element of emotion and the compass point of the West. The whale allows me to climb on its back so that I can swim without any effort at all. All I need to do is to hold on. If I am particularly unwell, my whale has a seat on its back where I can climb to ride the waters. One of the most powerful animals I have in my army is a tortoise. I was reminded a few years ago (at a Christian festival) of the story, 'The

How my river runs

Tortoise and The Hare'. Within this fable I see the bipolar
mind. If I feel my thoughts and ideas beginning to speed up,
I picture the tortoise clearly. I also have a small ornament of
a tortoise that I carry in my pocket. This immediately slows
me down. I have my swan tattoo on my upper right shoulder,
with the recent addition of a garland of leaves around it, in
every colour of the four seasons. This represents the turning
of the wheel and is a completion for my swan memorial. On
my right shoulder blade, I have a brightly coloured
hummingbird feeding from a pink lotus flower. This shows
my bipolar mind, drinking from the nectar of peace.
Opposite, on my left shoulder blade I have a purple and pink
passion flower, which reminds me that passion is a good
thing in a woman. It is a sacred thing. Moving down onto my
upper left arm, I have my elk, standing proud with large and
beautiful antlers. I wear these colours and these allies on my
body because they are part of my journey and they remind
me who I am, when all is forgotten and I start looking for
snow.

Helen Mary Barr

How my river runs

Chapter Ten
Confessions of a psychotic Shaman

My ceremonies involve calling the four compass points and the energies associated with each. I call on the elements, the birds and animals associated with each part of the life cycle and focus on new life and rebirth, sustaining and maintaining life, moving into a place of balance and letting go. Each quarter of the cycle has its power and a Shaman will set an intention which will manifest in the best way. Dreams and creativity form a massive part of the work I now do. Images of the tarot provide access into the subconscious laying the groundwork for a journey that will bring back insight, healing and knowledge. Working with the whole life cycle, celebrating every season in its time, is a beautiful and natural way of being. I allow this practice to sit upon the ethical knowledge I gained during my counselling degree and also the philosophy of art and identity I studied as part of my master's degree. I am not stupid enough to criticize the evangelical movement, I would simply show alongside the measured and considered therapeutic work of the Shaman, the chaos of a Wembley conference. I have four spirit allies and guides that I focus on for help and support. Both are devout Christian Mystics.

In my childhood, I was drawn always to the early mystics. At eleven years old I scoured the Radio Times to find programs about them on BBC Radio 4. I would never have believed that decades later I would write for BBC Radio. I wrote my contribution to the program, 'A Passion for Yorkshire', written and directed by John Godber about the tradition of Yorkshire pudding making and my work was chosen. I wrote a second piece about the railways in York and my Grandfather. I have put them here for you to read.

A PASSION FOR YORKSHIRE

My Grandfather lay in hospital.

He was a proud man who packed for Joseph Rowntree.

Those same nimble fingers forged exquisite golden links –

horseshoe chains for his family to wear.

I grew up in my Mother's childhood home listening to the sound of trains.

Our house backed onto the railway.

When the bombs struck York, hoping to destroy the train tracks, my Grandfather called for a nurse.

'Nothing to worry about' she reassured, 'The Minster hasn't been hit Sir'.

'I'm afraid my family don't live in the Minster', said Grandad.

My grandmother ran from her night shift in the Railway Goods Yard, freeing horses as she fled. She reached Great Granny's tiny terraced house where my mum and her brother were hiding.

Standing only four doors from the rim of a giant crater, hymn books fluttering like doves, Albany Methodist Church where Great Grandfather preached was missing.

Grandmother raced to the shelter and found no one. The end of the line.

Then she saw them, so covered in soot she had not found their faces.

 Grandfather made my sister and I a horseshoe chain each.

I gave mine to my daughter, who now works for the railways.

The piece that I recorded was about Yorkshire Puddings.

My mother, hers too, my daughter and I are all Yorkshire women

Born in York with a birth-right of hardiness and the

How my river runs

Ability to weather storms. We alone have the precious
ingredient found nowhere but here.

The Yorkshire air for our Yorkshire puddings.

My mother explained that for a true Yorkshire pudding to
rise, the bowl of batter must

be placed in the fresh, hardy air.

We ate our puddings righteously, hot or cold and I did not
forget the secret.

Aged eighteen and weathering storms, I cooked my first
pudding.

My fiancé, baffled by the sight of a pudding batter on the
back doorstep

Did not question as I explained. Yorkshire air.

I bore a daughter, another girl to grow amongst the daffodils.
I taught my child

The secret, as she weathered storms inside the walls.

Aged nineteen, she telephoned me upon entering the ritual
of pudding making

In her own home.

'How long do I leave the bowl on the doorstep Mum'?

'Until you learn to question everything except where you
come from', I whispered, smiling.

The batter is wet, but the humour is dry, and we weather the
storms and grow

In our precious Yorkshire air.

John invited me onto the stage at the Wakefield Playhouse to perform my piece in the giant, empty theatre. Empty apart from BBC cameras and Charles, sitting proudly in the t-shirt we made bearing our photo and the message 'I love loonies'.

Knowing that there were people in this world, albeit centuries ago, who believed in more than can be seen, who even walked between the worlds gave me the pain relief needed to carry on, despite the overwhelming hopelessness. My first mystic, Hildegard von Bingen, was born in 1098. At eight years' old, she became pupil to a Benedictine anchoress who lived as a hermit and in an enclosed life. Hildegard felt that she was different from the folk around her and she received visions, often relating to ordinary future happenings. At fifteen, Hildegard took the habit of a Benedictine nun and in 1136 was elected as the head of the all-female community. I discovered the life of Hildegard von Bingen quite accidentally whilst looking for spiritual music that drew me into ritual thinking. Hildegard is mostly known for her ability to weave celestial manifestation through visionary intent. For me, I read about her life, her love of green garments and her total commitment to the Divine in every single part of creation and to all intent and purpose, in my mind, she practiced as a Druid Priestess.

Green garments are often associated with the druidic life of a healer and visionary. A natural teacher, her life was filled with creative energy, manifesting through herb lore, crystal healing, art and music. Known for her flowing green dresses, Hildegard filled her life with the pure expression of God, through the painting of Mandalas and exquisite musical composition. The purpose I have in telling you about Hildegard, is to let you know that this fierce and devout Christian comes to my aid, yet the Christian Evangelical church would burn me as a heretic. Hildegard has become one of the most celebrated female Christian Mystics of all time and in Germany, 1179 was venerated as a local Saint. Today she has a feast day celebrating her life and work, and her understanding of the divine interconnected weaving within all life is as sacred as it comes.

How my river runs

The second guide who meets me to assist my healing and study is St Geraniums of Kefallinia, 1506 – 1579. Also a hermit, St Gerasimus is famed for his visionary work, both in dousing for water and as a healer. Finding wells beneath the ground, St Gerasimus also became known as the patron Saint of the mentally ill. His story calls to me on a deep level, as the element of water strongly represents emotion. The idea of a hermit locating water has many connotations for me, particularly when it is set amongst healing for the mentally ill. St Gerasimus was again as with Hildegard, a person out of time, before his time in fact. As a devout Christian, divination would be held as evil by most of the charismatic evangelical churches I have experienced. Yet my work is no different. The divination of Divine energy using the four elements of air, fire water and earth, the reflection within crystals and the potency of herbs weave the power of ceremony and ritual. This deeply sacred practice is neither chaotic nor prejudiced. The colours and image of the Tarot, take the hand of those needing guidance and support them though ancient and mystical counsel. I do not believe in the devil; I believe in the good within everything. I see an absence of light, a darkness that can be lit by the divine spark that lives within us all, a spark that can light a mind, a gathering, a nation. A bucket of vegetable oil poured over my head will not take that away from me.

I also have a third Mystic, who is extremely powerful for many reasons.

The Goddess Brighid has her feast day on the 2nd February. She is associated with candles and sunshine, a bringer of light. Her symbol is the snow drop – light of new life through the snow. Brighid, known by many variations of the name, weaves many traditions together and inspite of her Celtic status as a deity of light, she also becomes known as the foster mother of Jesus in Christian tradition. So much complexity and so many manifestations, yet one, uncomplicated face.

My most recent support has come from St Elisabeth (Princess Elisabeth of Hesse and by Rhine (1864 – 1918).

Whilst visiting St Albans Cathedral, I looked around to find the green garments of St Hildegard. I was feeling very low and knew that a sign from her would lift me up. I began to look at some recent sculptures and noticed a nun, who's clothing had a tinge of green about it and who also stood out to me as much brighter than the other sculptures around her. I researched the statue and discovered that Elisabeth, was a German princess who had chosen to renounce all her goods and care for the sick. She was martyred under terrible circumstances, having been thrown down a deep mineshaft, followed by two hand grenades. She could be heard singing even after, and so burning shrubs were placed over the entrance to the mine. The two men carrying out this atrocity were known to have lost their minds. It turns out that St Elisabeth was known for wearing a green butterfly brooch. When the sculptor worked on her likeness, an emerald moth settled on the figure and would not leave. Green was given to me that day, in the form of a wonderful saint who I am lucky enough to be able to see photographs and paintings of.

My first dabble with the Church of England, came in the form of innocent questioning. I was eleven or twelve years old with a mind stretched by fear. The chance to visit a church group excited me as I believed I might find a way to feel better. The youth group were a lively bunch and having just turned twelve, it felt strange to be doing something outside of my family. We met in the vicarage and talked about things that might relate to us from the Bible. At the beginning and the end, we held a prayer session. I was enthralled because the chance to somehow hand over the incessant voice and the fear booming inside my brain felt like a get out of jail free card. Every night when I went to bed, I didn't want the night to end. Even the nightmares and night terrors didn't stop me from wanting to stay asleep. As morning reached my bedroom it was strangled by the 'creeping mortuaries'. I fought with my mind and have done so for as long as I can remember being alive. I tried to talk away the fear and the dread but as soon as I had finished, ready to try for another day, the thoughts would start again. Originally the doctor thought I was suffering from depression caused by 'Obsessional Neurosis', now known as OCD. Looking back, I can see why they thought this and why in later years I chose to create projects aimed at sufferers of the illness. Cognitive Behavioural Therapy would indeed prove vital in my journey towards understanding the noise inside my head. Drug treatments for OCD, namely anti-depressants didn't stop my distressed thinking. In fact they made things worse. The crescendo in my brain touched fever pitch and I screamed silently because mania had me by the brain stem. I couldn't tell which fears were genuine which existed only inside my head. The battle raged day in day out. Very few things brought even a modicum of relief. Bright sunshine had the ability to hold my dark thoughts back a while, but most times the black would eclipse the sun and I lived inside my head, talking and thinking through the terror to try and make it go away.

Being a vulnerable teenager in a church youth group puts a certain kind of experimental religion upon your shoulders. Over the next year or so I continued to meet with the others on Friday evenings. One week, a young man with plans to join the Church Army, an organization belonging to the Church of England and not to be confused with the Jesus Church, a cult belonging to the free church and Evangelical house church movement. The man asked if he could pray for me. I relished prayer because for a couple of minutes, the thinking took a step back and went quiet. Asked if I had any questions, I was glad to have the opportunity to speak. I had begun to read the book of Revelations in an attempt at deciphering the future and feeling more positive about what was going to happen to the world. I decided to ask the chap if I would be separated from my family when Jesus returned and the world ended as we know it. He looked at me with a kind of scared look about his face. 'Yes', he answered. 'When the Lord comes back again our families won't matter as we will belong to God'. I was absolutely terrified. A few weeks later, after the weekly meeting I was given a card with an invitation written on it. The invite offered me a seat at a wonderful feast. I was confused and showed it to my parents when I got home. Both Mum and Dad were utterly livid. They were already angry about my being told that our family would be separated from one another but now this weird invitation was intended to make me want to be a committed Christian.

My journey began as a child needing to be saved, alongside my first meeting with a psychiatrist. I have waged war on my heart and soul ever since.

After experiencing the full force of the Jesus Church and being offered the small rooms as a place to live in, Francis and I had a lot to consider. We telephoned Paula who said that Keifer was not at all pleased that we were still in Northampton when our commitment to the community church necessitated our being there to drive the van and take Sunday school. This annoyed us a little but on balance the comment was fair. We met with the elders who had become our main point of contact and explained that we needed time to think about our plans. This was not taken well. I was still in some pain having fallen over during prayer at Wembley, also still shocked that no-one was in place to catch me. I had been given all manner of explanations about this but the most favourable one seemed to be that God wanted to make me listen. I'm not sure what he wanted particularly to say to me, I was bruised and also still a little worried by many of the things I had seen. The preference for young male addicts was undeniable, as was the likelihood that they would end up working for God on one of a number of farms, owned and run by the organization. I had watched as people fell to the floor, shaking with involuntary spasms and wondered how the elders might know the difference between slaying in the spirit and a full-blown epileptic fit. I understand the joy of letting go and being released from mental torture, more than most I would think, but this did not feel spiritual or healing in the least. Not even close. I also sat at the table in the main kitchen and watched the pastor, who wafted
quietly past the doorway. He was a charismatic and powerful preacher. I was present at a number of his meetings and was both incredulous and awe-struck in equal measure. Today, the Jesus Church continues its work on the streets and in houses. It provokes strong reactions from all who come into contact with it and will always be controversial in the way it goes about saving folk from their sins.

How my river runs

Chapter Eleven
Wild Horses

After returning to Whitly and picking up where we left off, life did not feel the same. We were given a lift back and we brought with us a young man who apparently needed the support of a family. Looking back now, I should have questioned this request but Francis and I had begun to accept requests that most people would simply laugh at. The man, James, was only to stay a few days with us and then move on. He did do this and was welcomed by the community church with open arms but on top of this, we gave him many of Francis's decent clothes and also a lovely watch, a gift from Francis's Father. It then seemed the right thing to give most of our other clothes away, mainly to homeless people who would need them more than us. Francis and I were in the town a couple of weeks later and we saw a man sitting on the street, he was wearing a beautiful grey suit and some smashing shoes.

I was bruised from my fall for quite a while, the back of my right hip turned from black to green to blue. Michael and Lucy seemed pleased to be back at school and I managed to embarrass Michael by going into the classroom because I had not given him a goodbye kiss. I was invited to go into school and listen to the children read, in the library. Supported by Paula, I felt that I needed to ask the teachers to remove all library books with an occult subject matter. As I think about this, I wonder how I could ever have become so fanatical. It is frightening to think that I slipped so easily into extremism. I picked out titles such as 'Casper the Friendly Ghost' (created in the late 1930s by Seymour Reit and Joe Oriolo) and 'Meg the Witch' from the early 1970's, (written by Helen Nicoll, illustrated by Jan Pienkowski). The teacher looked at me with horror and confusion. I am utterly embarrassed by this now and shocked at my ability to be so dangerous.

In the last few weeks of our life in Whitly, Francis and I were introduced to the ministry of Youth Work. A young couple were already putting together meetings and we started to go along, whilst Paula babysat for us. The first session was traumatic for me, as yet again the focus was on the sacred nature of virginity. I couldn't see how this would benefit the young people, or if at all, in a very few who wanted to listen. I was asked to lead the group and I was unable to do it. I understood the message behind the teaching but it didn't feel real to me, neither did the other youth leaders. I couldn't see a way of making the groups work. During our meetings, Francis and I were introduced to a young woman in her late teens and her two-year-old son. Melanie and Jack lived in a flat not far from our rented bungalow. It seemed that we were being guided into mentoring Melanie, because she too had led a 'sinful' life. I hated this with a passion. Keifer and I went to pray with Melanie and as we stood in her tiny hallway underneath the loft hatch, Melanie promptly fell on the floor. Jack was screaming and the loft hatch kept banging in the high wind from the headland. Keifer began to speak with the evil spirit he envisaged flying around the place and I just watched Melanie's eyelids as they flickered. What it is to belong. To conform with the special ones.

Melanie and Jack were encouraged to visit for tea and we did strike up a friendship. I was struggling with no psychiatric help at all and I believed that if I could 'save' Melanie then I too would find peace.

Melanie's step-mother owned a large black horse called Harold. I love horses, although I don't have a great track record, having been trampled in a gymkhana, albeit jumping in a sack in front of the horse. Francis could ride well so one weekend, Francis, Michael, Lucy and I went with Melanie as she walked Harold to a nearby field. Both she and Francis had a good gallop and I was beside myself with excitement for my turn. Sitting astride Harold, I walked slowly to the top of the field. I held a riding crop in my hand but refused to use it. Suddenly Francis realised that he hadn't shortened the stirrups for me but it was too late, Harold saw the straight ahead of him and took off like a rocket. I managed to hold on but losing both my stirrups sealed my fate. I knew I was going to fall and to be fair, it was very dramatic. I was launched onto the hard ground, rolling over and over, landing on my stomach, worthy of any leading lady. Harold galloped away, jumping the main gate and took himself back home. Francis, in his long dry as a bone drover's coat and Clint Eastwood hat with the red platting set off running after him. Melanie rushed to my side. I was obviously in pain and for a moment, I didn't open my eyes (although my eyelids flickered). I had wet myself which wasn't very graceful and my children stood over me. Michael looked at me and said 'Is it my turn now?' While Lucy simply added 'Is she dead'? Fantastic. At that point, Melanie decided she needed to pray for me. She placed her hands across the back of my right hip (I'm sure you remember this place) and started to pray. I just wanted to swear because my hip was truly knackered.

A few months earlier, I had planted all manner of seedlings and plants in the front and back gardens of the bungalow. I watered them and watched them. They became beautiful blooms but very suddenly they all turned black and died. I asked the landlord if he could explain this and he shared with me that he had filled the soil with weed killer before we arrived.
I asked Francis if he wanted to go home to York. He did.

Visiting the local council, we were told that a house could not be arranged for us in York, we would have to arrive homeless and move on from there. We were entitled to a house in the area of Whitly but we really didn't want to stay. It was time, we felt, to go back to our family and our friends. The day I was told that we needed to become homeless, was the day I experienced the first of many meltdowns. Sitting in the council offices I screamed myself literally inside out. Referred to a psychiatric consultant, I was given Prozac. I praised God because I thought it was a healing. It wasn't. I have never felt so ill. One minute, so high that I simply did not sleep and I walked the streets without telling anyone where I was. I could walk an area of five miles in under an hour, propelled by an energy I was beginning to do battle with. Within hours, I felt so bleak that I could do nothing but sob and wish for death. I now know that usual anti-depressants exacerbate the symptoms of bipolar mania, causing dramatic rises in mood and energy. At times, I felt as though I was sitting at the helm of a rocket ship. I saw shooting stars fly by me as I soared.

We stored most of our furniture in outhouses belonging to members of the community church and packed as much as we could in cardboard boxes. The day we left Whitly I climbed into the van Francis had hired with some difficulty. The pain in my right hip almost doubled me in two. I thought that probably Jesus was punishing me for leaving and had begun his punishment whilst falling on the floor with the Jesus Church. The day before, the whole church had got together to throw us a surprise leaving party. Francis and I had always been seen as the 'alternative' element to the congregation. We had been welcomed as this although the word 'sin' had occurred in far too many conversations for my liking. We had received prayer for the blessing of a pregnancy but we knew this was a long shot.

Arriving back in York, we took our belongings to my Mum and Dad. A poster had been stuck to the door with the words 'They are Back'! and a picture of the four of us. I knew that our return would mean an increase in time spent with the children and John so this made me smile. After settling Michael and Lucy at Mum and Dad's house, Francis and I walked into Acomb, where Lucy was born and I had been to school. My Uncle and Auntie also lived there still. As we walked past houses beginning to turn on their lights and close the curtains, I felt stupid because I found myself looking in the windows. I will never again underestimate the fundamental need for a place to call home. We had lost our home and now we were on our way to sleep on a friend's floor. There wasn't enough space for us to stay with Mum and Dad along with the children, so we opted for the floor and the homeless route.

We were offered a bed and breakfast for the four of us, two days later but within that time, we had found a four bedroomed privately rented house for us all. I would never have believed that this would be the start of the worst possible church experience, ever. Neither would I have believed that Mitch, the man who considered himself a spokesman for God in the community church we had just left, would herald our way into the worst pair of hell gates I have ever witnessed. To top this, Melanie and Jack were to follow us closely behind. The next stage of our spiritual extravaganza was just beginning and this time, Jesus had his gloves off.

Helen Mary Barr

Chapter Twelve
Blowing smoke and breaking mirrors

The night after my horse riding attempt, I had a vivid dream. Possibly down to the painkillers, possibly not. Either way it was a strange one. I realised that I was inside a cannon, the kind you might find at a circus. Nelli the Human Cannon Ball. Looking out of the black firing machine, I pulled my right arm free, squeezed my head to the right and lit the touch paper myself. Flying through the air, there was no doubt that I was entirely responsible for my own trajectory. Within the dream I found too that I was standing in front of a Catholic shrine surrounded by strange handmade wardrobes. The wardrobes looked like coffins and the house was open to a family who were alcoholics.

We had been in York a couple of days, most of which had been spent visiting the housing offices to try and get accommodation for the four of us. Francis's cottage in Nestleton had been repossessed, voluntarily and there were no funds in its sale. With parting prayers from Whitly still ringing in our ears we looked to God for guidance and seemed to have raised the interest of the great deity, as a four-bedroomed detached property came up for rent. Most importantly, no guarantor was needed so we could move in and pay the reasonable rent without much trouble.

When we arrived to view the house for the first time, we were struck by the obvious state of disrepair. The landlady was a woman of money who only ever wore green Hunter wellies and ate breakfast at MacDonald's every day. Her partner was a quiet man who repaired everything himself and was never far behind his 'friend' as he called her. Both were in their mid-fifties and had an oddly homely exterior that felt somewhat misplaced. Daisy and Alan bought houses as most folk might buy sweets. They popped regularly into their favourite estate agent to look at the goods on the shelf.

The house had been filled with tenants who were addicts and our landlady suggested to us that we might clean it up, given the low rent they were prepared to charge. When I saw the house for the first time, I tried very hard to see the good in it. It was situated on the corner of two adjoining roads not known for safety or peaceful sleeping. The area just beyond was good and in fact the Dolls House, where I moved to after Francis and I separated was only ten minutes away on foot. This large, run down property was across the road from a large Catholic Church and Alan had a fancy for building rather strange single, tall wardrobes. My Whitly dream had also contained hints of difficult people as yet not known to me, but who drank a lot of cider. This too was to become sadly prophetic. However, I had the reassurance that not even Jesus had sent me to this place, I had managed it all by myself.

The day we moved in, out transit van pulled up outside and we began to unload the boxes. Our furniture was still mostly in farm sheds on the coast, but we had plenty to unpack. The first time we heard a loud knock on the side door (which was exposed to every alcoholic and his wife, due to the nonexistence of a fence, a hedge or any other boundary), we thought neighbours had come to say 'Hello'. I went to see who was knocking and was met by a group of children, probably aged from around seven into early teens. The boys and girls, around six of them had come to ask if we would lend them some gardening equipment. It struck me as a bit odd and we explained that we didn't have any. I happened to look across to the road and flipped out as I saw a couple of adults and more children running between houses and the van, steeling our things. I felt so tired and so angry. I almost shouted at them to just take it all because I didn't care. We closed up the house and returned the van. Lucy went into the room we had chosen for her. She was jumping about, excited not to have to share with Michael any more. My parents were also in walking distance so all she felt at home in this weird house. Running over to the window, she attempted to open it and the entire frame came away, the glass falling towards her and breaking all over the floor. It was obvious why this house was so cheap. It was a pile of crap.

How my river runs

We had fish and chips out of paper and all of us went to bed early. I had just begun to take my new medication, Prozac and I awoke around five thirty in the morning with an insatiable urge to clean the bathroom. Because the house had been used as a drug base it wasn't safe really for Michael or Lucy. There was dried in sick on some of the carpets and broken glass in a few of the rooms. I went downstairs into the tiny bathroom and started to scrub. The downstairs of the house had two large rooms in it, a sitting room and a kitchen. One corner of the kitchen was walled off and in it was a small bath and a toilet. This was the only toilet. The bathroom sat just inside the main door, between a second main door so it felt exposed and cold. Another main door sat at the front of the house, and opened straight onto the garden. The house did not really have a front or a back as it sat at an angle, with the corner facing out.
After everything that had happened, I still believed we had landed at the house for a reason. I decided to try and pray to see what would happen.

That is when things got weird.
Without the backing of a church we felt out on a limb so I knelt down (avoiding any bits of glass) and asked for guidance as to what our mission was supposed to be. There didn't appear to be any great pillars of fire or angels coming down the chimney so I thought I would walk to see Mum. I locked up the house (fairly pointless), turning left to go along the main street. I idly looked into the gardens as I went and suddenly, one house with a minivan in the front garden leapt out at me as though I was suddenly seeing in 3D. The van and the house had the symbol of a fish in the window, the sign by which Christians recognized one another. Years later, I saw the first ever fish symbol carved into the rock at Ephesus in Turkey. I remembered this day, standing facing the unknown house and it made me laugh. I could see, standing in the heat amongst ancient ruins, that I had truly fired myself out of a cannon that day. Boy, had I ever.

I stood, facing the house, building myself up to knock on the door. Thinking that I maybe ought to leave it a while, I

walked on. I spent a couple of hours with my parents, mainly trying to explain that I was waiting for God to tell me why we had moved our family into such a Godforsaken place. Walking back home I felt really awful. My mind was racing and I began to think that I had jumped out of the proverbial frying pan into some Joker's hell. Only home a couple of minutes, there was a loud knock on the side door, next to the bathroom. I was angry because I thought the local kids were back, wanting to borrow something else we didn't have. I was surprised to see a tall woman with long straight blond hair and a smaller woman, also with long hair and large glasses. They introduced themselves as the Pastor's wife and representative of the Children's ministry belonging to an independent evangelical fellowship. Through the pathways of my brain surged a bolt of lightning. Jesus was here! He had sent his women!!! I invited Sandra and Gillian into the kitchen/bathroom. Sandra was the more talkative of the pair and explained that they were part of a local church currently meeting in a warehouse near town. Gillian, the Pastor's wife was more wistful as she spoke, and when she told me that she lived in the house further up the street, the one with a minivan in the front garden, I was utterly stunned. I did however wonder why the pair had stumbled across us. Had Jesus told them we had arrived? The explanation was almost as unbelievable. Whilst part of the fellowship in Whitly, Mitch, his wife Helen and their children had arrived not long before we left. You might remember that Mitch believed in only reading the Bible and knew that God had called him to marry Helen, who was some kind of fallen woman apparently. It turned out that this new fellowship, here in my kitchen, was the church that Mitch and Helen had left behind. Now, bearing in mind that Whitly is a village not at all well-known and a long way from York, this really was something of a miracle. Especially as nobody from the village was aware of where we had actually moved to.
A miracle from hell as it turned out.

Gillian invited us to the church service on Sunday. The four of us turned up to the warehouse which had racks of second hand clothes and household goods downstairs. The meeting took place upstairs in a large room with chairs for around forty people, divided into two halves. We sat down amid lots of noise and chatter, children running about and people reading from their copy of the Bible. A large man moved around at the front of the gathering. He was tall and broad with a big voice. Thomas was the Pastor of the Redeemer Fellowship. He started to speak and I was amazed by the tone of his voice which felt superior and a little condescending. The service started with a hymn, a modern song which I had never heard before. It was nice though. Thomas began to shout and to criticize the congregation. He bellowed at them, insisting that they weren't up to the job that God had set them. I didn't know how to take this. Having seen abusive preaching in the Jesus Church, on a much larger scale, this felt like a personal and scathing attack. I didn't feel at all comfortable. Michael and Lucy seemed unconcerned and Francis didn't say anything at all. When Thomas came across to us I began to wish we hadn't come. He shouted 'THIS is God in action. Can you see what happens when you follow the Lord's wishes for you? This family have been guided by the Lord to come here and work with us. They followed the Lord's voice and now they are here. CAN YOU SEE IT'? I looked around, shocked at this very public introduction. It was rather odd I had to admit, Mitch and Helen leaving this church to move to Whitly and join the Community Church, alongside our family, leaving Whitly Community Church to come to York and join the Redeemer Fellowship. I think it was this single holy transaction that finally convinced me that I was called by God.

Very quickly, Francis was given the use of the church mini bus. Once again he picked up church members and took them to the various meetings. Sunday was the busiest, with three meetings; morning, afternoon and evening. Thomas was a robust preacher and not afraid to terrify his flock with messages from God who spent a lot of time angry at them. I began to see a pattern. Most church members were vulnerable in one way or another. The people seemed to fall into two categories. Those who were desperate to feel loved and wanted by God and those who were desperate to speak on God's behalf. Tithing was expected, even from those on benefits with little money. Our house became a focal point for church members to hang out. Once again I began to notice separation between men and women. Men were encouraged to be strong in the Lord with loud almost aggressive control whilst women were moved into subtler, supporting roles. This isn't to say that there weren't outspoken women, who also believed themselves to be leaders of men. Sandra was one such woman. Her home was the centre for the children's ministry. I found her to be strange and overtly sexual in her manner, particularly when around Thomas.

Gillian, Thomas's wife however, was a gentle and unassuming lady. I liked her a lot. Twice a week she ran a soup kitchen for the homeless people in York. Several shops donated their sandwiches and yoghurts that hadn't sold that day and Gillian handed them out also home-made soup. Thomas made it perfectly clear that as member of the church, God required us to lead by example. We were to eat the food that was left from the soup kitchen. God had provided the food for us and it was severely frowned upon to go shopping at a supermarket, even a budget one. Four months into our work with the church, I watched myself sitting at the kitchen table with Michael and Lucy, eating packets of out-of-date stuffed vine leaves and yoghurts that needed to be eaten two days before.

I was reminded of a friend, a new age traveller who drove about the country in an old ambulance. He had taken me 'skip raiding' round the back of our local supermarket one night and the fun I had, rescuing hundreds of packets of carrot cake and steak to feed his dog showed me just how much food goes to waste every single day. I wasn't too sure though, when John and I were woken at three in the morning by our friend who was leaving strings of sausages and blocks of cheese on every doorstep in the street.

Sitting with the slightly dry sandwiches, horrible as they were made me feel good somehow. I was living for God and by his instruction.

Life at the house was very hard, not least because it had become a centre for the troubled families in the area. Once the word got out that there were committed Christians in the street, children began turning up with messages from their parents that they were unable to give them lunch and needed to leave them somewhere safe. Michael and Lucy appeared to like the kids who walked right into the open garden and through the back door. One day I had been visiting Gillian, who lived in the house with the fish, Thomas and their two children around fifteen houses away. When I got back, Michael was holding court in the living room with five or six other boys. Each of them had a big cup of juice and were munching on apples and bananas. It took a while to dawn on me that most of these children had never eaten fruit

I managed to get Michael and Lucy places at the Catholic school in town.

I don't know at what point I realised that I was losing my mind. It could have been when I allowed Thomas and Gillian, plus the many people who frequented the open-door policy to look after my children whilst Francis and I went to central France with our landlord and partner. Yes, that's right. They took us to France.

Francis had been asked by Daisy and Alan to help with the maintenance in some of their houses. I don't think I have ever seen stud walls go up so quickly and so often, ready for numerous university students to stuff themselves into little spaces and write essays. As an honest God fearing Christian, Francis would not take payment for the work because we were claiming unemployment benefit. Daisy came up with the idea that we should go to France with herself and Alan, just for a few days to maybe look at a bit of work on the two cottages they owned. For me, events were spiralling out of control. I hated the house. I hated the constant stream of people needing support, I wasn't trained or protected against any mishap and the majority of the families coming to us were either in the grip of addiction, drug or alcohol or with severe learning difficulties. Years later when I gained a BA (hons) in Counselling from York St John University, I realised just how dangerous the life we had led for those seven months had actually been. I suppose that looking back, I am proud that we put our lives where our beliefs were and made a difference to many of the families, but I am also disgusted that our beliefs were misguided and abusively created. If hell exists (and I am sure it is of our own making) then this was it. Out of the cannon and straight to hell. The only good thing I can say is that we made it out alive. I almost didn't.

The day we got in the car with Daisy and Alan was so surreal that all I wanted to do was scream and run. I trusted Gillian to take care of Michael and Lucy but I was also bereft at leaving them in the chaos of a Christian circus, led by a preaching bully. Thomas could be nice and sometimes was, but he was overtly charismatic with a rhetoric that in other situations might raise an army. His two eldest sons from a previous marriage had agreed to stay in the house to watch over it in case any more stuff was stolen. The boxes that had gone missing on the day we moved in, contained crockery and lace belonging to my own grandmother and Francis's grandmother too. We had seen regularly over the past few weeks, twin boys living opposite, who had discovered their elder sister dead from a methadone overdose. She was in recovery from heroin but had decided to give herself a farewell dose from the bottle that was measured out safely in smaller amounts. The boys walked in on her body lying on the kitchen floor. The twin's Mother was a kind woman but lost in an abusive relationship. Michael ran home after playing in the street with the boys one damp tea time. He shouted at me to get help. (Not what I wanted him to see whilst out playing at ten years old). I feel angry with myself for allowing the situation to happen, the whole of it. We didn't have to be there in that disgusting house, amongst people who needed better help than I could offer. The lie that we had been called by God perpetuated situations like this, because our neighbours trusted us and trusted the church. I ran over to the house to find that she was screaming about miscarrying a baby due to a beating. I tried to call an ambulance and calm her down but within fifteen minutes she had stopped crying and was seemingly fine, in the arms of her boyfriend again. It turned out that she had not been pregnant, she was also fully in the arms of the Mormon

How my river runs

Church, who had picked her up on a street mission. I had only encountered the Mormon street mission once, back in Whitly. I remember it with great hilarity. Keifer regularly walked the streets, knocking at doors in an attempt to tick more names on the walls of his bedroom at home. On one particular street walking session, Keifer had noticed that behind him, a street or so away, two Mormon evangelists were following his steps and knocking at the same doors. He was absolutely livid and when they followed him back home, without knowing they were at Keifer's own door, he challenged them to a prayer war, right then and there, accusing them of stealing his flock. I know that this was a massive thing for Keifer but I will never forget the look on his face as he shouted 'You pray to your God and I'll pray to mine, then we'll see'! I'm not too sure how the results would have been judged, but it was a sight worth seeing.

Early morning, June 1995, Francis and I climbed into the car driven by Alan, with Daisy in the front seat. We were to be away only three nights and I didn't know what to pack. I hadn't been on a holiday since I was fifteen, other than the odd family trip and this break was strange to say the least. I didn't feel at all happy leaving the children and I had packed a couple of jigsaws and some treats into the bag that I left with Gillian. I was sure they would be safe, it just seemed a lot of trust in a family we barely knew. We drove to the South Coast and boarded the ferry. Driving into the gaping mouth of the boat I felt as though I were being swallowed by something I couldn't quite make out. Driving through France into the rural Loire Valley, it was fascinating to look at the houses filled with geranium clad windows. We made a terrifying toilet stop and I couldn't believe that hovering over a hole in the ground was the accepted way of weeing. Taking a break at a small roadside café, I asked for a cup of coffee and grit my teeth at the thimble of black treacle I was given. As we neared the tiny village, six hours of driving later, Alan pulled over so that we could get some food from the small supermarket. I had never seen cakes like it, so big, rich and colourful. Daisy bought a large pear tart and Francis got some wine cheese and fruit. The last bit of the drive brought us into the three-house area of farmland. Daisy and

Alan owned a small cottage. There was an attic, which Daisy suggested I climb into to see what might be there, and I did find three French cotton lady's bonnets, but they were quickly snaffled away. When I saw inside the cottage for the first time, I was shocked. To describe it as a house was really saying something that was only loosely accurate. It was filthy, with straw and mice scuttling into the corners. There was no electricity so we hung torches around the place. The kitchen was unusable. It was a tiny building, with dung walls and dirt floors. Through a door at the back of the kitchen (which opened out onto the grass), the first bedroom was also full of the most horrible spiders I have ever seen. An old bed on which Daisy laid clean sheets backed against the rear of the room below a tiny window. One door from the first bedroom into the second, where Francis and I were to stay felt even scarier as Alan led us in with his torch. A small bathroom opened off our bedroom which consisted of a makeshift shower, and a chair in the shower for Daisy as she suffered arthritis and a chemical toilet.

Standing by our bed, I couldn't speak. I was so terrified. I looked at the spider sitting in a web that must have taken nearly as long to build as the house and it looked back at me. It was the size of a tennis ball. This place was the living embodiment of my night terror hell. Somehow I knew I would have to not be afraid and get some sleep. Francis poked the spider with a coat hanger, not to hurt it but to try and move it. It attacked him back. I forced myself to sleep.

In the morning, I realized how pretty the village was. I went around the back into the garden which had long grass and a pair of lovely goats that jumped onto the roof and the window sills. It was beautifully hot but not humid and although it was still very weird to be in that place at that time with Daisy and Alan, the sun melted my fear and I began to enjoy it. Alan cooked some bacon for us on a small stove and I watched a lizard skimming around the stone wall. We were introduced to the neighbours, who were friendly. I liked them very much. They had a small area of farmland worked mainly by the husband Pierre as his wife, Charlotte had lost her right arm in a harvesting accident. I soon learned that despite not knowing a single word of what they were saying, we could all make ourselves understood, even having a laugh and making jokes. I think at one point, Pierre made a

'Mother-in-law' joke and pointed to me. I laughed anyway as his laughing was infectious.

The second day of our trip, Daisy and Alan took us to another village where their second cottage was situated. It was here that they asked Francis if he would cut the long grass, which he did, happily. The dynamics of the visit had become odd. The previous evening, after spending time with Pierre and Charlotte; Daisy, Alan, Francis and I had walked back over to the house and Daisy brought the pear tart out of the cool box where she had kept it from the previous day. 'Now', she said sternly, 'You two sit down at the table here,' she pointed to the small wooden drop leaf table in the kitchen, putting the tart firmly in the centre. She then picked up a long knife and handed it to us. 'Put your hands over Helen's, Francis', she smiled, 'as if you are going to cut a wedding cake'. I must admit, right then and there I thought we were in for some bizarre ritual out in the wilds of this tiny little group of houses. 'You may conceive a baby while you are here and I hope you do', she announced. I looked at Francis. It was an odd thing to say. It was highly unlikely that I would conceive a baby on the trip as we had been told that only IVF would give us a child between us.

When Lucy was only three months old, John and I had become pregnant for the third time. The miscarriage was so traumatic. As an 'incomplete miscarriage' I was required to catch the fetal tissue in a papier machet bedpan so that it could be tested and verified. This I did and was in fact in the toilet doing this when my Mum arrived, chatting to the other women on the ward and jokingly asking them if any of them wanted a daughter. I understand why she did this; I think that another pregnancy so soon had pushed the boundaries of what she thought made her look like a bad mother to me. It was very mixed up and very sad because she didn't know how hard it was to hear. The baby hadn't been planned but I was losing it all the same. I don't remember anything nice about any of my pregnancies, or my weddings. Only my wedding day with Anthony holds wonderful memories.

Two months later, I was rushed onto hospital having haemorrhaged. I could feel the pressure from inside, pushing down with contractions. The gynecologist pressed his hand onto the right side of my lower tummy and I almost choked with the pain. Nobody had believed me when I said that there was another baby. My own GP snapped 'You have had a miscarriage Mrs. Hocking, what do you expect'. Days later he was at my bedside tripping over his apologies. My right fallopian tube was blocked and the pains in my right shoulder tip were a symptom of internal bleeding. The fallopian tube was glued to my ovary, my bladder, second ovary and bowel were all affected. Straight down to theatre, where the fallopian tube was removed and all my other organs separated to the best of the consultant's abilities although leaving extensive adhesions. I was grateful for my Mum's help with Lucy who was just starting on solid food. I began to see the part of my Mother that has blessed me for the last twenty years. Lucy needed to be fed and cared for while I recovered. Mum weaned her and bonded with her in a way that has never changed to this day. I do know how hard it was to understand me. Looking back, I would have struggled with Lucy had she been me and I was my mother.

Not that long ago during our year in Whitly, the slot rented TV proved to be my first scream at the world I believed was judging me, one mistake at a time. My guilty pleasure (and not something I would have told to good old Mitch) was daytime TV, particularly Neigbours. I had watched from the very beginning, when my own children were babies and I suppose I identified with the characters, laughing at them and crying inconsolably when one of them died. I had become angry whilst paying for my TV program, that Neighbours had begun portraying a young woman with serious pelvic inflammatory disease, as sexually promiscuous. Sick to the brim as I was with 'clean virgins for God' this was the final straw and I knew that I had been betrayed by a drama that I felt I could relate to. So I wrote to 'Points of View'. Barry Took was the presenter, I think, I could be wrong. I saw him being filmed in York once, meandering down through the Shambles. I did not skip out of the way into the Market. I stood and stared at him. I told Barry, that Neighbours had no right to make women suffering with PID feel as though they were being punished for promiscuous sex, when there were many other causes for this kind of damage. I think I was beginning to fight my corner for the first time. For myself, I explained, had been rendered unable to conceive due to an ectopic pregnancy and a miscarriage not thoroughly treated.

I would never know the children that had been in store for me, whilst still married to John and it was unlikely I would ever see a child from my marriage with Francis. If I remember rightly, I ended my letter with 'THANK YOU NEIGHBOURS FOR MAKING ME FEEL AS THOUGH MY SCARRED BODY IS MY OWN FAULT'. Something like that anyway.

Francis and I were watching TV, I think we were about to watch Friends (there wasn't much choice back then, especially on a coin operated TV). I was lying on the sofa, half asleep, when the angry voice of a woman I can only describe as very middle, almost upper class began to sound out the words I had written. I sat bolt upright, listening to a lady who sounded so utterly acceptable, tell the world how unbelievably disgusting it was to make women feel unclean. I laughed like a hyena on that sofa, rounding on the world that had allowed me to feel so responsible for what had happened to me and I heard my words fly across the land. Who knows how things might have been had Anthony and I made our connection without this, and the crippling insecurities that prevented me from being whole and responsive.
I remembered all of this, when cutting the pear tart. The best I could hope for was a miracle but the word was starting to wear thin.

On our last day, we sat outside a local café drinking beautiful cold French cider. An interesting looking road travelled up to the right and I could see a church so I thought I would take a look. Francis and I had no money at all. We had bought some gifts to take back but were now completely reliant on Daisy and Alan. It was lovely to be on my own for a few minutes and as I got to the church I could hear drumming and other kinds of percussion coming from inside. I love drums and had a strange drumming experience not long after Francis and I married.

Liff married the year after us, and she and her new husband Neil formed a band. Liff sang as often as she could, not only operatic pieces but contemporary even new songs written by the two of them. I heard them practicing one Sunday afternoon, but the guy playing the congas couldn't get the beat. In a rather heightened state of mind, I shushed him away and took over. It was great fun and they asked me to play with them at their first gig, in what is now a top music venue in York. The original drummer didn't mind (he didn't have much choice) and so we were advertised to play at 'Fibbers' music venue. My drums had a microphone but unfortunately the chap placed it right underneath my woodblock. Wearing my patchwork dungarees, my sister singing next to me and my new brother-in-law on keyboards, we also had a lovely man we hardly knew on guitar. As I began to hit the congas, and I have to say, my timing was out of this world, the terrible thoughts began to hurtle into my brain. The more I bashed, the more the fear rushed at me like a bull with nothing left to live for. Blinking out of the bright light, I knew that my turn on the woodblock was nigh and I knew that it lasted on one single beat for the whole of the song. In blind panic I held my nerve, as the paranoid thoughts entered my head I turned each one into a beat on the conga and then the woodblock, ordering them all in line, like a parade ground that only I could control. It worked and I successfully played the drums at Fibbers in York. I didn't do it a second time, but fortunately Liff and Neil went on to be successful musicians without me, alongside their teaching career in the family school. We did record my speaking in tongues one lazy Saturday. Several recordings later we played each version at the same time. I will never forget the sound.

Hearing the drum beats floating out from the church I casually walked through the door to see a group of people setting up for a concert of some kind. As I stood watching, an attractive lady in her late twenties came over to talk with me. She explained about the concert they were to give that evening and invited me to come along. The percussion looked incredible and it struck me as a little strange that this was the main part of the instrumental set up. The backdrop to the instruments was fantastic. As the lady talked to me I was aware that a number of the other people were looking at her as if to just check on who she was speaking with. At no point did I realize who I was talking to. I had no idea she was deaf, no idea at all.

I said goodbye and walked out of the church, saddened that I wouldn't be able to make the show.

Sitting next to Francis on the pavement outside the café, I looked up to see a large lorry pulling out across the road. In the front I saw the lovely percussionist and she waved at me. I smiled and as my gaze wandered across the lorry itself, the name 'Evelyn Glennie', written on the side, hit me between the eyes and I grabbed Francis's arm. 'That ...... that's the famous percussionist who is deaf'! I shouted. And it really was.

When I saw Evelyn Glennie play centre stage at our London Olympic Games, 2012 ... I was transported back to that unlikely day, in that unlikely place where I cut a pear tart and hoped to get pregnant.

The journey back was horrible.

Daisy and Alan had a massive argument. I still can't remember what about. They had brought back bottles of French cider and Daisy informed Alan almost by the minute every minute that she was going to crack him over the head with it. I slept on the ferry and couldn't wait to get back home, albeit to the house from hell.

A few weeks later it was my birthday. The house, situated as it was, alone and nasty, it was obvious that the church was holding a party there. The whole congregation poured through every room and out into the garden (such as it was). They were everywhere. Children squashed in and out of the bedrooms and the little bathroom almost burst. I had invited Mum, Dad and Liff. It was Sunday and the event took on a feel of ministry about it. I was sitting on the doorstep, flattened by the desperate life that was going on around me and I saw my family cycle on pushbikes towards the house. They looked at the scene and didn't stop, they kept on cycling. After a while, they did arrive and as my sister gave me my present, I could see my decisions, my choices and my dreams crumbling. I didn't want to be sitting in a concrete garden with everybody looking at me. There was no privacy. Non. Not anywhere. Not in my faith, my family or my house. Right then and there I could have simply walked off with only the clothes on my back, clutching my birthday gift. My parents found a space to sit down and the people I had come to accept as my brothers and sisters decided that they should ignore them and not make them welcome. The Redeemer Fellowship was a giant syringe, drawing the life blood out of any person unfortunate enough to belong. It was a fly paper, stuck to the dredges of heaven and offering a ladder to God. Instead, we were stuck with no way up and no way down. I had spoken a great deal about the things that caused me pain. Back in the mid-nineties, I had no idea what this really was and my sadness, my delusions came pouring out into the snatching hands of would be healers. Healing prayer became a drug that I would take as often as I could, which allowed those for whom a prayer ministry is vital for their sense of importance to breed. The more I spilled the darkness, the more the crowd around me grew.

One Sunday evening, I was particularly agitated. I often received a 'word' from god which would tie into the sermon and I had been asked to join the Prophet group. The Prophets were all female and would meet to pray with Thomas, the only male at the meetings.
A couple of church members, decided that my particular brand of mental illness needed more than just the good old hands on approach. Bearing in mind that I hadn't yet been correctly diagnosed with a psychotic illness, but with depression, I would have done anything to feel well and to lose the muscle spasms and overwhelming fear. The prayers began. A woman placed her hands on my head and the two men rested hands on my shoulders. Beginning in a quiet, calm fashion the three prayed for me to find peace. I began to shake. From head to foot, my whole body vibrated with sweeping, powerful jerks. I was unable to prevent my hands, almost touching across my front and facing inwards, from violently quivering backwards and forwards. The more my body moved involuntarily the louder the prayer and

speaking in tongues became. 'You will leave this Child of God, you will get out NOW', a woman screamed. Thomas attempted to calm the episode down by speaking more slowly, but the decision to pour oil over my head was already made. As the oil flowed across my forehead and down my face my mind began to bend, throttled into overdrive. The usual gagged sobs resulted which was a sign to my ministers that the demon had left the premises and had left a space which needed to be filled by God. By the time I reached the horror house, late into the evening, I was exhausted and confused. I must have been filled with a vast number of demons because the legion inside me kept the church busy for a good few months. It also took a lot of shampoo to wash away all the oil in my hair.

Life at the house became intolerable.
Opening my front door to walk down the street and visit the doctor was an ordeal in itself. One such morning found a couple of teenagers sunbathing in the front garden just outside of the doorstep. I carefully walked around them. After I returned from the doctor, a group of around ten young adults were playing football in the garden, all around the house on the concrete and the grass. I attempted to walk through them to get into the house but I was spat upon and intimidated. We were still getting children knocking on our door because their parents, mother or father, wanted us to take care of them while they were out. I rarely met any of the parents. Francis and I would let the teenagers ride around in the church minibus everywhere we went. I can still see my mother's face when we pulled up outside my parent's house in a van filled with nine or ten boys and girls. Just like the church elders, we had no training, no vetting and no qualifications or insurance to look after the young people. Nobody seemed to care and there was no way out. I was rapidly sinking and unable to hold onto my own children. Myself and another female member of the church decided to take the kids on a picnic by the river. I can see us now, running across the bridge pretending to be airplanes and singing the theme from 'The Damn Busters'. Unfortunately, the group of about six young teens decided it would be fun to jump in the river and roll around in the mud. We managed

to get them back to the house and took it in turns to separate boys from girls, running a bath for each child, giving them new clothes belonging to Michael and Lucy to put on. It wasn't just teenagers we were inundated by, but adults with problems ranging from alcoholism, drug addiction, childhood abuse, learning difficulties and mental illness. My attempts at keeping some kind of control over the situation were useless. We were eating second hand sandwiches, praying our way through a demonic army every week and coping with a house that was literally falling apart around us. Friends that came to visit, glad that we had returned home from Whitly were subjected to visits with the Pastor and church services. Anthony found himself dragged to a Sunday morning meeting. One Saturday night, he invited Francis out for a drink. Jumping at the chance of something normal, he went. I stayed at home to babysit. I remember watching a film 'Four Weddings and a Funeral' (which now seems eerily apt) and waiting for him to come home. Anthony had brought his motorbike into the kitchen for safe keeping. I stood by the window, watching. I watched and I waited, terrified to be alone. Eventually I went to bed. Francis turned up the following day, with Anthony and I could barely keep the anger from grabbing him by the throat. Not a phone call, nothing. I wanted out. Out from everything and everybody other than my children.

We took Michael and Lucy to see John and Clara. Every other weekend they stayed with their Father and Stepmum and I must admit that this was a good time for them to be away from the house. As Francis and I drove back towards the street, we could see smoke rising in the near distance. I knew, without a doubt, that part of the house was on fire. We were constant targets for the crime and poverty around us to manifest and so I wasn't surprised. We pulled onto the concrete and saw that it was the shed that had been set alight. I laughed because the only stuff that was in it was rubbish and drug paraphernalia. We kept the shed locked away from the children and I had refused to clear it out. The window was broken and that is where the fire had been started. We called out the fire brigade and it seemed that there had been needles and all sorts of dangerous stuff left to rot. The fire cleaned the place out and I was glad it had happened.

We began to try and do some constructive work with the local kids. Whilst living in Whitly we had been given the chance to live and work on a troubled estate in Hull. The Church of England had offered us a house on the estate and an old church for use as a Youth Club and meeting place. We tried visiting the estate and running some workshops which seemed to be positive. We were offered youth training and we did wonder if the move would be a good environment for Michael and Lucy. Paula was brilliant about the idea and babysat for the children while we tried the ministry on for size. The local children really enjoyed playing with art. An accomplished artist, Francis took along rolls of wallpaper and with art materials, we let the children free with drawing and sticking and model making. This went down very well so we agreed to take part in a youth disco. Arriving at the church we soon realized that things would not be as easy as we had first thought. We could not control the children coming into the disco. They were all ages and often unaccompanied by an adult which fell outside of the guidelines we needed to work with. In one case a very young child tried to enter, he was around four years old. The youth leader showing us the rules explained that the boy was safer on the streets than at home as drugs and prostitution were a large part of his mother's life. We also needed to check the children for weapons, particularly knives.

During the few months that Francis and I first attempted youth work in Hull, our leaving had been necessitated by the actual threat of violence. I was experiencing terrible pain and thick, heavy menstrual bleeding with a swollen stomach that made me look at least six months' pregnant. Our last visit to the church in Hull gave the mistaken impression to the teenagers that I was in fact pregnant. I did not correct them on this and used the situation to get out more safely than I believe I would have done otherwise.

Francis and I decided not to take the job as there would have been no boundaries for us living on the estate and with the expectation that we would be a safe house for troubled young people. I could never have put Michael and Lucy through such a life, although I inadvertently did, when back in York.

Here we were in York, again, with a house full of troubled young people. This time, along with the lack of training and support, we were 'appointed' by a church with no training or support either. The whole ethos of the church was an appointment by God without the need for worldly rules. We were soldiers for the Lord, appointed solely by him.
Very soon, a new prayer requisite found its way into our life.

It was September 1995 and Michael and Lucy were due to start the new year at their Catholic School. I had managed to secure them a place despite not being Catholic. I did this by joining a Catholic support and prayer group. My presence didn't go down too well because I explained to the small band of devout Catholics that the Virgin Mary had spoken to me about how sad she was when the young Jesus was lost and then found teaching on the steps of the temple. I told them how I understood this because my own son often went to stay with his Father. Years later, whilst a rather angry teen, Lucy insisted on wearing a pentagram necklace around her neck when going to Religious Education classes. Both Michael and Lucy refused to take part in many of Thomas's meetings, particularly Sunday school, where Michael would sing 'Barbie Girl' at the top of his voice throughout the lessons.

The day before the children were due to start school, I suddenly realized that I hadn't got anything ready for them. Their uniforms were still in the wash basket where they had been since school had ended in July. I had no bags or shoes and nothing for their packed lunch. As I stood in the kitchen, window sills crumbling, sandwiches on the table, my sanity on the floor, I realized, that I was in the middle of a breakdown.

Even then, my mind was to become further punched and kicked by God's righteous army, because it was decided that I would be blessed by Jesus, with a miracle baby.

How my river runs

In the final two months of our seven-month stint in the house from hell, we were asked if we would bring Melanie and Jack across from Whitly to live with us. It was felt by the fellowship by the coast that we could support them into a better life by giving them the chance to explore a city rather than a small village that was falling into the sea. Francis went to pick them up in the Redeemer van. We moved Jack in with Michael giving Melanie her own room. Things went bad very quickly. On top of all the responsibility for the local children and their often-damaged parents, we now had to cope with Melanie who had her own problems and four-year-old Jack. We introduced them to the Redeemer Fellowship and things seemed to be OK at first. When you are living in a crazy world however the crazier things that happen don't draw your attention. Life became one long blur to me and when Melanie began to date Thomas's son things became even more confused. I would stand outside the front door, sandwiched between the church controlled house and the thug controlled garden, not knowing where to run for safety. After two months of a living hell, I asked Melanie to leave after Daisy came up with a house for her. The walls were falling in on me and I had to get out to survive.

If our lives in the church had been all bad, I don't think we would have continued with any of it. I would have slipped quietly away (or not so quietly) into a spiritual community and more than likely come out lecturing on the Holy Spirit. As it was, Francis's parents were very supportive of our evangelical work and thought that our little family was being called to South Wales, to become the Youth Leaders for their Church.

Towards the end of our year in Whitly, pre-Jesus Church, we were invited to 'Greenbelt Arts and Music Festival', by Francis's parents (who couldn't make it themselves). They hoped that we night apply for the Youth Leader post in their local Monmouth Church. I felt I had finally found the place I belonged. Having never been to a music festival, I absorbed every last bit of it. The music was lyrical and not the strong charismatic verse I had become accustomed to, there were arts workshops, galleries, the most incredible food I had ever tasted and a night life filled with colour, fresh donuts and vintage clothes stalls. I thought I was in heaven and to this day, wouldn't turn it down as a possibility. We went on to attend Greenbelt for more than nine years and my last visit was with Charles. Both Michael and Lucy loved to go too. However, on this first visit, we were due to meet the Welsh Youth Group. We had arranged to wait by the notice boards filled with messages and invitations. As Francis and I sat by the gate, he in his bike leathers and I in my crown of flowers and maxi dress, we watched a group of youngsters balance on one another's shoulders. As they formed a kind of human pyramid, it suddenly became obvious that they were holding a large yellow card, with 'Francis and Helen' written on it. Francis and I looked at one another, and smiled nervously. 'Do you reckon that's them'? I grabbed at Francis's arm, 'I suppose so', he answered quietly. 'Shall we'? I asked, getting up and going over to the exuberant group of boys and girls, aged around fourteen to eighteen. I pointed to Francis and then to myself and waved at them. In one almighty rush, they came at us, enveloping us in a massive hug. It was terrifying, but everything I had ever wanted from working with young people. They were so excited and so were we. We spent much of the festival talking with them and their current youth leaders. It seemed that there was a flat available for us in Wales, with full training. Everything we had hoped for.

So why then did we choose to stay in a place where we were unhappy and move on instead to work with the Godforsaken Redeemer Fellowship in York? Perhaps it was the way we were made to feel by Thomas Pastor, that our journey back to York was at the hand of God. Perhaps it was the way we were told in no uncertain terms about our calling to the Redeemer Fellowship, its old sandwiches and its buckets of oil. In the end we didn't think twice about turning Wales down.

How my river runs

Chapter Thirteen
Swimming against the tide

It was the all-important final exam choice meeting at my school. I sat with my parents either side and a female teacher at a desk (who's name completely escapes me) – that is how important this meeting turned out to be. The nameless woman asked my parents what career I had in mind.

'Film Director' my mother replied.

Without batting an eye, or creasing even the hint of a smile, 'You'll need physics then'.

The following two years were a gradual descent into something closely resembling a living hell. I took physics. The first lesson I squirmed about on, clinging to the high science lab stool with my ankles, saw the tall male teacher (again no name) throwing the spinning black board high and laughing 'SHE NEEDS THE THEATRE IN HER LIFE!!!' (Cue mostly male class in fits of hysterics). I hated physics and to this day I can't wire a plug. However, seventeen years later I walked into college, a mother of two children and began two years at Media School. I played with cameras, made short films and went on to write, perform and direct a radio program that won me the title of 'Lifetime Member of the Millennium Association'. Tessa Jowell gave me the award for my work in the community with mental health and the arts.

The year 2000 turned over so many new beginnings and so many painful, writhing in agony experiences that I will try to give them to you in some sort of order. I think you know me enough now to work out what's coming next.

I began the new Millennium, in a field with three good friends. My very tall, very Gothic friend Don who wore a fantastically long black coat and big black boots, not to mention his purple and black dreadlocked hair gave me the most marvelous hugs. The moon hit the new Millennia with me wrapped inside his giant bat wings, out on the common away from home and my husband Francis. Francis was working nights with a newsagent. I had placed a happy card in his lunchbox but I was spinning so far out of our marriage at that point that even the sound of his voice made me want to run away. With us on the Common were Kate, my fellow media student – who was wearing a tall Christmas tree hat, and Matthew, a talented artist friend of Don's. We had been to Liff and Neil for a meal earlier on, and Don had become rather irritating to them as he wanted to hop off, and explore the night. Liff had given us all a glow in the dark alien toy as a gift. Don had forgotten his and so Liff posted it to him, not before sticking purple dreadlocks on it.

We came back to my house not long before Francis arrived home from work. (Don't feel sorry for him, he was not very nice to me). I went to bed.

The word 'gloom' is used for a reason. I began to notice the particular sense of dread associated with twilight. Every light in the house needs to come on, often both television sets and also the CD player. Anything to bring energy back into the house. The edge of curtains in the early evening, swaying slightly beside the bed, with the fading day behind them. Shadows. Then there was the time I ironed all night whilst Francis was at work, so great was the pressure of energy flow. So afraid of everything. I asked Francis to block up our post box because I thought that a little-known terrorist group would post a bomb into the house. He obliged (without really questioning me, which he ought to have done), putting a small catch to block it up overnight and opening it up for the postman. Often I didn't get to it in time and the post man didn't ever understand why he had to bash away to try and get the letters in.

My best friend Margaret was diagnosed with terminal cancer. She had been previously diagnosed and managed to go to University in the space of her remission. After gaining a fantastic degree, she again became ill. During this time, after I had finished my Media Studies (leaping also into five A levels, all grade A apart from one grade B), I was accepted at York St John University to study English Literature. I had been so amazed at my ability to study that I applied to University in a moment of madness. My work with mental health and the arts had also begun to do well and I was even asked to be the guest speaker at a Mind conference. On the back of this (and because the solar eclipse occurred right outside the Mind office as I visited) I changed my degree from English Literature, to Counselling Studies. Again, this should have rung alarm bells. The conference evening, which took place the week my University Course began, placed me centre stage. I had brought some of my paintings and even a list for people to order a book that I had not even begun to write. (I got quite a few names)! On each chair I placed a print out with the words 'Perfection is a horizon that is never underfoot'. When it was time for me to speak, I spoke without any notes and using my own poetry. At the end, everyone stood up and clapped. I couldn't believe it. I didn't even know what I had done. In the audience were representatives from two hospitals and during a very strange question and answer session, I was asked the best way to support a child with mental health issues. I remember answering, that the best way was to say sorry to them if you felt you had been wrong. That way they would not think of you as a perfect model that needed to be replicated. Francis was in the audience. He had tried to sit at the back but I had made him come to the front. I don't think he was very pleased. I flew.

I began Fresher's week in a glow with warm winds that whipped me up in a sunshine only mania can provide. I ran between tents, spending money from my grant and squashing into the café for coffee and cake with the students. My head turned inside out and I crammed as many leaflets as I could carry into my bag. I think, that day, I signed up for every possible society, pledging my time to minority groups, political strays and animals of the world. Most pleased though was I when I was given a large blue blow up chair in exchange for opening a student bank account. The account came with a mobile phone (my first). Armed with my chair, my leaflets, my phone and extra cake I danced home feeling a billion dollars.

After my two years in Media college, and the revelation that I could in fact go to university, I was contacted by my

Communications and English lecturer Alison. I loved Alison because she was genuine and kind. A few years older than me, she was a woman I respected for her skills but also for her confidence in the way she moved through the world. Alison wore short skirts and bright leggings; her hair was a chestnut red with one blond streak at the front. Her classroom was filled with tall green plants and the chair she used draped with purple and leopard skin print furry cotton. Alison had immediately taken me under her wing and we continued to be good friends after my college years were over. It was she who showed me that I could do or be anything I wanted to and not have to explain myself.

A good friend of Alison's, who also happened to be a BBC Journalist and producer had asked if she knew of anyone who might like to enter a call for submissions regarding innovative radio work. During my Communications study with Alison, I created a number of performance pieces relating to anxiety disorder. On one occasion, I feigned an anxiety attack during an unrelated presentation. Only Alison was aware of my intentions and it turned out to be a powerful experience albeit a hard one as one student had to be escorted to the sick room she was so upset. This gave rise in me however to put together a bigger project using photography, poetry and monologue. Eventually I also included drumming. The proposal was put forward, and the 'I Am' project took life. For the first time I found myself in creative conferences, all over the country. During most of the planning and creating I was so high that I literally had no fear of anything. I sought out highly skilled professionals in the field of anxiety and trauma, leaving messages with secretaries and asking outright for an interview. One day I was at home, and on a downward spiral. (It transpired in 2006 that my diagnosis of Bipolar Affective Disorder fitted the Type One Rapid Cycling presentation). It was not uncommon for me to be high, weeks at a time yet rapid cycle into a depression for an afternoon only. It was a dirty looking afternoon and I hadn't bothered to get dressed. The telephone rang and I considered not answering it. When I did however, a well-spoken man asked to speak with me. I soon realized that he was one of the top professors in the country, working in the field of anxiety and trauma at the

How my river runs

Maudsley Hospital in London, with several television programmes on the subject also to his name. Professor Paul Salkovskis chatted with me, putting me completely at ease. In my manic state I had thought nothing of contacting Professor Salkovskis, but now, as he asked me about my project I could hardly find the words. It was an amazing revelation to me that the Professor believed in the voice of the patient. He said to me 'The sufferers are the experts'. I was then invited to London so that I could interview him. Alison's friend from the BBC and I went on the train a week later. I managed to get stuck in the spiky turn style but we eventually got into the building. Meeting Professor Salkovskis was for me, at that time, like finding the Holy Grail. He knew so much about anxiety and fear and he picked up in the first five minutes that there was more going on in me than Obsessive Compulsive Disorder. My fears couldn't be controlled so easily with exposure therapy, the paranoia was psychotic in ideation and only just beginning to make its nature known.

The project turned into an hour-long radio soundscape, using the interview footage I had gained, some of my poetry and a monologue adlibbed alongside the wonderful weave of drumming. I remember sitting in the recording booth, watching Alison's friend and his wonderful drumming techniques, allowing myself to perform my poetry completely unrehearsed to the beats. I also wrote pieces gained from interviews with other sufferers of anxiety and added other monologues. By this time, I was well into my first year at university and had made lots of beautiful and amazing friends. I asked many of them to come and record some of my pieces for the project. We took two days to record and I was so high I don't think I said one coherent word. Wearing leather jeans and mirror shades, I completely took control, organizing my friends and colleagues into order of recording, marching about playing every inch the rock star. I shut my eyes and wince when I think of my behaviour yet my friends seemed to love it. The energy in the studio was like light bouncing from a crystal chandelier. I needed nothing, not medication not alcohol not drugs, I was the creator of my own destiny and no-one could stop me.

After the I Am project was finished, it was made the face of publicity for the first round of projects. I went to Sheffield for photographs and my picture appeared on all the posters and leaflets, under the caption 'Have you got something to say'? I was awarded money from supporting charities to fund the use of the project and asked for interviews from community media associations. During this period, I also went screaming, sky high into my first experience with Druidry. During my first stay with the Insular Order of Druids, I had my nose pierced with a ring that was really meant for a bellybutton. It even had a piece of crystal on it. The ring was pierced by a Druid piercer as part of my ceremonial intention to be initiated into the order. I make my decisions very quickly and every time I look at the poster with my face on it, I see the large ring through my nose.

The final part of my project involved going to London for a large media conference. I could take my husband and two guests. Francis and I met up with my media tutor. I also invited Alison, who was unable to go. I really should have invited the producer who had initially asked me to create the project but for some reason I was angry with him. He had asked me if he could buy the project (he had been paid by the charities for his input and to be honest, he was the genius behind it, and the studio) taking it away from the original funding source. I wanted to keep hold of the community branding however as I felt it was worth more.

As my mania began to slip into a phase I now know as the third, middle and worst state, my emotions became mixed and agitated. On meeting everyone for a film showing relating to members of the Redeemer Fellowship and a wonderful, powerful project created by a member of the congregation, I bought cigarettes and began smoking wildly around the people I valued the most. Blowing smoke everywhere, over the buffet, the people I admired, I couldn't seem to stop. I was agitated and aggressive. Possibly, this meeting which brought together two of the then most potent aspects of my life, the church and the media, fractured by my teetering on the edge of a life in paganism, wasn't the best backdrop for creativity. I was loud, brash and unrecognizable. Looking back, I hate the self that manifested that night, yet I know where she came from and I want to cry for her.

Arriving in London with Francis at the conference centre, (named the 'Hal Media Centre', no doubt because the year was 2001) I soon began to feel out of my depth. The ceremony loomed and Tessa Jowell, the then Secretary of State for Culture and Media was due to present the awards. My media tutor had come and I was so thrilled because I know how uncomfortable I had made him feel and we all waited for the arrival of our political celebrity. Unfortunately, Ms. Jowell was running late and so a couple of her colleagues handed out the awards. Half way through, they stopped. It seemed that there were no more awards to give out. I almost combusted and began jumping from one foot to the other, demanding to know where my award was. Then, the remaining few awards were found and when it was my turn (I was number eight out of twelve) my tutor and Francis clapped and cheered like idiots. I loved it. Every bit of it.

I was due to give a presentation about my project and Ms. Jowell but was completely thrown by the alteration of the day's events. Originally, I had decided to give my presentation wearing a sari, I am completely clueless as to why. All I can think is that the day I bought the sari (a gorgeous blue and turquois silk) I was with my friend who had strayed into the heady fever of Bhangra nights and the lovely men who when with it. I bought her a sari too, so she could fall in love with her secret pleasure even more. I do remember also, that the day had found me unable to speak very much as thoughts were ramming into my brain followed by more thoughts behind them before I could even speak the first ones. The hummingbird thinker, who's wings beat so quickly again they look still.

Hummingbird thinkers beat faster than sound.

By the time I was expected to give my presentation I could hardly stand, or speak. My body shook that much that I was terrified. I was supported by my fellow project winners who were amazing. One of the winners was a lovely young woman, wearing a sari and talking about her work with Ayurvedic medicine. When I saw her I was glad I had ditched the sari idea. I stood at the front, with some of my art projected onto the screen behind me. I couldn't see because of the light from the projector but had become as competent as a five-year-old. I shielded my eyes from the light with my hand and then I heard my tutor's voice … 'Just move to the left, Nelli'. I followed his voice and then gave my piece, with little intonation and next to no confidence. Everyone clapped but I hated myself.

As Francis and I left the building, a button fell onto the floor from my jacket.
I stood on the stairs and just broke down. I hated myself, I hated everything I had done and I hated my life. Francis just walked away.

In the second year of my Counselling degree during which I studied for a Teaching diploma, Alison agreed to let me loose on her current Media students. She would monitor and mark me for the observed teaching part of my course. During the first two years of my degree I had become fascinated with Gestalt therapy and Alison gave me free rein with it now. Sitting in Alison's wonderful chair, I worked with the students supporting them in a Gestalt sculpture. I had learned how to do this on my first university weekend away. I will never forget the weekend in the dales with all my fellow counselling students. The day was so bright it was hard to feel anything other than optimistic. I was flying very high because I felt so much in my element that everything was wonderful. Our group had taken over a local park, with a gorgeous stream and lots of grass. I often wonder what the local people thought of us, a band of adults playing like ten year olds. Our lecturer, Gordon, asked us all to get together and form a sculpture of a train. As we got together, some on the floor as wheels, some as coach doors and my new best friend Sandy standing tall as the driver. I laughed as one of the only two boys became the steam, standing in front of Sandy throwing his arms in the air. Gordon interviewed each of us to find out why we identified with the part we had chosen. I had decided to be a piece of track and when asked why, I found myself explaining that I was necessary for the train to ride over and to keep it from derailing. I didn't like the experience. Gordon then asked us to change our position into what we would like to be. I immediately became a window. When interviewed I said that I wanted to be the glass through which the people could see their world beyond.

The following day I was chosen to be the guinea pig in a Gestalt Dream Workshop. Again, we sat in the park, this time in a circle. Gordon asked me if I had experienced a recurring dream. I had been dreaming the same dream for a few months so I began to recount it one step at a time. As I told my dream to the group, Gordon began to ask me what each element of the dream felt like and what it was like to be that aspect of the dream. My dream was fairly simple. Francis, who by now worked part time as a driving instructor, was in his car, driving to a place with lots of industrial buildings. He stopped the car and a second car parked beside him. The second car was driven by a woman. Francis got out of his car, got into the second car and drove away. I then found myself at a station, with my possessions. I had all my possessions except they were halved, exactly. The only thing that wasn't halved, was a pair of red boots.
Gordon asked me how I felt about Francis getting into a car with a woman, and what my reaction to this was. I began punching the grass next to me, punching and punching harder and harder. 'Do you feel any better for that'? I was asked. 'I feel justified,' I answered. Actually, I felt worried because the clarity of the dream and the symbolism scared me. For many years I had experienced aspects of prophetic dreaming, particularly when it came to the emotion within a dream. Now, as a practicing Shaman therapist, I have been taught how to use dreams and interpret them, working to support change for the better in my clients. My dream, however, became eerily accurate in the months to come.

That evening we got together and played 'tag' in the park. It was the kind of half-light that summer brings and as children we stayed out playing as long as we could. I was flooded with childhood memories, the excitement of playing away from home and laughing at being caught. Sandy however, had remained the train driver both before and after the train

was built from our bodies. She began to form a strength in my life, someone who accompanied me through some very weird experiences. She was a loyal and extremely funny friend but always, always the train driver. Together we joked about some of the people we had met on our now joint quest to find spiritual meaning. We travelled by bus to a Shamanic Therapy meeting. I almost poked a woman's eye out on the top deck with my wand. Our meeting with the vegetarian Shamans (nothing at all wrong with this, nothing) caused me to imagine the shaman dancing with his drum, wearing a bear skin made out of cotton fur and large plastic teddy-bear eyes all cross-eyed and wonky. She came to my first ceremony at home, where only the two of us and Francis sat in a circle whilst I climbed over the sofa to make sure the circle wasn't broken. I wore and old white nightie as my robe. More serious experiences formed the initial part of my touching Druidry. Our course tutor came to take part as a number of us joined in Sandy's garden. I placed oil on their foreheads and we celebrated the Summer Solstice.
Some of my most favourite memories of beginning to work as a Druid were made with Sandy by my side.

The initial year of my degree at such a beautiful university in York, found me in an elective module – one we could choose from a different course subject. As a result of my experiences with cults and religion, I had initially wanted to train as an Exit Counsellor. A support for people leaving their dependency on a church, both physically, mentally and emotionally. The role had many of the elements of addiction within it, but I felt I could bring insight to the area. Both Sandy, my friend Debs and I chose to study 'New Age cults and beliefs'. The tutor, Chris was fantastic and supported the group of three we usually worked in. Also fascinated by the concept of the 'wounded healer' Shaman, I decided to research the field for my final essay. Instead of moving into the role of Exit Counsellor, I moved easily into becoming involved with my new area of study, Druidry. Attempting to find information on Shamanism, I came across Druidry time and time again. In 2001 I discovered seventeen different Druid orders.

How my river runs

After the success of my project, website and radio program in 2001, and riding on the back of my talk on Obsessive Compulsive Disorder for York Mind, I believed I could do anything. This is where Bipolar Disorder and skill, also confidence become intertwined. I was indeed successful in my work and my studies, and my confidence was real. A Druid or a Shaman – a Druid Shaman as I now see myself will use the highs and the lows as a natural part of healing and vision. I know that the pitch of my mood and experience was real, but it was also part of a chemical imbalance. I write here now, utterly conflicted, knowing that I can soar with my swan and run with my elk, but I also know that my medication makes my experience a much narrower emotional range. Yet it allows me to function in a society that demands 'normal' behaviour and doesn't tolerate me hanging from trees beating my drum. I will however, if blessed with a soaring wind, or a running elk, run and fly as best I am able.
My total belief that I could do anything at all with success, took me to some scary places, but places I survived and benefitted from.

At home now, in 2001 with Francis, I googled away on my computer. I had been given an old but fully functioning computer from a charity specializing in support for the mentally ill. It is important at this point, to recognize that I had a diagnosis initially of Obsessive Compulsive Disorder, Hyper-activity and depression. It was recognized that I had psychiatric problems but these had never been accurately diagnosed. Having come through 1995 – 2000, drenched in Evangelic Charismatic teaching, I was now ready to jump into something more meaningful and less restrictive.

Googling away, I simply typed in 'Druid'. Very quickly I found the details of a chap going under the title 'Arch Druid of Portsmouth'. I could feel my thoughts leaping onto the flight winds and I sent the Arch Druid a message. 'Hello, would it be possible to ask you some questions about your beliefs'? Again, the little seed from which a massive great multi-coloured forest grows.

The following day, the Arch Druid (known to his friends as Dylan) replied.
'No problem. Why don't you come over for a few days so that I can show you more about our practices?'

'That would be brilliant.' Again, the simple response, the all singing, all dancing forest began to break the ground and touch the sky.

Francis was in the kitchen with our seven cats, filling the food bowls. Lucy was at school and Michael, in the village he now lived in with John and Clara.

'I need to go to Portsmouth' I said. 'I need to go and stay with the Arch Druid of Portsmouth, to do some research.' Francis looked at me with the sidelong glance I had come to hate. 'Do I have to take you'? he asked. 'I'll find my own way', I replied.

My first accurate diagnosis was beginning to find its way to the surface and the anti-psychotic medication prescribed had given me a large weight gain. I hated the professional graduation photographs and the final two years of my marriage were gradually beginning to take shape.
Despite all these things, I walked onto the platform, proud to be a York woman who had taken back some of the life that had been missing. My Mum and Dad, Lucy and Francis were watching and Mum stood up, clapping and shouting.

It was the proudest moment of my life and I wore a pair of bright red boots.
Back now, to the first year of my degree in 2001.

Having decided to travel to Portsmouth, many of my friends and fellow counsellors were worried. A few tried to prevent me from going. Francis said very little and drove me to the coach stop to catch the bus at around six in the morning. Getting on the coach with my small bag and a bellyful of excitement I travelled to Bolton where I was to be picked up by two of Dylan's friends. As I travelled this first leg of the journey, the woman next to me saw I was reading a book about astrology. Bearing in mind that I was not long out of the Charismatic Evangelical movement, the woman terrified me. She began telling me that there was a 'den of vipers' waiting for me in Portsmouth and she then gave me her phone number to call her if I needed saving. I smiled to myself. At one time this intervention would have been evidence for me that God was watching me, and I would have jumped off the bus and gone home. I didn't feel that way. I was a little un nerved but I believed that the lady was not intended to halt my adventure. As we pulled into the bus station, I was instructed to ring the mobile phone belonging to one of Dylan's friends. I didn't know what the two chaps looked like, so I telephoned the number. Immediately I saw a smiling man with a long beard waving at me. Feeling more confident, I walked towards him and we got into his car. I found it difficult to control the moods inside me as I swung from elation to depression and also through agitated fear. Having no diagnosis at this point, I trusted my instinct and travelled to meet the second man. For this, I needed to go into the man's house. I didn't like this so much and didn't feel as confident. The fact that I was in a house I didn't know with two strange men wasn't lost on me and I began to formulate an escape plan should I need it. I got back into the car with the two men however, and set off to Portsmouth.

The journey wasn't too bad albeit long, and we stopped at a service station for a burger. Sandy began sending me messages roughly every half an hour to make sure that I was still alive. Eventually, we arrived at Dylan's home. I got out of the car, it was just getting dark and I looked carefully at the front door as it opened. Dylan was about as tall of me, with long light brown hair and he wore jeans and t-shirt. I wasn't sure what an Arch Druid would look like but he seemed fairly safe. (Not that jeans and a t-shirt can't be dangerous). Dylan's friend who had driven us most of the way, winked at him and I decided to take this as a good sign. I even harboured thoughts that this might be an enchanted friendship that would take me away from Francis, because Francis couldn't give a toss about me. We walked into the house, and I was utterly silenced.

The house was large, and it was filled from top to bottom with all kinds of strange and amazing stuff. On first sight I saw a suit of armour, shields and books upon books. The house had belonged to Dylan's grandmother. I was shown into the living room. At first I felt a little out of place. I wore bright coloured leggings, a lace top with a silk fringed scarf slung around my hips and a turquoise velvet cap. I soon lost the feeling however as the first thing I saw was an enormous and beautifully decorated throne. The throne was in dark wood and beautifully carved with acorns and leaves with lots of other Druid symbols. On the walls were all kinds of wonderful pictures and carefully placed pentacles made from twigs, just the same as the one in the film 'Blair Witch Project'. Dylan's girlfriend then appeared from the kitchen asking me if I would like some stew. When she saw me looking at the twigs she began to laugh. Apparently they had been put there as a joke for my benefit. I smiled as I saw the joke, but as the night wore on, I became so tired that my illness rose up to try and kill me.

How my river runs

Chapter Fourteen
Exit Strategy

After seven months of living in the hell house, I knew that I had to take the children and get out. The final straw came one Saturday night whilst I lay in the tiny bath, in the corner of the kitchen. The window was old and cracked, looking out onto the shed which had been burned. As I lay in the warm water, with the hope that I might somehow feel a bit better, I heard the older teens outside the window. Everyone and anyone walked into our garden, there were no boundaries at all, either physically, emotionally or with decency. They banged about and stood underneath the window. 'Get the petrol', one lad yelled (the same boy who had burned the shed). 'Get it over here, chuck it on the window'. I ran out of the bath, half naked I grabbed Francis and I screamed at him 'You have to get us out of here'.

A week or so later, Francis's eldest sister came up good. She offered to stand as guarantor for the rent on a new rented house. Francis and I looked around at a few places and settled on a mid-terrace, salmon coloured three bedroomed property, with tons of daffodils in the garden. The house had a long kitchen, a walled secure garden, a garage and two reception rooms. I loved the house as soon as I saw it. Using the church van to move our stuff, we couldn't have found a more different place to live than what we had left behind. Our bedroom was enormous (I remember it well because we lay there, in that wonderful place the sad day Princess Dianna died). Michael and Lucy had a bedroom each. The house had belonged to a group of students and evidence of their fun was right through each room. On the living room ceiling, bright green handprints had been walked from one end to the other. French windows looked out over a small patio and grape vine. Bright yellow winter flowering jasmine framed the doorway and the garden backed onto a primary school, one I had visited as a schoolgirl, to play the clarinet in an orchestra. I couldn't have been happier.

Francis and I continued to work with the church but we tried to keep ourselves a little more separate. We bought food without discussing it with Thomas, but we became involved in many other pastoral situations. Prayer had continued long and hard, for me to fall pregnant. I knew that IVF was our only option and we had recently received a letter inviting Francis and I to the first meeting, in Hull. Gillian and other women in the church regularly bought me items for new born babies, in fact they often brought me double of everything in the belief that God would manifest this faith into a twin pregnancy. I didn't know what to make of it. On the one hand, I believed that planting an intention, fuelling it with faith so as to result in the desired manifestation was a real and true thing. I still believe in this way of working with the creative forces, I just go about it differently these days. Something didn't feel right about this somehow. As baby things were donated to the church, many of them ended up in my dining room.

First, I went into hospital to see if it might be possible to rectify the damage in my remaining fallopian tube. The doctor who explained to me that this wasn't going to be possible, was heavily pregnant. I began to feel like I was being tortured.

A date was then set for me to have my remaining fallopian tube removed, so that an attempt at IVF would not result in another ectopic pregnancy. How I would have coped with all this if we had remained in the hell house, I do not know. Because my investigations had begun in Hull, I was referred to Hull for the surgery. Francis and I travelled to the Princess Royal Hospital and I was checked in, ready to meet the surgeon and anaesthetist.

I lay on the bed and Francis sat next to it. He had become more and more morose about the idea of more children, even though at that point, he didn't have a child of his own. He told me that he regarded Michael and Lucy as his own and didn't really want to go further down the baby route. I had recently joined Francis' sister in her Dorling Kindersley Family Library franchise so I too had another focus. I could feel the restlessness and my realization that Francis didn't want to have IVF. The surgeon arrived, and sitting on the bed he talked about the operation I was due to have, whereby my fallopian tube was to be completely removed. 'I don't want to have any more children', I looked at him, full in the face. 'Please will you do whatever it takes to put my insides right so there isn't any more pain or heavy bleeding'? 'What has brought this on'? my surgeon asked, looking equally intently back at me.

'I have a new job selling books, a son and a daughter who need my love and support, and my husband doesn't want any more children'.

'OK. Do you want me to make a judgment call when I see how things are inside'?
I agreed. I began to shake, but kept it to myself. Francis drove back to York in the church van and I had my last meal before surgery. Looking back, I know that I went into shock. I don't believe things would be done this way today, but I have to say that all the doctors and nurses were amazing. It was a strange week, but they were wonderful.
I was given a portable cassette player, to listen to calming music. I hadn't had any counselling at all for what was to come. The nurse who had been ready to observe my operation was now replaced by another, as the surgery had become more major.
I went down to theatre late morning.

When I woke, my head was throbbing. The room was dimly lit and I had lovely pieces of cold damp sponge on little sticks to suck. I saw a nurse walk through and I tried to speak with not much success. She understood me though and came over, putting her hand on my head. 'Did they do it'? I asked.
'Yes' she smiled.

Something inside me crumpled in devastation.
I had been given a hysterectomy at twenty-nine years old. The operation took place on a Friday. Sunday, coincidentally, was Mothering Sunday. Francis brought my parents and the children to visit me. I was very down. Mum had brought me a gift which I didn't understand at first. It

was a shiny box, around the size of two packs of butter. The parcel felt very light and felt empty.

As I read the card attached to the gift, I began to understand. There was so much love but also sadness around my bed. The shiny box, tied with a blue ribbon said it all.
'This is a gift that cannot be opened because it is endless. Inside this box is a mother's love. It is here for you always, should you need it'. In an envelope too, Mum had placed her favourite handkerchief, sprayed with a perfume I recognized well. These two simple items, on that day, broke down years of pain and a chronic lack of self-worth. How quickly things can be repaired when we choose to listen and to stop judging. Francis too tried hard to make me smile. He gave me a bag and told me there was an Easter egg in it. When I opened it, there was a fluffy chick stuffed toy. 'It must have hatched' he joked.

I returned home to our safe house, but the church was still eating into my sanity.
The Elders were not at all happy that I had opted for a hysterectomy, despite it being the best way forward for me. I received a number of visits from small groups of church members, who sat in my room with the green hand ceiling and spouted nonsense. One day, the cat was sick in front of them, all over the carpet. I loved it, especially as I had bought them cream cakes to eat.
Francis and I had become very disillusioned with the church, particularly the pastor. Relationships were unhealthy, particularly between himself and the children's worker. In fact the whole church had taken on a quality I had seen before, at the Jesus Church. Messages were flying about from God left right and centre. Our pastor began to shout louder and louder, becoming more animated as weeks went by, with his message that God had left the church due to the lack of faith in his flock. Tithing was always a big subject and an already vulnerable congregation, mostly on benefits, offered ten per cent of their income to fund God's plans. It didn't seem to matter what ridiculous sermons the pastor spouted, he was always believed. The meetings became

chaotic and often emotionally dangerous. No training, no support, no insurance.

I had chosen to stay away from the meetings, after my hysterectomy. It had taken me longer to heal than expected and I had also been rushed back to Hull from York, by ambulance after a haemorrhage. (Largely brought on by pulling a box of books across the floor during my first Dorling Kindersly selling event. My own enthusiasm).

It seemed as though my operation flew in the face of the plan, the church members believed God had set out for me. I was angered and insulted.

I had heard enough. I was unable to stand in front of the church myself, but I wrote a statement, outlining my objection to those who questioned my medical situation and believed that God had ordained that I would give birth to at least two children. Francis, Liff and I discussed long and hard about what we felt should be said to the church, the following Sunday morning. We decided that the gloves were off as the pastor had gone too far in his rise to some sort of unrecognisable holy status. We discussed the inappropriate behaviour between the pastor and his children's worker, also the unethical way the pastor's wife had been side-lined. We even used bible passages, the very ones the pastor himself used regularly to condemn many of his congregation. Liff agreed to represent me, and to read my statement.

The following Sunday arrived. The pastor had no idea that he was about to be challenged in his own church, the way he had always encouraged (but had never received).

Liff and Francis entered the warehouse and climbed the stairs where they could hear singing. As they entered the room, they calmly asked the pastor to receive their challenge. He stood to one side and readily gave Francis the lectern. I was never more proud of Francis.

After everything was said, the pastor simply stood aside and pointed to Liff and Francis. 'Do you believe them, or me?' he boomed. Believing himself to be a 'Moses' figure, the pastor genuinely thought of himself as above criticism, no matter how much he attempted being humble.

It didn't really matter, it had been said.
A few weeks later, Francis received a phone call. 'I wondered if you would like to come back to the church?' the pastor asked. 'I have a role I think God is calling you to'. I was fascinated because there was no mention of me in God's plan.

It turned out that the pastor had created a new job. 'Conscience of the Church'. Having not actually been banned from the church for having a hysterectomy, I was enthralled by this, so I chose to go back to meetings for a while, mainly because I was now drawn by the psychology of what was happening. What I saw will never leave me. Francis was called up to the front of the church, to stand at one side of the pastor. To the other side, stood the children's worker. She too had been chosen as a Conscience of the Church. The pastor explained that Francis and she would need to work closely together on this new ministry and there must be no gossip about this. Shortly after this happened, Francis received a phone call from the pastor, suggesting that he had a 'disruptive' wife and ought really to think about what needed to come first, his marriage or his role in the church.
I think I spat my sandwich out.

I would like to leave this chapter with one final story about the Redeemer Fellowship.
In devastating circumstances, a young boy, part of a large family who mostly belonged to the church, killed himself. He had been the victim of abuse (from a known peodophile) and his abuser was out of prison, taunting him on the streets. The young boy committed suicide.
One thing the church did well, was to support families in times such as these. It is true to say that the Redeemer Fellowship went into areas that other more mainstream churches would walk away from (despite the Gospel of Christ). True to form, the church supported the whole family brilliantly, mainly due to the steadfast work of my friend Cathy, who's outreach into the community was inspired.

A while later, in 2000, as I finished my final year at Media College and I heard about a film that had been made by a former member of the Redeemer Fellowship, now a talented media student.

The film was due to be shown across the country but we were being treated to the initial showing. The film maker, was the older brother of the boy who committed suicide and the film was about his brother's life, how he had been bullied, and what could have been done to help. Quite rightly, it began to win awards.

Francis and I had left the church a long while earlier, but were invited to the screening due to my media connections. We arrived at the cinema and it was very strange to sit alongside my fellow media students, yet behind a full row of church members. Most of whom ignored us completely.

The film was brilliant and to some degree my faith in the church was restored.
A while after this, I happened to have 'Songs of Praise' on the TV. I'm not sure why as I hate the program, it makes me feel really low. I was drawn to the announcement that a boy from York, had make a film about his brother who had killed himself, and would be talking about his work and sharing his church with us too.
The world stopped.

There on my screen, the pastor sat in a lovely Christian family sitting room. The sitting room belonged to the children's worker. The scene before me was nothing if not contrived. Contrived. This is probably the best word I can use to describe my life in The Redeemer Fellowship. I gained a great deal of insight into people and manipulation and I also gained a great friend, Cathy. On hearing about my return to hospital in Hull after my hysterectomy, Cathy came straight to see me and left the church along with her daughter. We are firm friends to this day as are our girls. Cathy was to be my matron of honour when Charles and I had our wedding blessing, nine months after we married and her daughter was a beautiful bridesmaid when Lucy tied the knot in 2016. I heard that the pastor left the church along with one of the singers and her six children. I don't know how true this is.

Chapter Fifteen
The School by the River

At an early age, my cousin was my playmate and the two of us pretended that we owned a fish and chip shop. Jo, fifteen months older than me had a short blond elfin haircut and my hair was auburn, swept to the side with a bow and a clip to hold it in place. The day of my wedding to Anthony, Jo rang her glass with a spoon and shouted a toast to all of us sitting in the beer garden. Jo is an amazing woman and lives her life in an outstanding and beautiful way. I have met many people who live with tragedy. Jo lost her eldest son a few years ago to an accidental drug overdose and within months she was also diagnosed with breast cancer. Now a survivor, she shines so brightly that she can lift an entire beer garden with her laugh and a single spoon.
Through her, her lovely son David lives on.

 I will always remember her as my playmate in our fish and chip shop. Our parents, (my mother and her brother, Jo's father) share a history that makes me think with great clarity, how Jo and I almost didn't make it to this life.

In April 1942, the Baedeker raid on York found my mother and her brother hiding under the stairs in my great grandmother's house. The house is just round the corner from where Anthony and I now live. The blast (aimed at the railway), blew the front door across the under stairs and all the adults, my mother and brother were trapped inside. A brave friend and Warden came in and pulled the door away. The whole group of seven had survived. On escaping from the house, which was only four small terrace houses away from the large Methodist Church, they were face to face with an enormous crater. The Church had taken a direct hit and was completely demolished. Only the fluttering of hymn books falling to the ground remained. Just a few metres further and neither Jo nor myself would have been born at all. Mother and her brother moved back into the house newly built and bought by my grandfather and grandmother. The house is one street away from Albany Street, where my mother survived and lived to become a teacher and

business owner. Salisbury Road is the house I was born
into, along with my sister. Mother has lived there all her life
and lives there still, with my father. It can be a strange kind
of life. As a successful local business woman, who has
taught most of York's young women the art of touch typing,
often over two or three generations, she is sometimes asked
to support local events. I recall very clearly, going with her to
open a local jumble sale. Mum had written down the story of
the York blitz which caused so much damage to the area in
which we lived, she tried to tell the people waiting to buy
their toys and clothes for pennies, but they seemed
indifferent to the tale. I stood in the crowd with Michael, then
a baby and wished that the locals would care more about
their history. To this day I can't find information about Albany
Methodist Church and I want very much to place a plaque
commemorating its presence.

 My mother is someone who will always get involved in local
events and has been foremost in saving the wildlife in a local
green area, which is just over the back from my childhood
home. In 2003, after studying Druidry for three years, I
performed the naming ceremony for my sister's one-year-old
son. A large group of family and friends gathered on the
green land and I dressed in a green and gold robe. The
ceremony makes me laugh uncontrollably to this day. I was
not at all well at the time, struggling with a deep bipolar
depression. My nephew's favourite cartoon was the 'Blue
Cow'. My Mum drew and painted a large cow, colouring it in
blue, and we placed it in the circle. My brother-in-law, a
musician had also put together a song consisting of his son's
favourite cartoon theme tunes. Bob the Builder and Noddy,
formed most of the song. Everyone was given a song sheet
and we led the way so that the friends and family could sing
the song as a sort of hymn. I remember looking at Kath, my
friend and also the shorthand teacher from our family school,
we could hardly contain ourselves. At the festival of
Lughnasadh (August 1st) we placed a basket with corn,
rosemary and lavender. As I entered the circle to lift my
nephew up into the air, the ceremony became deeply
sacred. I called out 'Universe, this is Adam James, he is part
of your magic, Adam James, this is the universe, you are
part of its magic too'. I will never forget the beauty of that

moment. Forget the fact that I had cut my fringe badly, and resembled and extra from Star Trek, forget the fact that I had gained three stones in weight as a result of wrongly prescribed medication and forget also the fact that Francis was on the cusp of ending our marriage. None of these things mattered, because in that moment, I felt the power turn and I saw myself in the turning.

All my life I have sought to find peace and to feel of worth. I am only now beginning to find my place within the scheme of things.

On visiting 'Eden Camp' museum North Yorkshire with my nephew, Mum found herself in front of a class filled with young schoolchildren, explaining how she experienced the war as a child. The teacher did not have too much on the subject to hand, so Mum stepped in. After this, she became in much demand by local primary schools, with her bag of ration sized chocolate, and her tales of the Blitz.

As a baby, I struggled to sleep and to be calm. I screamed round the clock and needed constant attention. My mum used to put me into a rocker, and would rock me with her foot whilst working. At one stage, I had made myself sick so many times with crying, that there were no clothes left for me to wear. I think it was at that point, that I was handed very sharply to my dad, because Mum had had enough.

As I grew older, the incessant chatter grew with me. At eighteen months' the doctor felt it wise to treat me with Phenobarbitone, a medication used in the treatment of sleep disorders. I remember clearly riding behind my mother on her bike and deciding to throw my knitted rabbit on the floor, because my thoughts told me that I needed to do this. Over the years I have watched many scenarios unfold because the urge to make things change overwhelmed me.

When my sister arrived in 1970 I did not take the arrival very well. Liff was placed in her carry cot onto the blanket box in the bedroom I would soon be moving into. Mum brought out a large orange teddy bear and a panda with harlequin coloured legs. 'This is a gift from Elizabeth to you', she

smiled giving the orange teddy to the four-year-old me. '…
and this panda is for you to give to Elizabeth'. I looked at the
baby in front of me and replied 'What would SHE say if I said
I didn't like it'. Now my mother often regales folk of this tale
which I find upsetting, as my sister and I have become
closer than sisters and better than friends. It is a devastating
thought that it took violence to bring us together. After the
attack she suffered, Liff and her boyfriend (first boyfriend)
came to stay at Warthill for a few days. I watched the
dynamic of our family shift. My sister had lived the role of a
daughter who never failed and I had always believed myself
to be the opposite. What a burden it was for her to feel that
she must not step across the line. Perhaps because of my
as yet undiagnosed illness, it seemed as though I was
always the disruptive influence. I cannot remember the
things that caused this angry response from my parents, and
if it was confusion as to my seemingly chaotic behaviour
then I accept it. I know that I did not drink or take drugs, I
wasn't violent or a thief, but somehow I was always in the
wrong. The highs must have been a terrible thing to bare for
a parent, especially when there was no apparent reason for
it. When my sister was harmed, the two of us became
somehow connected to life in a similar way. It was me that
she turned to for support and I felt blessed by the fact that
she needed me. I had never been able to support my sister
before and taking care of her was a privilege. She became
perfect to me. A fragile and lovely person who no longer had
to endure my fractured spirit without insight. We had both
been damaged in the same way and there was no need for
words. I am devastated by the means, but I am glad that we
got there.

I think that acknowledging a child's reaction to a new sibling
is precarious.
Certainly Michael struggled with the birth of Lucy in 1988. I
struggled with the birth of both my children. When Michael
was born in 1986, my mental state took a nose dive and I
was terrified that something bad might happen to him that I
couldn't control. I was so low that the doctor suggested I go
into the mother and baby ward at Bootham Park Hospital.
John was not at all impressed by this and he did what he

always thought of as right, he stood in the way of my being taken into hospital. Over the coming years he would stand between myself and a stay on hospital many times. When Michael was a baby, I would often go into the pub and steak house, next to the big pond opposite our house in Warthill. There was no shop in the village and I would drop in for chocolate often in my bed clothes, with my baby in my arms. The pub was the only place where I could buy chocolate and more than once I have confused the steak diners as I appeared, pyjamas and wellies, hungry for a Yorkie Bar. One sunny afternoon I was walking with the pram and I recognized a girl I knew from school. Sheila was one of the bullies who had tormented me with salt in my drinking water and taunts. As one of my Mother's students it could be very confusing as during the Saturday morning lessons Sheila would be nice as pie. However today, she called me over in a state of near panic. Now an adult she had become a genuinely nice person. The boyfriend next to her told me that he and Sheila needed to get away. They then asked me if I would do a house swap (both our homes were Council owned) so that they could leave. I talked to Michael and we agreed. At four months' pregnant with Lucy, we moved back to the heart of my childhood and school life. Our new garden backed straight onto the playing fields were I painfully played hockey every week. Our neighbour Sam became a great friend, and we shared some hair-raising experiences. Lucy was born and I immediately flew into severe mania. I know that this is what caused the madness, but back then, in January 1988, the doctor did not pick up the signs. My mood rocketed and the doctor left after visiting, happy at my elevation and secure that I was truly well. He couldn't have been more wrong. I was never more in danger.

Eighteen years earlier, in 1970 my Mother took over the floor of a building which sat on the banks of the Ouse. Premier Commercial school gave both my sister and I a place to deflect our personal pain and a kingdom within which my Mother was the queen. Peacocks would wander across the main road, from the Museum Gardens and up the flights of stairs to visit and snip at the polo mints Mum kept around for them. At around the age of thirteen, it was my job to collect the money from the students as they arrived for their classes. Saturday morning was the busiest. I loved arriving at the school and walking up the stairs past the long line of students, who were queueing for typewriting and shorthand lessons. Quite a few of the students were girls from my own school and for once I had the upper hand, although this did not extend to my secondary schooling. In the small office I sat at a desk with an ancient, long till. I would count the sheets of A4 paper into lots of five, using a rubber thumb and sell these too for a few pence. As I got older, I used a stop watch to start the speed tests and measure the time until I shouted 'STOP'. I learned how to teach touch typewriting, also shorthand. I loved using a stop watch to time shorthand dictation and even progressed to teaching Pitman Script. The scariest time however, was Saturday lunchtime when all the students had gone home. It was my job to stay behind and clean the rooms, also the stairs leading up to our floor. I enjoyed being on my own, sweeping and mopping, hand scrubbing the stairs and dusting the typewriters, (apart from the one time I discovered that a student had done a poo in the actual toilet cistern), but I always had a sense of unease when alone. Sometimes, Liff cleaned the school and we both felt the strange presence. Neither of us would use the vacuum cleaner because we believed that we could hear faint voices coming from it. We didn't realize it, but we were both doing anything we could to avoid the noise, even so far as using sticky tape wrapped around our hands, to pick bits up from the floor. I loved the school however, the paper and pens and of course the stopwatches. During a particularly difficult few months, sixteen years of age and living in a flat of my own, a friend and I took an acid tab each, to see what would happen. I was due to work that evening and I rocked up to the school wearing no underwear at all(a skirt and a top thank goodness) and the inability to understand a word anyone said to me. The students' mouths appeared to be out of sync with their words. Mum put me in a taxi and sent me home. It took three days for the muscular spasms and the nightmares to stop. Not a good idea.

In my late teens, the York Archaeological Trust was given permission to excavate the grounds of the school. Sitting on the banks of the river made it quite possible that there would be a burial ground hidden beneath the stone flags. This turned out to be true. Two nights a week, we held lessons in the evening. On Mondays and Thursdays, I would often help out and as the nights became darker, the digging became scarier. There were no lights to speak of down the slope and into the dark courtyard. When the dig was in full swing, medieval skulls and other bones were laid out within a foot of the door to the school. My first proper boyfriend also worked for the trust. One evening, we were invited to a camping barbeque in the disused grounds of a private psychiatric hospital. As a joke, he led me in the dark up to an old wall with bricks bursting from ivy. I was wearing a full length white muslin skirt that I had found in a vintage clothes shop and my feet were bare. (I sometimes think that I should retitle this book 'My feet, a sole bared'. Anyway … the arched doorway was pushed open and I was told to cover my eyes for a surprise. I walked forward and the door slammed behind me. Suddenly, I found myself standing on the side of an enormous abandoned swimming pool, empty, dead and filled with dry leaves. It was like a nightmare. The pool belonged to the hospital and the old treatment ideas involving outside exercise for patients. I walked gingerly towards the changing rooms to my right and saw a dirty, stained towel. The whole place made me feel sick and a rising panic began to threaten my ability to stay calm. I hammered on the door and to the sound of laughter I was let out, shaking both with anger and fear.

The offices always felt odd. A few years later, when I had begun to practice reading tarot cards, Liff and I did a reading in one of the classrooms. I can only say that we ran from the building. In 1992, when Francis and I got together, I had developed tarot reading using techniques, that I really should have stayed clear of. In the late 1980's and early 1990's I began to read, whilst still married to John. I also, stupidly took up using a Ouija Board. Before I was born, my dad brought the board (made by Waddington's) home as a game for he and my Mother to play. It was only used once, and my mum began speaking to her mother, telling her about Grandfather's marriage to Gladys. The plastic pointer flew around the board, agitated and took flight, crashing against the wall. A device after my own heart. My Mum has since said that she felt completely 'taken over' by the experience. The Ouija Board was pushed under the bed that was to become mine, the same bed that had belonged to my Mother. As I grew up I became curious about the box, wrapped in plastic. I would pull it out and scare myself by looking at the cover, which had an image of something resembling a ghost, plus letters and the plastic heart shaped pointer. The pointer was cracked from its smash with the wall. I progressed into putting the heart onto the board and waiting for it to move. Whilst still with John, in 1991 I asked my Mum if I could have the board. She was a little reticent but to be fair, it should really have been destroyed years before.

My sister and I, also a couple of friends had begun to attend the York Spiritualist Church. The whole Spiritualist movement fascinated me and was the first experience that had ever harnessed the chaos inside my head, with any strength. We got together, usually in mine and John's house, practicing meditation and contact with the spirit world. The meditations were fantastic but some of the results became scary and didn't sit too well with my friends or I. We were encouraged to practice 'physical manifestation' and it was at that point, I decided to halt the meetings and stop the study. However, everything I did I took to my Mother to try and win her acceptance. I never jump into puddles without wanted to splash them around completely and utterly over everyone else in splashing distance. Liff, myself and a couple of others decided it would be a good idea to hold a buffet at my house, where Mum, Dad and others could experience the Spiritualist Mediums from the church for themselves. We made homemade coleslaw, bread and all kinds of stuff. My parents duly arrived to share the experience. Before long they were discussing Spiritualism and my Mother was receiving spiritual healing for the arthritis in her hands.

Now, I am going to tell you of my experience with Tarot cards and Ouija, but this is not to be confused with the work I carry out today. I now understand the role of cards in the therapeutic process, and that they are deeply psychological symbols which mark the way towards healing and good counsel. A tool to use and for me, the best addition I have alongside stone and crystal divination, and my Degree in Counselling Studies.

In 1991 however, my use of Tarot cards exploded into something that blew my mind completely out of the water. My friend, Sam, asked me to go round to her house to do a Tarot reading for her. This I did. I placed the cards in the layout known as the Celtic Cross, and began to look at the images which showed me the influences on Sam's past, present and future. As I read, I looked at Sam and she seemed to have gone a bit distant, her eyes didn't look as though they were in focus. She began to shake. 'I don't feel well', Sam said and I could see that she was genuinely out of control with the experience. All of a sudden, she began to wince in pain. 'Somebody is walking through me' she panicked. I continued to read, not at all sure of what was happening. As I watched Sam's face it seemed as though somebody else was moving into her body. This was becoming more and more painful for her and I didn't know what to do. The feeling seemed to settle down but Sam was changed. She seemed very shaky and described wanting to do things that were completely alien to her. If it hadn't been so scary it would have been funny. Sam wasn't a fan of ironing, but she was unable to prevent herself from dragging the ironing board out. I had thought it a clever prank at first, but the experience didn't ease up, continuing across the next few days. In fact, Sam had become very distressed by the whole thing. On the second afternoon, I thought we might try some automatic writing to see if we could get spiritual guidance as to who it was that had taken up residence with Sam. I opened up a big role of wallpaper, gave Sam a pen and tried my best to communicate with the spirit involved. Sam began to write and to write and to write, without tiring or stopping. I looked at the sweeping irritable lines, making out some words and also some familiar names. I was able to interpret the messages but Sam was providing the physicality of the episode. Eventually I became convinced that the spirit attached to Sam, was the Mother of the boyfriend who had become the Father to Sam's child. The lady had not known about the child being born. Once we realized that this was the person who had been called to visit, it became easier to work with but she showed no signs of leaving. Liff came to help and was able to smell Catholic incense. The lady had been a strict Catholic. I tried to photograph Sam and when the film was developed, around her body could be seen what appeared to be cotton wool, pulled thinly around her silhouette. Looking at the negative showed more clearly the image. I kept the photograph for years, until the first destruction of my spiritual belongings by the Charismatic Church.

Liff, Sam's boyfriend and I attempted to pray for Sam. In all honesty I felt out of my depth back then. We helped her to lay down on the bed and I placed some different crystals down her body. I have never seen anything quite like it. Sam began to buck and to convulse. I had given her a clear quartz crystal to hang around her neck and this disappeared only to resurface broken, on the front doorstep. It was truly terrifying but I needed to see the whole process through. I felt responsible. The three of us managed to calm Sam down and she laid on the floor. Suddenly, she began to experience what I can only describe as contractions. As Sam had given birth to her child without the knowledge of her boyfriend's Mother, it almost seemed like the lady wanted to get close to this experience. It also transpired, that Sam's boyfriend had not managed to make it to the hospital before his Mother passed on. As Sam lay on the floor, I suddenly felt it right to ask her boyfriend to lay his hands on her and to say his goodbye's properly. This he did. Sam became still, her vision returned to normal and all urges to iron everything in the house subsided. During the whole experience, so many things had happened to Sam that were out of character. I spent every day with her, even sleeping over to help her keep safe as at that point, she was not married to her boyfriend. When I left to go and pick up Michael and Lucy from school, Sam would come out into the front garden and wave me off. Such an eerie sight, and not something Sam would ever contemplate. During this time, I also continued to use the Ouija board, almost obsessively, trying to find answers. At one point, I called for the help of the Spiritualist Church but they refused to get involved. I then took things to another level by asking a well-respected medium from Leeds to come and see what was happening. He came to Sam's house but made it clear that he could do nothing. It was I who had opened the way for the spirit to come in and I who must support it in its leaving.

Dangerous energy bounced around our two-bedroomed house and John was frequently faced with my urges to give our things away and to move furniture around every single room. One afternoon, I was alone apart from the children who were three and four years old. A loud knock startled me and looking out of the window I saw a largish truck. When I opened the door I was face to face with a Romany Traveller lady and a couple of children. There were two men sitting in the truck. The woman, in her late thirties with long dark platted hair asked me if I had anything that I might give them, for the children. She wouldn't come into the house because apparently it is bad luck to enter the home of a non Romany. So I opened the door wide, I made the whole family cups of tea and they sat in the front garden, whilst I packed up bag after big bag of clothes, toys and house-hold items. So many in fact, that after around half an hour I had filled the truck and they asked me to stop. When John came home, I was confused by my decision to empty the house into a Gypsy truck. But it had just made sense to me at the time and I was bouncing off the walls with excitement.

My marriage to John wasn't doing well. We had married very young and our emotions were only starting to unfold. We loved each other very much but didn't know how to manage our lives together. As parents to two small children, we tried really hard to make a safe and happy home, but my as yet undiagnosed illness and John's restless depression meant that we never quite made it. These days I see John as a truly lovely person and a good Father, he is my friend and I know we share good memories. Our lives apart however had been better, and his choice of Clara as a wife and subsequent mother to his second son, was the best thing he could have done. Unfortunately, my marriage to Francis was not so well planned. He gave us many good years as a husband and father to Michael and Lucy, but he failed to be the right choice during the latter part of our time together. Useless in fact. I no longer admired Francis as I had once. He revealed himself to be a bully. Life with Francis was a rollercoaster of colour, sound and new ideas. We embarked on the most outrageous of projects together, throwing our hats into the ring without a thought. The first couple of years were really lovely. Riding coal sacks down the Daleside and revelling in our first village Christmas were closely followed by holidays to arts festivals and trips to the East Coast. A holiday to Prague which took place not long before our split, and the first time I had flown abroad ought to have provided clues as to the coming nightmare. Looking back now, I can see the love that drained away but the idea of moving on, so ill, seemed unthinkable. Sometimes those we love can't handle our illness and choose to shut their eyes to it, annoyed at the suffering they don't or can't understand. But I found love again and Anthony is by my side even if I am rolling around on the floor in pain from medication side effects. It takes strength to hold on when the demon is invisible but so obviously tearing your loved one apart.

Life with John twenty-five years earlier, was a different matter. John was bursting with love for the children and we tried our hardest to give them a happy life. Lucy was a fire-cracker however and very nearly sent the pair of us over the edge! At two years old, she began to demonstrate the skills of escapology known only to the best in the business. I first realized this skill when I came downstairs early in the morning to check on the children as they were playing in the living room. Straight away I noticed the front door slightly ajar, with the baby buggy pushed against the wall to allow for opening of the lock. Michael was alone with his Lego, and he looked at me innocently. Immediately, a knock came at the door and a police man called in to me. Flinging the door open, there was Lucy, in her night-dress, held by a policeman. She had managed to open the front door by climbing on the buggy and had run to the local newsagent, where she had attempted to steal a chocolate bar. I couldn't believe it. John and I fixed a stair-gate but there again the following week, Lucy was outside the front door, sitting on the curb of the main road, with a bus hurtling in her direction. I became an Olympic hurdler that day, leaping the stair gate

How my river runs

and grabbing my daughter out from the coming bus. We realized that we needed to sort out the locks on the front door, so Lucy stayed with my parents while the work was done. This didn't stop the problem though. I was upstairs in the bedroom and John had decided to and buy cakes from the local corner shop. I heard the door shut and went downstairs. 1991 was a good year because my sister turned twenty-one. Our family and friends had got together to organize a surprise 1970's themed party. I had cut posters of Garry Glitter (not such a great choice) and Elton John (a good choice). We had all dressed in 1970's fashion, I wore a leather mini dress and large felt hat. The evening was brilliant with the right music and home-made food. My parents were babysitting for us and the following day, we were all tired but happy at the way the party had gone. Michael was watching TV when I realized that Lucy wasn't in the kitchen. Thinking that John had taken her with him, the short distance to the shop, I wasn't too concerned. When I heard the handle turn on the door, and saw only John come in, panic grabbed my throat. Lucy was not with her dad.

Immediately I ran next door and we went through our back gardens, calling and pulling back the hedges. I began to run, in the direction of the shop, stopping every person I could see, people on cycles, people walking, folk in their front garden. As I barged through traffic, a lady on her push bike said she had seen a little girl, of Lucy's description, running towards the sports hall. I couldn't believe that no-one had stopped her. I was beyond frantic as I was also aware that a pedophile had been discovered close by the area in which we lived. Running through the sports hall, I demanded that they shut the doors. Lucy was three years old, wearing a red velvet dress, a white bib, a nappy, tights and slippers with monkeys on the front. The memory of those slippers has stayed with me all of these years and was probably the reason why as a vulnerable adult, I bought some for myself associating them with safety and rescue.
By this time, my neighbor had called the police. I daren't tell my parents and I could barely see straight, such was my fear and adrenaline. The police asked me for a photograph of Lucy and as I travelled slowly about in my neighbour's car, I

watched as they showed it to every house in the very long street. Women, mothers themselves looked at the picture and then at me. I saw them look at me with an indescribable pity and a tangible relief that this was me, my child and not them and theirs. The pond of a neighbor a few doors down was investigated and in the end, all we could do was wait.

Around half an hour after Lucy had followed behind John and run in the opposite direction, we saw a policeman carrying her down our path. My instinctive reaction was to grab her and check her from head to foot. She was holding a chocolate in a piece of kitchen roll and was smiling all over her face. The police were wonderful and kind, compassionate beyond what was expected. A strange feeling came over me and I began to feel that my baby might not be my baby. She had been away from us and I began to experience a strange sensation that Lucy might not be my Lucy. The only other time I have ever experienced this, was during a manic episode when I couldn't be certain that Charles was really my Charles. I looked at his face and listened to him speak but I just couldn't be sure.

Lucy had run and wandered a good half mile away. The policeman simply held out the chocolate and she had gone to him. Now safe at home with John, I rang my parents and told them what had happened. It felt like a confession to bad parenthood, but I needed them to know. John suggested I go and sit with our neighbor for a while, so that he could tell the children a story and settle them down. I walked into my neighbor's living room and became quickly hysterical. I was given a glass of whisky, which I had never drunk before and launched into a mixed state of mania and darkness. I became uncontrollable, drinking more than half the bottle of whisky, reliving the recent miscarriages, the surgery and the fact that I would almost certainly never be able to have children again.

John and I lived in the little two bedroomed house for almost four years, ending with the explosion of psychic energy and dangerous spiritual experimentation. I was addicted to change, of any kind. I couldn't keep still either physically or in the decisions I made be it giving away everything I owned or starting new businesses. My floristry work did well but I was continually agitated, needing to explore everything I could turn my hand to.

Things returned to a sense of calm and a year down the line, John and I exchanged houses with a family from a larger house, which we needed. Not long after the exchange, the couple asked us to swap back. Apparently their young daughter was experiencing terrible nightmares and they believed the house to be haunted. I felt terrible, but unable to do anything. The house needed clearing. Something I would know how to do today without any problems at all, but not then. I remember these things well and I never forget to show respect and to hold sacred any sort of spiritual activity at all. These days I am able to clear and make safe any space and I and I wouldn't go near a Ouija board for love nor money. I read the cards as they were intended to be read and I have learned what it is to walk other worlds in both safety and for the good. The questions remain. 'What is this energy that runs circles round me. Is it part of mania and episodes bouncing with manic activity? Is the energy, psychic and spiritual, that which we can explore and work with, existing in every living thing? What is it to be mentally ill, yet also spiritual? Is this the Shaman, crazy and able to see the high and the low? the wounded healer'?'
 I believe all these things are right. I know that in some societies, the manic depressive has the creativity to express the intangible, and this brings suffering along with it but often healing for others.

The cathartic experience resulting from handing over fear into the hands of a shaman has proved to be my salvation. As a practicing shaman myself, I feel the catharsis build, then burst into a thousand possibilities for change. Acknowledging fear and paranoia, seeing it for what it is and then choosing to hold love in its place instead, is the most powerful practice I have ever experienced.

As Francis and I began our relationship, I was moving away from irresponsible practices. It is probably not such a bad thing that The Nestleton Rambler wouldn't advertise my

Tarot reading service. It has taken more than twenty years to learn the true art of divination.

During the later stages of my days with The Redeemer Fellowship, I became more and more drawn to the safety and authentic divinity of the Mystics. So much so that I allowed myself to want to be as much like them as possible.

During a trip to a Christian Arts and Music Festival, I met a group of Franciscan Monks and Nuns. Every day they offered free food and drink for those who had run out of money. I loved sitting on the blanket outside their tent, sharing fruit and laughter. In our talks, I discovered that there was a level of the order that I could join myself. The Tertiary, Third Order. Here, I would be given an advisor and helped to create a rule of life for me to work at and change as the years went on. This idea appealed to me greatly and I chose to go ahead. Unfortunately, my mania took up the wind of excitement and ran away with my lovely ideas. First of all I attempted to stich myself a brown pinafore dress (the colour of the order). I am not known for my sewing skills and the dress was a rather odd, oversized creation. I then gathered every item of clothing I owned, including boots and coats, with the intention of giving them all away. The largest amount I gave to Clara, but she wisely held onto them for me knowing I would need them back.

My overwhelming desire to be a Franciscan Nun came at the expense of much hilarity from the church. However I know where my heart lay and I also know I had the courage of my convictions.

Chapter Sixteen
The Black Egg, Pain Across the Sun

After an excitable rampage through a healing fair at
Coventry Cathedral I found myself huddled in the back
garden of the Coventry home Charles and I bought. My
Sister inexplicably telephoned, it was a Saturday night and
nobody telephoned me then, in fact few friends telephoned
me at all now I had moved away. Kathleen was staying with
us overnight as we had all been drinking. She tripped down
the path to give me the phone, seemingly unaware that I
was half naked and clutching the gate. Liff spoke to me for
five seconds and then told me she was phoning for an
ambulance. As we talked, the ambulance appeared down
our back lane. I was carefully loaded, a half-naked, woman
with a crazy language. I was checked in at the hospital and
assessed for alcohol addiction. I tried to explain that I wasn't
a drinker and had psychotic symptoms. They ignored me. I
didn't even know which hospital I was in. I tried to ring
Charles on my mobile but got no reply. There was one
doctor, a lovely man who spent as much time with me as he
could. During the night I wet the bed, and the nurses
continued to misunderstand. The doctor popped in to see
me and told me to 'keep holding on'. He made up for
everything else. Eventually Charles arrived bringing clothes
with him. He brought one of his tatty sweat-shirts with
cigarette burns in it and a pair of his jogging bottoms. At that
moment I felt like a real tramp.

Something must have fallen into place somehow, as a
psychiatrist came to see me. By this stage I was unable to
stop crying and vomiting. The psychiatrist looked amazing, a
bit like Einstein. He simply looked at me, smiled and said
'You have Bipolar Affective Disorder Type 1 Rapid Cycling. I
will give you Lithium and it will change your life'. This was
eleven years ago, and on the whole, he was right.

I began to notice the different stages of my illness and I
realised that they were more identifiable than I would have
guessed. Until the year 2000, my mania, depression and
paranoia played a large part in my inability to socialize well. I

found it difficult to be amongst Francis's friends and family. Francis had a family that were incredibly successful and no matter how successful I became I don't think I would ever have felt confident enough to jump in.

After meeting Charles however, my new found manic confidence pulled me into doing things I would never have considered had it not been for what I now know was a diagnosis of Bipolar Affective Disorder and Schizo-affective Disorder. My confidence didn't manifest into lasting success because with every few steps forward, bipolar depression slapped me back further, giving me a good kicking into the bargain. Bravery took me back to university later in 2012 in the gaining of a Masters Degree, whilst taking powerful medication. This is my greatest triumph, albeit terribly hard as Charles began to slip away from me, by the end of 2013.

Long before this, just after my marriage to Francis ended in 2005, I went on a night out with a few friends (something I hadn't experienced for more than eight years). One of my closest friends, Clare, looked at me as though I was losing my mind. We were standing at the bar in a very loud themed pub. I had just embarked on internet dating and was meeting my first interested man later on that night. Clare said warily, which then I couldn't understand, 'Your eyes are really sparkling, it's amazing'. I was a little taken aback. I felt really good, I was aware that I was talking a lot, and very fast, but my brain seemed to be set at full throttle. For as long as I could remember I had experienced pressured thinking, thoughts that entered my head and left again so quickly I couldn't cope. I had struggled with school, not least because alongside the fizzy sherbet head, as I had come to call it, there was the dread, the 'creeping mortuary', the depth, the black and the dead. I was treated for Obsessive Compulsive Disorder and depression, despite the obvious manic presentation. I do understand that mania does not always come to light because the symptoms make for such elevation that they are almost desirable. The episodes of deep depression are so dangerous that these receive more attention. Who wouldn't want to feel like flying after wishing yourself dead and buried? At twelve years old, my parents were recommended to speak with a psychiatrist. I recall two doctors visiting our home, but not what they said to me. The recommendation was that I go and stay in an adolescent unit for an undefined length of time. My Dad refused and the meeting did not end on the best course of action. I often wonder whether going into the unit would have saved me so much pain, multiple marriages and bullying, or whether I would have become institutionalized. I will never know. What I do know, is that round the age of twelve, I began to develop screaming night terrors. From a deep sleep I would hurl myself up and run down the bed. The injuries could be nasty, especially if I skidded on the carpet or ran into the wall. By the age of thirty-four years old, I had tried just about every kind of anti-depressant known to man. Most of which exacerbated both the highs and the lows. Nobody seemed to acknowledge the obvious.

I think that paranoia was the worst. Apart from the need to block up my letterbox as I was constantly afraid that I could be heard speaking and my words misinterpreted, I was also afraid that I would become the target of a terrorist organization. I would walk for hours up and down the street with Michael and Lucy, asking them to listen for me in case I couldn't hear well enough and had missed a stranger's conversation that might mean we were in danger. I pulled my Mother into many a conspiracy checking session. Occasionally I would have an overwhelming need to make sure that neither Michael nor Lucy had inadvertently eaten one of my tablets. I would then ask my Mother (as nobody else would understand the importance of it being an accurate investigation) to ring the chemist and make sure that one or two or three tablets wouldn't harm a child under ten. On one occasion I asked the man fitting our new gas fire, if he had planted a microphone behind it. The dangerous aspect of this paranoia became inflamed when mania jumped in the way. This created a 'mixed state' which I very soon realized was incredibly dangerous. All the energy of mania with the thought processes of paranoid ideation. With hindsight I can see the point at which I began to lose insight. During those painful days and nights there didn't seem to be a way out as my thoughts became more and more disorientated. Manic thinking was strange and overwhelming in a different way. I became obsessed by Francis, begging him to come home from work almost hourly. Leaving his coffee cup ready for his arrival, I also accused him of having affairs with everyone he knew. I was thought of as eccentric because my plans and schemes held little in the way of practicality, despite being explosive with creativity. The explosions melted away into the ground however, mostly, as nobody could back my ideas. Francis went along with much of it but he opted out, choosing to say nothing at all of good use. When the diagnosis of psychosis finally came, he just seemed resigned to it and began to hate me as my medication caused my whole body to balloon.

I had heard that it was a good idea to put carpet down in a garden to suppress weeds. Our garden was approximately fifty feet square and I had begun to create a Druid Grove at the bottom of it. I planted trees, made an altar from stone Michael had found beneath the clay surface and built a cobble fire with which to hold my ceremonies. It seemed like a brilliant idea to put down some carpet to make the rest of the garden easier to maintain. I began telephoning carpet suppliers, to ask if they had any old ones I could have, from houses they had newly carpeted. They were more than pleased to help. The first truckload arrived and Michael, Lucy and I carried the large rolls between us around the back of the house. Another two truckloads arrived after that. We began to lay them out neatly, all over the garden, cutting holes around the trees. The cats were very confused at their newly carpeted wonderland and had a great time scratching and rolling. Francis came home from work and just looked at what we had done. Michael and Lucy were quite confused and I began enthusing about all the hard work that would make the garden perfect. He just walked into the house.

When Clare came round for coffee the following day, she looked out over the garden from my kitchen window. 'Are you going to mow that or hoover it?' Clare always made me feel special. Not long after that, I had my first admission into Bootham Park Hospital. When married to John, in 1990, I had been offered a space on the day ward where I could learn to cope with Obsessional behaviour. The first day, I walked through the door and took one look at the large group of patients, some of whom had come as inpatients, some of whom shook, unable to focus on anyone else. I decided to run. I turned for the main door but a nurse asked me to step inside a quiet room. She asked me if I would like to telephone home to check that everyone was safe. All I wanted was to be back down the long sweeping drive, through the gates and back on the street opposite the Register Office. If I could make it there, onto the footpath outside where nobody knew me or could hear my thoughts, then I thought I might be safe. I ran. When I reached the outside, the ranting was still shattering my skull and it was so loud that it seemed more than likely that passers by could hear it. I wanted to try again on the day ward, but crammed inside the small kitchen at lunchtime, eating sandwiches sent over from the kitchen filled me with terror. I managed around a week at the hospital. I found myself sitting again in a circle, only this time we were throwing a sponge ball to one another and I think the idea was to cope with the attention when it landed. I hated this. I felt stupid but it was also very difficult to manage. My whole body tensed when the ball came at me. I remembered this experience when studying my Counselling degree. Between 2000 and 2001 I had no problem at all with attention. As the mania's ebb and flow ran through me, I directed my radio work, gave presentations and lectured in Druidry. The lectures went really well for a couple of years, when my thoughts were so elevated, triggered by the opportunity to study and talk and to feel of worth. Looking back however I can see that I was flying by the seat of my pants, reading up on the subject one day and teaching it the next. In one lecture, given to first year theology students I found myself saying 'Aren't trees brilliant'? As soon as I said it I was mortified, yet the group of around thirty university students thought me incredibly funny in my referencing of the popular comedy 'The Fast Show'. It was a terrifying way to behave and to think. More terrifying now that I see it with balanced eyes. Manic thinking gives rise to some incredible and inspired ideas but it is also dangerous, on so many levels. A sense of ultimate freedom and a rise above life as it is usually lived, gives way to the feeling that anything can be achieved, or experienced with complete safety. In fact, the idea of safety is incredulous. The mind and the body sizzles with inspiration and water fizzles, turning thoughts to popping candy. My body and mind tremored with the excessive pressure. Normal rules of living simply did not apply. I could have or be anything I wanted. And yes, obsession did flood through my veins. Any object of the right colour, in my case a turquoise green or a pastel pink. I became fixated on a can of pineapple chunks that my Mother had kept in the kitchen when I was a child. I thought about the blue green wrapper and the yellow chunks on the label. My earliest memory of colour and shape fixation takes me back to primary school. At six years old, I asked a fellow pupil, (Mandy), who incidentally had only one leg having lost one in a traffic accident, if I could have a painting she had done. I asked this (not because of the missing leg) but because I wanted to own the pink splodge she had accidentally dripped onto the paper. When visiting the aunt of a girl I had become something of a friend with, I couldn't stop staring at or wanting to hold a perfect and wonderful orange sitting there in the fruit bowl. After talking non-stop about the orange and breaking the aunt's washing line by swinging on it, the fruit was given to me and we quickly left.

The scary part of all this, is how quickly I can become utterly helpless. Sitting in the middle of chaos, waiting for help to come, or believing that help will not come and that I will disappear if I try hard enough. Recently I was lucky enough to have a fantastic spa treatment in Leeds. Leaving the spa to get the train to York, I called into Primark and stuffed the paper bags with all kinds of shopping. As I reached the station I realised that the bags were way too full and were about to burst. Holding up the escalator I stopped to try and get a grip on the many packs of underwear and other things I had bought. As I got to the platform, everything exploded. The bags were torn and unusable. As I sat amongst the knickers, slippers and nightclothes, my train pulled into the station. I began to shout at the guard, pointing at the train. Right at that moment, I needed someone to come and make everything right. The guard was fantastic, he bundled me onto the train, squashing all my stuff into a plastic carrier and making sure I had someone meeting me at the other end. Sure enough, Anthony was there with his big rucksack and utter absence of condemnation. Anthony is amazing.

How my river runs

Years down the line and as an adult, I began to pick up items that were 'special'. By the time I left home after my marriage to Francis, I had packed a bag with numerous special items, ranging from a guinea pig poo, a monster much crisp and a multi-coloured crayon I had stolen from the day ward. I still have this bag with me today and it has followed me through my swimming and my drowning. As my friends have come to understand some of these traits (maybe not understand, more like collaborate) some of them have begun to give me more special items they think I will like. In fact, the monster munch was given to me after a lecture, by my lovely friend and mentor Alison. I love this, because it makes me feel as though I am not alone with my thoughts and that if my thoughts can be heard by other people, they are tolerated and even welcomed.

I struggle with practical situations. For years, I thought that the way to work a drinks machine (one of those with leavers, where a glass would press against and trigger lemonade or something) was to push it with your hand first. For decades I got a wet hand, trying to push the leaver and fit the glass in also. Hot drinks machines are also an enigma to me. Whilst working as a Saturday girl, for Presto supermarket, I attempted the machine in the staff room, only to cover myself with scalding hot coffee. I didn't say a word and sat down soaked to the skin, until someone asked me why I had poured coffee over myself. I couldn't answer. Neither could I answer when my work on the bacon counter came to an abrupt end because I tried to sell customers lamb.

In 2000, at the start of my university degree, a student counsellor seemed to have the insight to identify what was happening to me. My best friend Margaret, was dying from terminal cancer.

I decided that I would visit the counsellor to find some bereavement therapy. On my second visit, I found myself feeling incredible. My energy levels were so high that it impossible to sit down. 'I feel so well, it's amazing', I laughed. 'Everything is perfect, there's not a thing wrong anywhere and today is shining'. My counsellor stayed seated and very calmly asked me to sit as she wanted to tell me something difficult. 'This is hard' she began, 'I don't think you are as well as you think. In fact, I think you are quite unwell'. She looked at me deeply and continued 'I think it might be the case that you have a psychotic illness. Has anyone ever suggested that you might have Bipolar Affective Disorder'? Right there, in the year 2000, I felt as though I had been smashed in the face. Suddenly I began to cry uncontrollably because I knew that she was telling me a true thing. I told my doctor what the counsellor had said. My treatment was changed to an antipsychotic medication from anti-depressants which had sent me sky high. I was so sedated that leaving the house for studies or work became a nightmare. Several times I landed in the psychiatric hospital in York, as my medication both swamped and suffocated me, but I was not given the full Bipolar diagnosis until my arrival in Coventry, 2006.

How my river runs

Chapter Seventeen
Life Raft

During 2002 when my mental illness raged at break-neck speed, I began to experience even stranger adventures. My journey into Druidry was in full swing and I was never to return to the Evangelical Church. A fellow I had met on my journey to Portsmouth, travelling overnight in a car with two strange men, turned out to be one of the most damaged people I had ever met. I decided it would be a good idea to ask him if he would be part of my case study project, something I needed to do for my degree. He agreed, and I paid for him, his girlfriend and his girlfriend's son to come to York, from Portsmouth. Meeting them at York Station I called 'Welcome to the pretty city' and I hugged them all tightly. Francis didn't say much about the visit. I had filled the house with all kinds of foods I thought my new friends might like and made a comfortable space for them in one of our three bedrooms.

When it came to tea time, I cooked a large stew but Colin couldn't eat it, choosing instead to go to the shop and buy sandwiches. A pattern soon emerged that he was unable to take up my hospitality and the idea of a person being nice to him, accepting him, made him physically sick. Colin had experienced life as a child that even the many current autobiographies around the subject of childhood abuse would never be able to match. He had gone on to carry these traits into adulthood, finding his safety compromised every single day, so little was the worth he placed upon his life. Yet his flat at home was spotless, the only place Colin was able to experience any sort of control.

On the second day of Colin and his girlfriend's stay, I decided it would be a good idea to take him in with me to a lecture at university. I cleared the visit, but didn't explain what my motives were. High, I was filled with a desire to show Colin that he was an intelligent and valuable human being. When we walked into the lecture, none of my fellow students batted an eye (as only counselling students are able to). As I encouraged Colin to answer ideas with his

239

own, my friends nodded and listened. I felt I had done a good thing. I didn't realise that I had become a rescuer and not a therapist.

That night, Francis and all the children were fast asleep, when Colin's girlfriend began screaming. I ran to the bedroom door to see the beginnings of a trail of blood, running from the toilet, downstairs and into the living room. Francis held the children back calmly in their room and I walked through the blood to find Colin. At this point in my journey, I was still terrified of blood, sure that at some point I would catch something terrible as a result of my own early life experience. I believed it to be unavoidable, as unavoidable as walking through this terrible and never-ending red puddle.

For years I had taken myself to free clinics offering testing for blood contaminated diseases. I must have had at least six tests for HIV, without any reason at all to have them. Every time, I went to a new location and used a different name craving the reassurance I received with every visit. My addiction to reassurance is one thing that has never left me, even today.

I looked at the stairs and put out one foot and walked.

Reaching the living room, I found Colin lying on the floor with his head in his girlfriend's lap. Using our sharpest kitchen knife, he had cut his wrists so hard that his hands were nearly off. Taking over, I telephoned for an ambulance and held his head in my own body. 'I refuse to let you die on my floor' I shouted at him. The paramedics arrived, and I gave as full an explanation as possible for the situation. The three of us climbed into the ambulance and I told the doctor at the hospital that I was Colin's counsellor.

Initially I was just glad to see Colin get the help he needed, in some ways it was a relief to hand his care over to the professionals, but I soon realized that he wouldn't be given much in the way of compassion.
As the young doctor cut away Colin's shirt, I saw for the first time, the self-abusive words he had cut into his own

stomach. With a look of disgust, the doctor quickly explained that Colin had cut through some tendons and needed immediate surgery. He was bound up and then left. As the doctor walked away, I called after him 'Please show this man some respect, he has seen more of life than you probably ever will'. Turning round, I saw Colin, attempting to get up from the bed and get away. I tried to get him back on the trolley but his girlfriend was still hysterical. Realising we needed psychiatric support, I ran around Accident and Emergency trying to find the person on call. There was nobody.

Since this time, I have myself been admitted to Accident and Emergency, where the Crisis Team were on hand and amazing. However, this night, in 2003, nobody came to our aid. I telephoned help-lines from a public phone box to no avail and eventually, decided there was only one thing for me to do. I ran to Bootham Park Psychiatric Hospital. The sweeping drive I had once run from was lit, making the large Victorian asylum even more stark. Ringing the bell to the right of the enormous wooden doors, I received no response. I hammered on the doors, and still nobody came. So I returned to York District Hospital where Colin had been taken into surgery. It was almost five in the morning.

Colin's girlfriend agreed to wait at the hospital and I got a taxi home, to find that Francis had cleaned up the blood and the children were still asleep.
I was due to teach at the family school the following day, but having not returned home until almost six, this was impossible. Mum stood in for me.

My lecturers at university were wonderful and suggested I take some time out, which I did. When I went back, my new medication had kicked in and it seemed that my fellow students hardly recognized me. It was as though the spark had gone out and they referred to me in the past tense.

At home, I had a large picnic basket filled with dolls and puppets. I had intended to specialize in working with children from an abusive back ground. I had collected everything, from glittering princess dolls to shark hand puppets. Despite it all, I graduated with a 2:1 honours degree.

The same day, I emptied the picnic basket and began to give away the dolls and puppets to friends and family. I rescued them.

I also tried to rescue a number of other people. In my volunteer counselling work for rape crisis, I became traumatized by my first and only client. Working as a teacher for the family school, studying and volunteering, also a full-time mother to my daughter Lucy I was run off my feet. All I wanted to do was to make pear chutney from the trees in my garden. I didn't recognize the signs at the time, but the over active lifestyle I was leading and the stress were brewing a dangerous cocktail of mania and mixed states. One Thursday in the summer of 2002, I was canvassing for our website design service. I decided to sit in a café in Malton and have a pot of tea. As I sat there, my mobile phone rang with the details of my first client. I confirmed the lady's telephone number by repeating it and writing it down. It was when I ended the call that the fear began to grow. I looked around the café. There were several people sitting chatting and one older man on his own. I became convinced that the single man had heard and remembered the phone number. I believed that he would telephone my client and arrange a bogus meeting with her, probably raping her again or killing her. The thought became so strong that the energy of it took my breath away.

On arriving back at the school, I paced the floor with such gusto that my sister had to ask me to stop and to sit down. I was carrying my nephew in my arms, then a few months old. I swung him backwards and forwards (not dangerously) but enough for him to be taken from me and given to his dad. I remember that day well because when I went on to meet my client, I tried very hard to take her mobile phone whilst she was in the toilet. I thought that if I smashed it, the man from the café in Malton wouldn't be able to harm her.

How my river runs

These thoughts are now incredible to me. Impossible to understand. The overwhelming fear of being either at risk or responsible for the risk of another saturated everything about me.

My first admission to a psychiatric ward happened at Bootham Park Hospital in York. I was in bondage with my thinking and couldn't get up from the floor. I was an outpatient at the hospital and my diagnosis was not entirely clear although psychotic ideations were agreed upon. Michael and his friends were upstairs, between eighteen and twenty years old they were a good group of youngsters but I was tied to my fear and allowed them to smoke in the house, so long as it was cannabis. My reasoning for this, was that I imagined cannabis to be less of a fire risk, because it burned slower. I did not want to ask them to stop smoking in the house because I thought Michael would go away again, as he had over the previous few years. I wanted to hear them laughing and having a happy time. I wanted to have a smiling family house. I think that Michael's friends might have thought me a little eccentric. Inviting one friend over for tea, I took to cooking bundles of nettles in pans on the cooker. Nettles are good for you and I thought them appropriate.

When Michael turned eleven years old, Francis decided it would be a good idea for him to move in with John and Clara. This seemed like the obvious solution as Michael didn't seem to be happy at home with us. It was a dreadful day. One of the worst. John and Clara arrived, shocked at the sudden decision and I sat on the sofa sobbing. I gave Michael a photograph of me (he was only moving a couple of miles away) but it felt as though my heart had been ripped out. John and Clara made a lovely room for Michael and put my photo on the wall. In fact I began to see Michael more often, going to the cinema and out for food on weekends. He seemed to be permanently unhappy and nothing I did could shift it. I think now, after talking with him about it, my son felt that he had been somehow banished.

Two Feet Away

Helen Mary Barr

I am on standby
If I were to call my heart and soul
I still could not find you
If I were to stretch every inch of my bone
I still could not reach you
I am silent
My words fade before they are spoken
You stand two feet away
But they might as well be broken
I am screaming
But sound does not ripple the air
You came from within me
Your eyes and your hair
Share the colours God gave us
The ones I wear
The ones I wear

I am not connected
If I were to cry my spirit now
It still would not move you
If I tore myself into strips of anguish
And built here a bonfire
You see no flames
I see shadows and hear muffled sound
You stand two feet away
But my search is leaving you unfound
I am savage
A mother whose cub has grown wild
You were a part of me
That part has died
Died from longing to hold you
My lonely child
My lonely child

For the next five years, Michael's life appeared to be chaotic, despite anything John, Clara or I did. As his sixteenth birthday arrived, Michael chose to come back home. I fell over myself to make our home a happy one, but I was too poorly myself to cope with the fallout. I felt increasingly guilty because of the spiralling in my mind and terrified of everything around me. I believed that I had made a terrible mistake, bringing Francis into our lives so quickly and that Michael had never properly adjusted. The well crafted home we had created did not seem to make up for Francis's appearance as a Father in our family. I blame my mania for my sudden change of husband and thought that I was doing the best I could. However, space between my thoughts might have changed the outcome.

So I welcomed all of Michael's good friends into our home. I loved having Michael back but I failed to recognise a lie despite being told with love. I could hear the group in the front bedroom, popping down for mugs of tea and chatting as they passed me. I was sitting on the floor by the front door, in the hallway. Suddenly I picked up the phone and rang the hospital. After listening to me, the doctor asked me to come to the ward. The house split away from me and I was separated from the very things that should have been a grounding force. Telling the boys I was going to hospital for an appointment, I called a taxi.

When I arrived at the imposing main door (Bootham Park Hospital is a purpose built Victorian asylum, in the same vein as Broadmoor Hospital), I pushed hard and walked to the reception desk. Sent on to Ward One, the floor beneath my feet spread from wall to wall with original blue and brown tiles. The arched roof reached forever upwards, a Victorian masterpiece extending towards heaven and flanked by gorgeous stained glass windows. The building was so cold though, so cold and detached from the very reason it was created. Reaching the locked entrance to the ward, I pressed the bell. I was so desperate to get inside, to sit on a chair or a bed and feel nothing at all, free from maintaining my paranoia and able to ask for help without the sticky mess of my life wearing me out.

On one occasion, having split up with Francis and now living in the doll's house, my body took the toll from stopping my antipsychotic meds so quickly (done in order to lose weight and find a new husband). I decided to have a bath and dye my hair red. Suddenly my stomach was wracked with nausea and I couldn't stop the vomiting. My stomach contents swam about my legs in the water and I tried to slide out of the bath onto the floor. A knock at the door gave me hope that somebody might be able to help. Wrapping the towel around me, now stained with red hair dye, I went to the stairs, promptly falling down from top to bottom. Managing to open the door an inch, the Kleeneze man went white with shock, seeing the red towel and presuming I had cut myself badly. I managed to tell him to leave a catalogue and picked up the phone. After six attempts I was able to dial my sister's number. She immediately arrived in her car and took me to Bootham Park. I was unable to stand and I also wet myself. I was admitted onto the ward but I was still determined not to take any more antipsychotics. I was so wrong but so sure I would get better.

One too many intrusive and damaging therapy sessions had left me with no-where to go and the feeling that I would never be understood. Had it not been for my parents, my sister and my friends Clare and Xanthe I would not have made it through. The simple things brought the greatest support and healing. Clare had me thinking that the Crisis Team would be a band of six muscle men who would put me on their shoulders and carry me home, running as they went. Xanthe listened to my longing for a ham and cheese sandwich, just like the one I had seen on TV whilst in hospital. When she turned up to bring me home, in her hand was a bag with all the bits to make it. Tulips brought by my dad when I couldn't even stand the sound of another person's voice.

Kicked it down

It was a long thin room, you sat at one end
Your waistcoat was red and so was your pen
It twitched in your hand like a hound on a lead
With the smell of the chase and the prize of the bleed
I saw you look down at your watch
Your mouth didn't smile as you narrowed your eyes
You had twenty long minutes to categorise
As you cut me with questions and bottled my blood
Stripping everything naked like no rapist could
Same time next week?

How my river runs

I stooped for my coat and the tattered remains
of dignity, wondering what I had gained
I had craved a cure awkwardly, loneliness lost,
Now a file with my name bore a boot shaped hole cost.

You kicked in my head, you had kicked it all down.

Sitting in the large lounge filled with soft plastic armchairs, I
looked out at the beautiful grounds. A nurse came in to see
me and suggested putting on the radio. Her words stung and
made me want to scream. I couldn't handle noise I just
wanted to sit and stare. I stayed in the room for about an
hour or so and when I looked again at the hedged area close
by, with shrubs and a pathway, I saw my Father. He
appeared lost and was carrying a bunch of tulips. I watched
as he walked up and down the footpath, then looking for a
nurse, she went to find him. My Father visited me often
when I was an inpatient and the doctors got used to him
ringing the bell and walking towards my room, wherever that
might be. They treated him with respect and kindness and
always made sure that he had a chair to sit on in my room.
It was unusual to be allowed visitors in patient's rooms, at
the Bradgate Unit in Leicester, where I was an inpatient a
number of times. Visitors were not allowed in patient's rooms
and were asked to meet in the communal area. I can
understand this when managing patients sharing a room, but
not so understandable with private rooms. Bradgate was in a
state of flux however and has probably changed since my
time there. I felt very safe in the Bradgate Unit. Being a
psychiatric patient however does put a person slightly at
odds with the rest of the world.

On my last visit to Bradgate, just before Charles died, I was
in a twin room with a lady who was very depressed and very
unwell. Our beds were facing one another and the room was
bright, on the ground floor and looked out onto greenery. I
was sitting on my bed, it was around mid-morning and the
curtain was slightly closed. As I sat there, quietly, I heard a
'bang bang bang' on the window. I got up and pulled aside
the curtain, to see a workman hammering across the lower
window. I stood, almost nose to nose with the man, staring

at him as he hammered but he didn't once look at me or meet my gaze. I expect that he had been told not to interact with the patients, but right there, in another place and time, we would have laughed together. The sense of 'otherness' permeated the whole place.

Yet Bradgate was light and airy, with pictures on the walls – something that Bootham Park didn't have.

My first visit to the unit was intended to keep me safe from a particularly low episode. On arrival I was asked a lot of questions, mainly about my mood but also practical questions about my date of birth and also other important dates. I suspect that these questions are used to determine concentration, memory and focus. Charles waited for me outside the room and he then said goodbye because I was taken to my bed. On my first visit, I had with me my large black and white shopping trolley which has cats all over it. I had filled the trolley with as many books on art as I could fit in. On the top I had pushed my teddy bear 'Bigrigg', which Charles had bought for me on our journey with my Father to his childhood home. I had a separate bag with clothes and toiletries. Charles walked from the ward and I watched him leave. He turned around for the last time, and put his hands on the clear glass door, two other clear doors away from me. I waved but couldn't stay, it was too painful. I turned around too and joined the nurse who locked the door behind me.

Burning Lazarus

Here on this bed I have stacked the wood high
Holy incense and smoke is bruising the sky
As I burn in the night, thick black as tar
Vincent pours yellow embalming the star
Starry nights lie to us truth is untold
We watch as a fiery meteor unfolds
And hold on to faith in those that we love
When light years ago they were dying above
You need no telescope to see this sky
You know I am flickering, desperate and I
Know you raised up my cross with a vinegar smile
My bonfire is blazing, raging yet while

How my river runs

I am bathing these sores in proud starlight gold
I fall like an angel, awkward and cold
Praying for feathers too close to the ground
Hummingbird thinkers beat faster than sound
Come running to halt all my secret release
Bound and determined, they piece after piece
Will bind me together, captured too soon
I met my defeat in that lonelier room
The room where now earthbound, life flickers on
Riding my nightmares to my funeral song
Trolley bells pierce the deepest of sleep, with
Rare animation we jostle like sheep
Hummingbird wings beat much faster than sound
Appear to be still those wings up and down
A silent crescendo a voiceless choir
Build up the pyre and fan the flames higher
You know my tragedy whispering bright
Scars on my pillow, soaked through in the night
Tragically shuffling we rise to be fed
Watched as we swallow, the sad living dead
Queue for our custard, all standing in line
Jesus in sorrow turns blood into wine
Speaks with the hummingbird, knows me by name
Calling me Lazarus over again
Like sick Hokey Cokey, we live and then die
He saves me my shroud for some future time.

One morning, I was standing alone in the ward. I had
decided to make an abstract film about my experiences and
was in the process of photographing the smoke alarm on the
ceiling. George, one of the psychiatric nurses walked past
the doorway, did a double take and then walked backwards
to ask me what I was doing. When I explained that I was
making a film, the nurse nodded and carried on. I was due to
leave hospital that afternoon. At lunchtime, I found myself
accompanied by George. Afterwards, he took me to one side
and said 'Don't shoot the messenger'. 'OK' I thought, that
doesn't sound too great. 'We don't think you're quite ready to
go home just yet. It won't be long, just a few more days
probably'. I unpacked my books on art and arthouse film and
got back into bed.

I remembered the absolute raging joy when I had begun my career in creative healing, 1998. Seven years had been a long time to arrive at this awful place. Sitting in my bed, the curtain around me and my wall of books for protection, I thought about the day when I bounced into college with no idea if I would be able to sustain even a single thought and learn something.

The first lesson I took in 'Writing for Radio' which turned out to be a professional route for me, gave me the space to act in an utterly appalling way. High as a kite, because of the new experiences, I convinced Ruth to complain with me about the standard of teaching. (What a bloody awful thing to do). It was a bit hit and miss but I couldn't seem to stop myself. Ruth and I went to the Head of School and complained. He listened in a rather bemused way and gave us the day off. Ruth and I went to the cinema to watch the new Woody Allan film. I felt awful the following day having spent all night convinced the lecturer had killed himself because of what I said. As the two years went by, I learned a lot from the teacher I had complained about and loved every second. I had an enormous crush on the Head of School and spectacularly made this known at the final exhibition where I had quite a bit of work exhibited. By then, I had been granted a large sum of money to create a project to raise awareness of mental illness through the arts. Both Joseph Rowntree Foundation and The Commedia Association funded the work which was amazing in itself. For my final piece I had begun to construct the project. I had painted, written poetry and also a monologue to be recorded as a sound track. The turning of the millennium hands seemed to flood me with both crazy and also creativity. I had begun to dislike my husband, Francis. He seemed stuck, nasty and oppressive. I asked Ruth to sing on my recording and so the day of the exhibition, I bought us both black velvet dresses and flamboyant gloves. We arrived to finish our stand. I had chosen to represent mental illness with handcuffs (which had raised a few laughs). Ruth's singing and my reciting could be heard and both my parents, and Liff had arrived to see the work. Francis also came, bringing Michael and Lucy. Despite the rocking and the rolling with sanity, I graduated

How my river runs

from college with five A levels, all grade A apart from one grade B. My marks for the project were only three below perfect and my Head of Course wrote across the bottom of my mark sheet, 'Wild Women don't worry, Wild Women don't sing the blues'. How I loved that man. How I loved my time at college. I was on home territory despite crunching up my results for radio work one semester and throwing them at my tutor's head. (Thankfully he laughed). I have to say that I am still rather ashamed of my behaviour on that evening. I made the mistake (an almighty mistake as I would come to realize over the years) of drinking from the free wine stand. I was so high that I couldn't get any higher, and believe me, I tried. The poetry I had written was very stark and revealing, around a subject I had never and still haven't really discussed with my Mother. I found my voice within the words but could not handle the circumstances. What should have been an incredible finish left me on the floor once again, praying for the memory of my actions to disappear.

Tree

It all felt so wrong
Wrong sad and dirty
I began to grow tall
Tall as an Oak Tree
 (I have your roots and I am growing upwards)
I will always be guilty
Guilty and endlessly,
Endlessly trying
And trying to punish me.
I cannot answer
Or speak the truth openly
All that I hope for
Is that one day they will see
(There is a poison spreading into my branches)
Twenty years later and
I have a daughter
She notices boys,
Like all her friends taught her
And I wrestle when
I'm accusing her now

As my Mother did then
Questioning innocence
(I am breaking small branches before they can grow)
With words I have learnt
That I should have burnt
Not saved for my girl,
For the next generation.
A lifetime ago
My past it was stolen
Daffodils golden
Daffodils taken,
In guilt we awaken
Then left in the wake
With a poisoned tree
We grieve for the loss
Of our tender years
And our Springtime too
Sabotaged by our fears.
If I had known of
This poison before
(I would have chopped the tree down, as it is, we have …)
The truth to restore
We will start now by
Planting acorns and daffodils
Three generations
The lie of some man
One day we women
Will know that we can
Laugh beneath the branches
Of a tall and healthy Oak
(… strong roots to bind us, and we will rejoice in our
womanhood, together).

Both in York and Leicester, hospital team meetings could be
a scary affair. When it was time for my situation to be
evaluated, I was invited to walk from my room on the ward
into another room, where approximately ten health
professionals sat in a large circle. I was invited to join them.
On a couple of occasions, looking back, I fitted the image of
a wandering mad woman quite well. I wore my long pink
night dress (which was made from heavy cotton so looked

more like a summer frock) and I always had bare feet as I was afraid of slipping. I was known for my bare feet. Being part of the discussion was hard as I was asked all kinds of personal questions. I didn't ever complain though, as I have always realised how lucky I am to receive such great treatment.

One particularly dark week in Bootham Park Hospital, two new patients arrived. A young woman who was certain that the whole hospital was out to kill her and an enormous wild eyed man who's jacket and trousers were so short that he looked like Frankenstein. I could see that the young doctors were very wary of taking his bloods, on arrival. He was very frightening. He was brought into hospital by two policemen and eventually he did calm down for his blood taking. I sat outside his room, on a window seat in the plush refurbished Victorian splendor. As he passed me, he turned his head and in the most polite voice you would ever hear, he asked 'Excuse me, do you know the correct time'?

Dinner time became more dangerous. I was sitting alone in the canteen when the man walked in and sat at another table further away from the food. Close behind him, the new girl walked in and sat facing him at the same table. 'Don't eat it', she hissed. 'It's poisoned'.
The man picked up his plate and returned it to the canteen. Walking out, I could hear the woman goading and winding him up. The atmosphere took a turn for the worse.
I went to bed early. I hated my room. It was like a prison cell, with dirty wood chip paper. I could see small splashes and marks on the wall and I wondered who or what had made them. Suddenly I heard a commotion outside the bedrooms, getting louder and louder. The young woman, followed by the massive man were kicking in the bedroom doors to 'free' the patients. As fast as they kicked the doors, the nurses locked them from the outside. (I never did quite get over my room being locked from the outside).

If I walk two worlds, then two of them must be the patient and the counsellor. I see my own slide into a frightening lack of insight and I am lost in psychosis whilst understanding the behaviour of my fellow patients. Not long before Francis and I split up, I decided I would train as a psychiatric nurse, even passing maths exams to qualify. When I was accepted at interview stage, I skipped out of the university grounds, down the side of a busy road clutching the cup of water that was given to me in the interview room. I wrote to the Royal College of Nursing for a bursary and was awarded two thousand pounds. Only after a training day, at Bootham Park hospital did I tell my consultant what I was doing. She simply shook her head and said 'No'. Within two weeks I had taken my first overdose and landed on the same ward where my training would have taken place.

How my river runs

Chapter Eighteen
Riding the Whale

During a journey meditation, when I was particularly distressed and fighting to stay afloat amidst the swell of emotion, I saw a whale swim slowly towards me. The whale was a blue whale, I think, and he arrived at my side in the midst of a lake. The sun was setting over the water and the salmon pink sky melted through the lavender blue. I climbed onto the whale's back and off we set, moving effortlessly through the water. My whale comes to me when I have no strength to swim against the tide. When I am particularly tired, he arrives at my side with a seat on his back, not unlike one would see on the back of an elephant. My favourite memory of the whale however, is the time he arrived with a ladybird on his head. The ladybird showed me the way home in safety, in full knowledge that my house was not on fire nor my children gone. Recently, whilst writing about my whale, a beautiful ladybird landed on my desk. It had more spots on its back than I had ever seen.

Both whale and ladybird are my allies, but not my power animals. They come to me for a special purpose, whereas my Elk, Stag, White Hart, Swan, Hummingbird and Tortoise form my energetic army and surround me as sure as the salmon pink sun rises and sets every day.
I now know that these things are real. They are expected and they are not the stuff of delusion.
Back then however, after my university counsellor stopped me in my ecstatic tracks with her insight into my manic behaviour, I gradually lost the ability to judge what was real and what belonged inside the walls of a hospital. The first year of my degree in Counselling had been one long joyous scream. Voted to represent the year in anything and everything, the chosen voice of year one, I would rise to any magical occasion with tingling and inappropriate timing. I breezed through the months, slimmer than before, confident in everything I said and wrote, ready to hold a party at the drop of a hat. I dropped a lot of hats in 2001. The energy flooding every part of my thinking and dripping with fizz into my veins saw me through the 'I Am' project. I designed the

cover of the CD, using the image of sound waves as they appear in the word 'perfect', the title and captured in letters, PERF, on the top, with ECT stretched beneath. The project did explore Obsessive Compulsive Disorder and Anxiety but it became clear as I cruised into 2002, that other forces were at work, bubbling beneath the surface with a menacing poison. My work with Druidry was rapidly becoming the main focus and I held the first Samhain ceremony in my living room, with my fellow student Sandy and also Francis. My experience of the Divine was fast becoming an almighty fist, shaken at the restrictive and ignorant times when the Spirit had been used and abused by a few to suck life from the many. Feeling the power of creation and freedom around me was beyond wonderful, the apple tree was exalted for sure, but amongst this energy I made rash decisions not based on any good reasoning at all. My dear friend Ruth was due to come over from Scarborough and take part in the Samhain ceremony but out of the blue, I reared at nothing and simply cancelled the meeting. I didn't know why I had done this; I wouldn't even speak to her. I decided to cut the evening off and not speak to anyone at all. This hurt Ruth very much as she had bought presents and was looking forward to taking part in the ceremony. I look back and see these events, sprinkled across the years, and I feel terrible because I don't know what my reasoning was. All I could do was understand that my illness was causing rash and disordered thinking. The thoughts are one thing and the energy is another. When the two collide, the results are anyone's guess.

Many times, I officiated ceremonies that were magical and profound. In 2001, a group of around thirty people, mostly from university, joined me in my garden. I cast a large circle with Cornish pebbles in the centre to form a fire pit. A large cauldron of honey wine simmered and the Celtic New Year (Halloween), Samhain, breathed new misty life across the dark night. Each of us spoke the name of a loved one who had passed over and I called in the energy of the Goddess Ceridwen to stand between the worlds as a bridge for us to both connect and also leave behind that we needed let go. As poetry invoked power, madness melted through the words and danced with light, taking the sacred form of the wounded healer.

How my river runs

Away from such magic, I often invited celebrities over to my house without letting Francis know what I had done. Thankfully none of them ever showed up. Ideas were catapulting around my skull and if the mood was low I was in danger. If I drank alcohol, as I wanted to in the days when my illness was unrecognized, I experienced a rush worthy of riding a horse in full gallop. The sparkle rose up and I moved so much faster than those around me, I am sure that they could only see a blur and hear a hum whilst I spun my observations and ideas around the room thinking that I made some kind of sense. I shared my million thoughts about God and how everything in my life was a communication to me from heaven. Every word, every book, every program on TV linked beautifully together in a seamless message and the message crackled and fizzed through my veins, linking me directly to the source.

I would like, just as an aside to share something that always makes me laugh.

My sister, as I have told you lives in a fairly remote part of the Yorkshire Dales. One Halloween, a family were travelling to their bed and breakfast for a short break. It was a dark night and there appeared to be nobody around, the road was empty. Occasionally, sheep can be found close to my sister's house stranded on their backs. This is known as riggwelter (a name taken by a particularly strong brew of local beer also). Without knowing about a local Halloween party, or even any locals – the family were suddenly terrified by the sight of a woman and two children in the road, dressed as vampires and pulling at a riggweltered sheep.

I love the Yorkshire Dales. I love my sister.

The difficulty in all of this is, that I do believe, absolutely, that the Creator speaks to us all and if we can slip ourselves into the right wavelength we can hear and see and gain insight. I also know however, that despite revelatory experience, the same energy that comes from within my mind and body becomes overloaded and confused. This is why I believe Shaman are wounded healers. They see above, into the higher vibrations of the sky world, they exist in the mundane and link with those who need their medicine and also travel below, to the world of power animals, green forests and ancient song. Moving between worlds is the way of the Shaman and those who practice Shamanism, necessarily feel above and below what is usual. This is a subtle line to walk though as the energy bounces back bringing mania, depression and the mixed state. Using herbs and oils is a deeply intuitive art, but when I am soaring and not sure where to go, alcohol fuels the pure addiction of mania. Many people with bipolar affective disorder and other psychotic illness self-medicate with alcohol or drugs, leading to the dangerous 'duel diagnosis'. It can then become a trade-off where addiction can't be treated until the psychosis is addressed, but equally, psychosis cannot be helped until the addiction is under control. My pattern under these circumstances was and still would be, the same. Identical no matter where I am or who I am with. First the soaring, the dancing on tables and the deep healing sessions with those drawn to ask for help when seeing a chaotic but insightful person. Then the drop, the painful screams and the vomiting. From spirit into matter with one fell swoop. Sleep follows for roughly an hour, then the waking terror. My muscles wrenched in every direction, the pain of spasm and the overwhelming agitation, the need to find a way out back to the waves of golden spirit. I can raise my arms and fly, feeling the power move around my body as my arms beat their wings. If there are those around you who have stayed the course of the evening and are still around you despite the vomiting and shouting obscenities nobody understands but know them to be obscenities anyway, then they will keep you safe. If they manage to get you through the next few hours without losing you to a sharp piece of glass or a bottle of tablets, then they might help you into a warm bath, the first of many. Only lying in a warm, not too hot bath will bring any kind of relief. It will clear the sick from your hair and ease the painful muscles. Then, sleep will come. The following day, you will want to die even more.

My visit to Portsmouth, although dangerous had set my thoughts in motion and I would hold Druidry in my heart forever, despite a couple of episodes resulting in evangelical gun-powder.

After my initial race-track thinking as I arrived with my two companions at Dylan's home, I had skidded to a halt when fear crept in later that night. Dylan gave me his childhood bedroom to sleep in. The house had belonged to his grandmother who now lived in a home. Dylan still cared for her but the house was filled with every flamboyant sundry you could imagine. In the bedroom, I had a single mattress on the floor and behind me, was a full-sized painting of the 'Iron Maiden' as is part of the rock group with the same name. The window was cracked and a bare light bulb hung from the ceiling. I plummeted to earth and it seemed that I had broken every bone inside my head. As I lay there, afraid, I telephoned Francis on my mobile. He was at work on the night shift. Sobbing, I begged him to drive down and get me. He refused, telling me I would just have to deal with it. I felt so ill and sick, I didn't know what to do. I managed to sleep and the following day was bright so things seemed better. I managed to find the toilet which was hidden amongst bathroom tiles and appliances, and I washed my hair in the sink. Dylan's girlfriend Bella suggested that the two of us walk into town and visit the tattoo shop owned by a member of the Druid Order who also practiced piercing. I had already decided to have my nose pierced and to do it here, in Portsmouth seemed fitting because it would mark my new spiritual journey with a ritual. Piper's nose was filled with silver rings, he had three along the septum and piercings just about everywhere else. He agreed to pierce my nose. I sat in the chair, knowing that Piper would pierce my nose using a needle instead of a gun. He began to recite some ceremonial words and then told me he would count down from three to one. Piper began at three and slowly moved to two and then put the needle through without reaching one. I was so surprised that I screamed, glad it was over as it really hurt and laughing with hysteria.

Back at Dylan's house, Bella cooked a chicken stew and I talked with her two children, a girl of around ten and a boy about seven. They were beautiful children from an earlier relationship. Dylan had no children of his own but was a good step-father. He had been brought up by a stage magician and showed me his close-up magic which was incredible. I made my mind up that one day, he would come to one of my parties and I would show off this colourful, amazing new friend. Two years later, Dylan did come to my birthday party. He died two weeks later from heart complications. I didn't find this out however until I had moved to Coventry and connected with the Druids there.

Being taken into hospital is a war between two emotions. On the one hand it is a sign of relief that echoes through your whole world but on the other, it can feel like a straight jacket. It is tight across your chest, invisible but you feel the buckles and ties all the same.
In February 2005, two years after the end of my degree, the lead up to the end of my marriage with Francis became particularly tough.
Wanting to begin studying again as a psychiatric nurse despite being very poorly, I was on the rescue warpath yet again.

Before realizing that training as a nurse was not a good idea, I needed to make space for my studies. Michael had recently returned home so I had lost the office I used to work for my degree. It seemed like a good idea to get rid of our double bed and replace it with an Ikea adult cabin bed, with a desk underneath. On boxing day, 2004, I asked Francis to take me to buy the bed. I suppose the reaction whilst pushing round the trolley 'I'M NOT SUPPOSED TO BE HERE' was a giveaway that things weren't as they should be. A few days later, in silence, Francis put the bed up. Michael and I helped but neither of us dare utter a word. It was when the ladder finally reached the top bunk that I realized the mistake. At almost sixteen stones in weight, due to my antipsychotic medication, climbing the metal ladder was near impossible. We did climb it, and as we lay on the bed, the ceiling was around six inches from our noses. I silently slid down the ladder and went to sleep on the sofa. My inpatient stay at Bootham Park hospital followed within the month.

How my river runs

Out of Time

I don't belong even to silence
Even shadows may crawl on the floor
And sunlight might dance in its freedom
Sliding effortless under the door
I don't feel the transient moments
Nor the movement of shadow or sun
Now currently twilight unending
With no sign that the morning will come
The world stares at me without owning
I am lost in the lack of its gaze
My name is 'Perpetual No-one'
I slip unseen through fragments of days
These walls watch the light and the darkness
All the years which have travelled from me
The seasons bring nothing by changing
And their changing brings nothing to me
I once went to town as a voter
And I travelled by bus with a card
I wore my best boots in the Spring-time
Growing flowers and herbs in my yard
Don't give me your clocks and your watches
Now those faces mean nothing to me
Like Dali they pour through my fingers
Broken hour-glass of insanity

Helen Mary Barr

How my river runs

Chapter Nineteen
Water Babies

Sometimes, the person you expect the least causes you the most pain. It is unthinkable to say to your son 'You hurt me and it has made me feel like dying'. I have felt this and I have said it. This doesn't mean that I love my son any less, in fact the love I feel for my child becomes intensified with every wound and every nightmare.

Charles and I discovered that Michael had become involved with hard drugs, not long after we moved into our second home in Coventry, 2006. Michael had been experiencing some health problems and was worried, so he rang me to ask for advice.

The previous year, whilst living in the doll's house, I had arranged for a drug counsellor to visit Michael at home to help him with his cannabis use. Most days, unless I was able to give him money for it, he would become aggressive. This trait has disappeared over the years and yet I wish that some of this fight would have resurfaced during the last ten years, when things got really tough.

During this same period, I began to stockpile items and to spend all my spare money. I bought three computers in one week and gave two of them away to people I barely knew.

I arranged for Michael to come to Charles and I in Coventry. I will never forget the day I met him at Birmingham New Street. It had only been six months since my leaving and yet I couldn't recognize him anywhere. When I heard him call, I swung round to see my boy, a face I had never seen and a haunted look that chills me to this day.

It was pouring down and the link from Birmingham to Coventry had been suspended, so a coach was laid on. Michael was quiet and uncommunicative as we travelled. It was only a few weeks since Charles had been operated on for throat surgery so he too was unwell.

During his stay, I tried to encourage Michael to visit my new GP, which he did, and was given some tablets for anxiety.

However, we ended up shouting in the street and I couldn't stop crying. I hated my life that month.

The day before Michael's twenty-first birthday, he and I returned to York to try and organize a permanent place for him to live. Our friend Basil agreed to meet the pair of us at York Council offices to offer support. It was a weird feeling to be arriving at York Station and then travelling through our old haunts to the center of town. I dragged my pink suitcase behind me and felt I belonged to neither York nor Coventry. I had dreamed, a few years previously that Michael had gone missing and his body had been found in a trailer by the river. The dream came back to mind as Basil, Michael and I sat in the same spot for a drink after our appointment. Michael was eventually given a nice flat but surrounded by people that weren't too good for him. He seemed happy, even inviting Charles and I over for a meal one weekend. However things began to turn sour, and Michael needed to leave.

Charles and I had moved to Barwell and we tried hard to convince Michael to move in with us. I hated to think of him being so vulnerable, even though he had family around in York, drugs were not the kind of subject that could have been broached with my parents. This has changed in recent years as life had forced us all to look at pain in a different way.

The day Charles and I drove to York to collect Michael will stay in my mind forever.

We had agreed to take on a small black kitten at the same time. Already rescue parents to two ginger siblings, we were suggested as a good home for Jackson, a three-week old little boy who had been dreadfully abused. Jackson, who was rescued by a car of young girls up on the Yorkshire Dales, where my sister and her family now lived, running a pet shop after the forty-year school finally ended; had been living in the James Heriot funded rescue house.

A gang of boys had thrown him out of their car (witnessed by the girls), and had attempted to run him over. He had lost his tale, but had been found and saved on June 25th 2009, also coincidentally, the day before my birthday and the day Michael Jackson died. (Hence the name).

How my river runs

Jackson had only a stump left and was very traumatized. When he came to us, even the slightest upset caused him to scream, not in pain, but fear.

The plan was, to collect Jackson first and then pick up Michael before heading home. When we arrived at Michael's flat, we squeezed as many possessions as possible into the boot, squashing push bike parts, cooking equipment and an old desktop computer alongside Michael. Giving Michael the pen with Jackson in it to hold, I pushed my front seat as far forward as it would go. We set off, Michael and Jackson falling asleep, Charles arguing with the satnav, and myself carrying a bottle of methadone.

I cried a lot that day. When we took Jackson out of the car, he stared at us from behind his cot bumper with large round green eyes. Meeting the gaze of someone who has been abused is a whole other level than hearing about them. Michael was exhausted too and so we simply put everyone to bed.

Charles decided to change Jackson's name, to that of his favourite late uncle, Albert. For a while we referred to him as Albert Jackson, and he and Michael were inseparable. Lying together on the sofa.

Tragically, a family member belonging to our neighbour was murdered, leaving behind a little girl. Anne, seven years old, refused to speak. One day, Albert wandered into our neighbour's garden whilst Anne was visiting. She began to pick him up and to talk with him. After his, Anne wrote letters to Albert and posted them through our door. I wrote back to her, with cards and pictures from Albert.

I decided to send Albert's story to the Angel Animal organization and as a result, he won second prize for bravery as 'Albert Jackson, wounded healer'.

Albert is now eight years old and still mesmerizes with his eyes, his little stump of a tail and his uncanny ability to bring calm amidst chaos.

Michael was with us about a year on that particular occasion. It was never easy living with both Charles and Michael although we all gave it a really good go. For me, in the end, the only respite came from a stay in hospital.

Michael sent me a card filled with all the things that he had achieved and also made me proud. An award he had won whilst playing guitar in a band and also my favourite photographs of him as a little boy.

When I returned home, I telephoned the Jeremy Kyle Show. I knew that the programme often aired special editions where illness or disability would be discussed. I noticed that the show didn't ever offer a special session focussed on mental illness. I honestly thought that a frank discussion around issues of Bipolar Affective disorder would have been beneficial and popular. I tried twice and was turned down both times. I decided then, that somehow I would raise awareness of the pain associated with mental illness, and I would crack it wide open without hype, or celebrity.

After Charles died, Michael came back to Barwell to live with me, which was wonderful. The company was great and my family were pleased that I had somebody living with me that they trusted. After Anthony and I got together, it was lovely too to have a supporting voice, when Charles's Coventry family (most of them anyway) decided I was in the wrong to plan a new marriage only a year after losing Charles. The difference being, that my new fiancé was Anthony and no matter how much I explained to them about our friendship it didn't seem to make any difference.

What I didn't realise was that Michael was still a heroin user. Whilst staying with Anthony in his flat, I discovered via Facebook about Michael. I cut short my visit and returned to Barwell. Michael met me in the car at Hinckley Rail Station. I immediately asked him to show me his arms, which I realized had been hidden for a long time. I told my son that I wanted complete honesty, and that we would all work together, Anthony too, to heal his addiction. I had been aware that money had been dropping out of my bank account for quite some time but Michael had convinced me that this was due to all sorts of things, none of which were true. I didn't see the classic signs of addiction, mainly because I was coping with bereavement and my own issues. After collapsing in the toilet several years previously, my doctor had told me to always call an ambulance if I suspected anything was wrong with Michael. Michael had

taken to staying in his room for large periods of time and my parents had warned me never to go in if I couldn't make him hear me. My neighbours too (who had been good friends to me and had even accompanied Charles and I on holiday to the Yorkshire Dales) offered their support.
One dark morning, I couldn't make my son hear me knocking on his door. Exhausted by it all I called for an ambulance and asked Tony to help me bring Michael out of his room.

Michael could now hear very well and refused to come out. As the ambulance sat outside the house, everyone could see what was happening. Tony managed to get Michael to leave his room and walk into the ambulance but he refused to go to hospital with them. The paramedics checked him over but told me they couldn't help as he appeared to be OK. If he had gone with them, I knew, he would have received proper rehabilitation support.

I remembered Christmas a couple of years earlier, when Michael and Lucy had come to stay. It is so exhausting attempting to lift the atmosphere into something close to festive when nobody cares enough to join in. I was pleased with the gifts I bought for Michael and Lucy however. Lucy loved her 'London Experience', a meal, tour around a theatre and a stay in a city centre apartment. The gift was for two people and I was thrilled when she asked me to go with her. We went to the Tate Modern together and had a brilliant time. Michael was really into his music and had wanted singing lessons for some time. I thought that his confidence might grow with some lessons, so I bought him six lessons, by far the most expensive present. Placing the voucher into a box, I added a glass pebble, with the word 'faith' written on it. A few weeks after Christmas, our neighbour knocked on the door and told Michael that he would buy the lessons for half I had paid for them. I wasn't supposed to hear but was standing behind Michael in the hallway. Years later, despite the missing lessons, I discovered that Michael had kept the 'faith pebble'. Out of everything, I would have wanted him to keep this, if only one thing could have survived.

Helen Mary Barr

The afternoon came and I knew that Michael had chosen not to work with us in getting clean. I understand now, the entrenched secrecy and habitual lying made this impossible, but I love my son and I would have done anything to help him. Over the years I have even followed people I suspected to be drug suppliers, hiding behind hedges and outside shops, tracing phone calls and asking unwelcome questions. All in the aid of a happy family life and to save my son from pain. I had known for many years about Michael's drug problem, but heroin was a whole new concept to me and not one I wanted to grapple with. I wasn't given the chance to opt out of the grapple, because I wanted Michael to be safe. I would have done anything to bring Michael back to us. I was angry and my hands were tied. I wanted our intelligent, gentle and sensitive son to come home but I knew that heroin was one of the worst demons we would need to face. The afternoon, saw me asking my son to leave. I couldn't think what else to do. It absolutely crippled me in every sense of the word. I had been advised to do this before by counsellors but I could never take the risk, believing that a safe house was best. It wasn't, and the safety enabled the survival of Michael's drug use.

I gave Michael the car, a mobile phone and some money. He packed his things and left.
Facebook brought me the news again. My son had sold the car the same day and put all the money into his arm, having chosen to stay at the house of a woman involved in the same lifestyle, literally just round the corner. He had on him, opiate blocker injections and the woman injected Michael, saving his life. For this, I will always be grateful to her. As a result, Michael was taken into the rehab system in Leicester. Because I had been enabling his habit, his leaving was the best thing that could have happened. He didn't make our wedding, but Michael now lives happily with us, in the little house Anthony and I bought in York.

Anthony's brother drove us to Leicester so that we could pick him up. By that stage, Michael had been given a flat in a high rise block next to the station. The rain was torrential that day and Mark waited in the car whilst Anthony and I waited at the bottom for Michael. I decided to go up, through

How my river runs

security to the floor where my son had been living for a while. Michael had owned enough furniture and happy belongings to fill a house three times over. I watched him come out of the door carrying three carrier bags and a rucksack. The bags mainly held cooking equipment. I looked past him to the large window and the view was terrible. All that could be seen was the roof of the station. Just black. No furniture. Nothing happy. I was filled with joy as Anthony and I put the bags in the car and we drove home. We had made Michael's bedroom as homely as we could for him, bought him a new guitar and some pictures. I can't explain how wonderful it is to prepare for your son's return, knowing he has made it through the evil alive.

Michael knows the boundaries and he is growing into a fine man, a healthy man. He is clean and we are more proud of him that I can say. John and I saw our boy come home. We all did. All the family who love him dearly.

Lucy was married this year, in a lavish and happy setting, which used to be the old railway offices. Both my mum and sister worked there, and Anthony worked for twenty-six years as a railway man, not forgetting my dad and Rhodesia Railways (British Rail).

In most ways her story has already been told. She was at my side as I fought to find my self worth when my marriage to Francis ended, and Francis did not treat her well.
The best thing I can do, I think, is to give you the speech I wrote for Lucy's wedding. John and I sat together and Liff read it for me, starting by telling the whole room that she was in fact Lucy's real mother! (This is not true)! I held my daughter's hands. John had planned to wear Charles's shoes to walk Lucy down the aisle but unfortunately they didn't fit.

'What can I tell you about my daughter that you don't already know?
Beautiful, dedicated, funny.
Yet my girl is so much more - allow me to tell you.

Helen Mary Barr

When Lucy has made her mind up about something she
puts everything behind her vision.

As a little girl, of around 5 years old, she demonstrated this
determination by making me believe that the clothes I had
chosen for her to wear were all worn out.

At first I found it a little odd that the dresses had all torn in a
similar way - but I didn't question any further. However,
several tops and skirts later I discovered the reason for the
terrible quality of Lucy's clothes. Caught red-handed, there
was my daughter - destroying all her most hated clothes with
a pair of toy scissors. A mischievous glint in her eye as she
ripped away, then coming to me with her 'rubbish' dresses.
Watch out Nicholas .... if Lucy's clothes begin to wear out in
sudden and inexplicable circumstances - causing her to
need a whole new wardrobe, be a little suspicious!

I have been privileged to enjoy several Mother/Daughter
holidays. Many times, our Mother/Daughter roles have been
reversed and Lucy has again showed her focus
and strength. On a recent holiday, my girl decided I should
not eat puddings as they were bad for me.

Rather afraid of her death-ray stare, I obliged but snook a
pudding onto my plate when she wasn't looking. I was even
more afraid when I picked up my Kindle to discover a
healthy eating book downloaded which I had never seen
before. However, I went up to our room to find Lucy working
her way through a family sized bag of penny sweets. I have
never forgotten the look on her face and it makes me laugh
to this day.

I could regale you with many such tales, however, I will
leave you with just one. My favourite.

Lucy and I travelled to Berlin and decided to track down an
abandoned theme park, to take some great photographs. I
will never know how Lucy found the way there, jumping on
and off trains, and walking quite a way to arrive at the eerie
sight.

However we soon discovered that the park was surrounded
by a large wire fence and guarded by a scary man and
his even scarier dog. Ready to turn around and leave I
suddenly saw my daughter drag up the fence and shout
'Come on Mum, we can roll in under here'! I don't know what

was scarier, Lucy's determination to get in, or her suggestion
that I should roll around on the floor!
Charles took great delight in winding our girl up with
incorrect historical information. Knowing, that she would
race onto the internet to prove him wrong. 'Our little squab'
he called her... curled up on the sofa with wide and
vulnerable eyes, yet an unshakable knack to see everything
through to the end.
Strong as anything. Someone you would definitely want on
your side, be it starting a new diet, or breaking and entering.

Lucy is my daughter, but I rely on her as my friend. She has
supported me in ways she will probably never know. I am
more proud of her than I could ever say.
My girl comes from a family of strong women, I think Clara
and I would agree.
We will always be there to support her and surround her with
love.
However, today we hand our girl over to a strong man.
In Nicholas I believe my girl has met her match. I know
that Nicholas will be beside her because he has married one
of a kind. Lucy too, has married one of a kind, and we love
him for his strength, vision and gentleness.
So, I would like to raise a toast
To Strong women and their Strong men.

I would like to share just one story out of the hundreds in my
mind, where my children have worked together to make me
laugh.
One day, I was very poorly in bed. In the next bedroom I
could hear Michael and Lucy playing with the dog Joss.
Curious that they were safe and fine (aged five and six at the
time) I went into their bedroom to check. My babies had
decided to make me breakfast. They mixed flour, water and
red food colouring, putting all these things into their toy bun
cases. However, Joss had eaten the breakfast. This was
funny enough, but not so funny as the colour of Joss's poos
when we took him for a walk later that day.
Whenever I feel sad, or I wonder if I have been the mother I
ought to have been, I just remember 'red poo' and I realise
that life is about fun, if you can get it.

It feels as though I have said only negative things about Michael here, and I don't want you to think that this is the only aspect of my son. It is simply that his drug addiction has made such an impact on my life that it must come into this chapter with a fair weight.

The truth about my son is far more than this.

He is funny, with the dry wit of his father and clever, intelligent far more than he knows. As a little boy, he would write me letters to tell me when he had done something naughty and often put 'Can we sort this out over a pot of tea'? When his dad and sister were asleep, and my four-year-old boy was awake, he would sneak downstairs and we would share crackers and strong cheese. He preferred tea to sweet coffee, and I made it for him.

Michael has also been my rescuer over the years although he doesn't know it.

When pregnant for the third time, I visited the midwife with Lucy strapped to me in a sling and Michael by my side on reins. He would have been almost two years old. I was so exhausted and suffering from the bipolar come down, after post birth mania following having Lucy. As I stood in the room with the midwife, I found I could not stop crying. Concerned, the midwife placed her hand on my arm. Immediately, Michael grabbed my other hand and shouted 'Mummy, the door. Go'.

Over the years, the mis-medications and diagnostic nightmares I came up against, Michael never flinched from being at my side through the vomit and the shaking. In spite of the path my son chose once, he has always been there for me. He may have behaved tragically when in the grip of his addiction, but he is a true and lovely person who would give his last pair of shoes to a homeless man with bare feet. (Something he actually did once). Either that, or he sold them for drugs. The answer will remain one of life's mysteries.

Watch 'A Street Cat Named Bob' and you won't go far wrong.

Both of my children have lacked self-confidence and it distresses me to think that they don't always see their strength, their kindness and their beauty. Michael is incredibly talented at art and cooking. He could have been a chef or a draftsman. However, the world is now his oyster and he has stopped it in time to find a different and fulfilling path. He is now thirty years old. At thirty-two years old, I entered college for the first time and changed my life. Yes, I had two beautiful children, but I had not come to terms with my own issues and problems until after turning thirty. He has all the time he needs.

I now have a wonderful step-son, courtesy of Anthony, and a gorgeous step-daughter, brought to me by Anthony's ex-wife Tessa (from her first marriage). We are a lucky family indeed. Anthony and I have seven cats; George, Charles, Henry, Lotte, Luna, Mabel and Albert.

My parents live close enough for me to take round a tin of rice pudding and for them to be able to hug me when my life is sliding down the river bank.

Helen Mary Barr

How my river runs

Chapter Twenty
Pond Skater, (Like pond skaters on the surface)

I landed back in York on July 24th 2016, less than one minute's walk from my parent's house, in sight of the church where my sister was married and I first found God. I live in the house which belonged to my dear friend Kath and her husband Mick, before she passed away. Kath, my shorthand buddy, was one of the few people to see that I was drowning and to take me to one side, and tell me that she saw it. I have been stable and my boat has not rocked in five years despite events over the last three years. I finally learned how to take care of myself and recognise the signs of being unwell. Medication is the main mast I hold onto. This can change as my life moves, rocks and rests. Lithium is the foundation for my recovery. Sometimes it can be hard work to balance my highs and lows, my fear and paranoia. Some anti-psychotic medication feels like amphetamine. Dancing in the red ballet shoes is painfully relentless. Projects start at a second's notice and are rarely finished. Recently I painted all the kitchen cabinets by candle light, at night in less than two hours. I am amazed by what I can do, but when I am unable to sleep and this goes on for weeks, the agitation is beyond description. Quetiapine is sedative and the opposite to my 'fast meds'. I want to sleep all the time and painting my kitchen would be a challenge even with a month to complete it. There are things I can do to catch the episodes, before my brain starts to wobble. Sleep is the main element, as is drinking plenty of water to counteract the lithium in my blood. Lithium toxicity can be fatal. I take the right medication and see my nurse weekly, I have a clear and productive relationship with my consultant, and we speak openly about my state of mind and how best to support me wherever I am in my stability. I also have psychological input to help me navigate my thinking. My consultant treats me as an equal and with respect. My regime consists of both anti-psychotic and mood stabilizing elements. I stay away from alcohol because at best it magnifies either high or low thinking, at worst it is a portal to hell. I need to pull on my red boots and walk.

Best of all I can practice my beliefs in complete safety, sure in the knowledge that I will be aware if I am being exploited, or disappearing into a world of fantasy. My shamanic practice is everything to me and I love working with other people to help them move through their own pain. The wounded healer is very much alive and well, as is my ability to see vividly the things around me that are too high or too low for most people to recognize.

The house we bought is over a hundred years old and the street travels straight down to the river and the large grassed flood defence. I can close my eyes and find my way to the water by instinct. In December 2016, the river rose so high that it threatened to tumble down upon us and into the houses around. During the night, at around three in the morning, after a loud bang at the door the army told us that we were at risk of flooding and should think about emergency preparations. Having taken my medication three or four hours earlier I was sedated and also scared. Anthony was downstairs and so I felt my way around the bed in the dark, holding on to keep myself from falling. I found a small shopping bag and filled it with my boxes of medication. Pulling a jumper over my pyjamas, I threw in a notepad, pen and a scarf also. I made it to the bedroom door and began to shout for Michael. 'Flood. Flooding!' I yelled. Michael was quite unconcerned but still I stood on the landing with my tablets, my notepad, pen and scarf. Anthony ran up the stairs towards me and took hold of my elbows. 'There is no need to be afraid', he said firmly. 'Let's get you back into bed'. I kept my jumper on and my bag nearby but I lay down in faith that I wouldn't drown. I could hear suitcases on wheels trundling down the street as folk abandoned ship. Anthony came back into the bedroom, 'Our bike is the only vehicle left on the street', he laughed. 'We don't run'.

I fell back into a sort of sleep and in my head I saw everything I owned, swirl around in a kind of whirlpool. Everything drifting away, my life behind me, everything I owned and all my fears. I woke fitfully several times and began to realize that Anthony was walking to the flood banks, every hour on the hour. The pumps were pulling back the river and the water had reached just eight inches below the top. I rested my mind, and knew that for the first time in

my life I had found peace. My husband was keeping me safe and my son was not afraid.
They say that when you drown ……

My biggest hope in writing this book, is that it may fall into the hands of someone caught in the undertow. Someone who wouldn't be missed, who might drown and not leave a space in the lives of others. Someone who thinks of themselves as without family or friends, whether true or not. Someone who believes that nobody sees them. Someone high and someone low.
Be vigilant but know you can survive.
As I watch Michael ride off on the motorbike we bought him for his thirtieth birthday, I know that I made it.
Swim. Swim.
If I can do it, so can you.

For all of you who need to be heard. The walking wounded.
Let them hear you.
You are not alone and you are not to blame.
You are worthy and you are whole.
You are healed.

Helen Mary Barr

www.ingramcontent.com/pod-product-compliance
Lightning Source LLC
Chambersburg PA
CBHW031150270326
41931CB00006B/208